THE OPENING ACT

BY
CHRISTINE HAMER-HODGES

THE LOVE STORY OF AUGIE AND MARGO RODRIGUEZ

Copyright © 2024 by Christine Hamer-Hodges

All rights reserved. No part of this publication may be reproduced, distributed, or transmitted in any form or by any means, including photocopying, recording, or other electronic or mechanical methods, without the prior written permission of the copyright owner and the publisher, except in the case of brief quotations embodied in critical reviews and certain other noncommercial uses permitted by copyright law. For permission requests, write to the publisher, "Attention: Permissions Coordinator," to the address below.

Studio of Books LLC
5900 Balcones Drive Suite 100
Austin, Texas 78731
www.studioofbooks.org
Hotline: (254) 800-1183

Ordering Information:
Special discounts are available on quantity purchases by corporations, associations, and others. For details, contact the publisher at the address above.

Printed in the United States of America.

ISBN-13: Softcover   978-1-964148-86-1
          eBook   978-1-964148-87-8

Library of Congress Control Number: 2024911738

Table of Contents

AUTHOR'S NOTE.....i
INTRODUCTION.....iii
CHAPTER ONE.....1
CHAPTER TWO.....13
CHAPTER THREE.....21
CHAPTER FOUR.....28
CHAPTER FIVE.....37
CHAPTER SIX.....45
CHAPTER SEVEN.....53
CHAPTER EIGHT.....59
CHAPTER NINE.....69
CHAPTER TEN.....80
CHAPTER ELEVEN.....88
CHAPTER TWELVE.....100
CHAPTER THIRTEEN.....111
CHAPTER FOURTEEN.....121
CHAPTER FIFTEEN.....139
CHAPTER SIXTEEN.....149

CHAPTER SEVENTEEN 161
CHAPTER EIGHTEEN 172
CHAPTER NINETEEN 181
CHAPTER TWENTY 192
CHAPTER TWENTY ONE. 204
CHAPTER TWENTY TWO 214
CHAPTER TWENTY THREE. 225
CHAPTER TWENTY FOUR. 234
CHAPTER TWENTY FIVE 242
CHAPTER TWENTY SIX 248
CHAPTER TWENTY SEVEN. 258
CHAPTER TWENTY EIGHT 265

AUTHOR'S NOTE

It's ironic that the first chapter of this book should be all about a final act, when the title of the book begs to differ. It *is* a final act, but it is not a final performance. This year, there will be many more.

The couple about to dance in this closing act has been opening performances for 32 years. They opened shows in North America and around the world from the 1950's through to the 1970's, for just about any famous person that one can name.

This is a story about two people whose determination to succeed as professional dancers eventually resulted in the significant role they played during the shaky beginnings of racial equality in New York.

The story chronicles an important point in our history, but it is primarily a love story about a couple of kids from working class areas in the city, who in the beginning had almost everything going against them except for love; the love of their families, their love of dance and, above all, their love for each other.

Their passion for the *mambo* took the dance to a level of artistry that retained its authentic rhythm and style, but they added such a powerful technique and dynamism to the dance that people of all colors and ethnicities were driven to go and see for themselves. The convergence took place in Manhattan, where a person named Maxwell Hyman was willing to go out on a limb and allow the worlds of music, dance and segregation to collide inside his club, the famous *Palladium Ballroom*.

Christine Hamer-Hodges

His experiment was triumphantly successful, and it is true to say that from that time on in New York a cultural revolution began, which welcomed blacks, whites, Latinos, Asians and everyone in between, to mix and mingle without fear of reprisals.

Thirty years ago, the couple retired as professional dancers, but they continued on with their own production company, where their legendary skills and popularity remained with them. So much so, that after I began writing their biography, they were invited to dance for the world famous *Cirque du Soleil*. Augie and Margo Rodriguez are about to complete their own full circle.

From their very first professional opening act in the *Waldorf Astoria* in 1955 for Harry Belafonte, they are now closing one of this country's most famous and spectacular shows in Las Vegas. I wish Augie and Margo a wonderful, successful year and I already know that, as in the past, this extraordinary couple will thrill hundreds of thousands of people as they continue at *Cirque* to create their own Circle of Sun around each other and everyone they know.

Christine Hamer Hodges
April 30th 2006

INTRODUCTION

"*I want you to meet some old friends of mine,*" Richard said to me. I had recently met Richard through a Club I had joined. "*I think you will find them very interesting,*" he continued, "*they are retired now, but they used to be professional dancers.*" "*What kind of dancers?*" I asked. "*Adagio,*" he said. "*Oh, how nice,*" I replied, not terribly impressed.

Perhaps I should make it clear that for the past seven years I have lived in Southern Florida. Dance Halls and Studios flourish here, mainly frequented by elderly couples who enjoy waltzing and fox-trotting as a form of exercise. The term *adagio* was familiar to me as a word in music, meaning slow and leisurely, so naturally I assumed that Richard's friends would be ballroom dancers. Rather slow now, but very game and still able to put on a good show together, twirling shakily around the dance floor for several turns before collapsing, fatigued, at their table alongside the wall. Rather like some of the elderly couples I knew in a local retirement community, only perhaps a notch or two above.

I expected to meet a charming couple, certainly, but I had imagined they would be quietly living out their years like the other retirees I knew, with minimal activities during the day and evenings spent snoozing in a chair in front of the TV. Fred and Ginger I thought, they cannot be.

I got three things very wrong that evening. *Adagio,* when it is referred to in dancing, means, and I quote from Webster's Dictionary, '*A sequence of well-controlled, graceful movements performed as a display of skill. A dance by a man and woman emphasizing difficult technical feats.*'

Christine Hamer-Hodges

Retired means *'To be no longer occupied with one's business or profession,'* which I imagined incorrectly would be the case with this couple, and *Elderly* means *'Advanced in years',* which correctly or not conjures up a vision of measured movement, failing memory and a visible depletion of energy.

When Augie and Margo Rodriguez opened their door and welcomed us, I immediately knew there was nothing 'elderly' about this couple. Both in their 70's, both agile and slim, with smiling faces, incredibly sparkling eyes and young, eager voices, they looked and sounded the epitome of health and fitness, putting many people in their forties and fifties to shame.

It was an unusual evening for me from the very beginning. I am used to being the one in the group who talks and keeps the conversational ball rolling - whether I need to or not - and on this occasion I just sat and listened; at least, I did until the end of the evening when questions just sort of kept pouring out. At the start of our meeting Augie and Margo spoke for the first hour or so with Richard, who is himself a professional musician, about old friends in 'the business'. There were names I had never heard of before: Noro Morales, Joe Vega, Cuban Pete, Benny More.

At one point, Augie turned to me and asked me to forgive them for talking 'shop'. *"It's all we know"* he said, *"reminiscing about our old friends and hearing all the latest news about them - when we performed with them, what they are doing now, are they still alive?"* He made the last comment with an impish smile which Margo spotted and immediately burst into squeals of laughter.

As the evening wore on, I became completely enchanted with Augie and Margo. I learned they played tennis every morning, if the weather permitted and Margo's knee was not hurting too much. They both displayed an amazing zest for life and clearly enjoyed hearing each other relate random dancing memories or tales of old friends. I began to form a picture in my mind of the life this delightful couple must have led.

They started to talk about places they had danced: *The London Palladium,* New York's *Carnegie Hall, The Savoy,* and *The Waldorf Astoria,* and also several famous hotels in Las Vegas and night clubs in Havana and around the world. People whose names I knew were mentioned as their stories expanded and became more detailed. Frank Sinatra, Dean

Martin, Johnny Mathis, Lena Horne, Milton Berle, Petula Clarke, Danny Kaye; the list went on, and on. They danced for President Richard Nixon and for President John Kennedy at his Birthday celebration in 1961. They toured the American West with Jerry Lewis and Liberace and they went to Hong Kong, Australia and Japan with Sammy Davies Jr. All their stories were told with a complete lack of egotism and huge amounts of pure enthusiasm.

Augie rarely sat down as he talked. He became so involved with his stories that he continually had to demonstrate a dance step or mime an event. All the time he was talking, he either walked around the room or stood still in a true dancers' pose and waved his arms about, completely immersed in his tale. His agility astounded me almost as much as his memory.

Margo was also totally fascinating to listen to. I loved her bubbly personality, spontaneous spasms of laughter and recollections of her life; from the very detailed start of her passion for dancing to the hilarious and sometimes scary situations she and her husband became involved with. I was mesmerized and fascinated with the entire account of their amazing career, but it was when Margo started talking about "*Roseland*" and "*The Palladium*" that realization dawned on me, and hit me like a flash of lightening.

This was the famous couple who had started it all - the Latin dance team whose performances at *The Palladium* in the early fifties started a cultural phenomenon in this country that has never been seen since.

I knew about the trend towards Latin bands in the late 1940's and early 1950's when, in an effort to erase the memories of years of sadness and grief after the war, peoples' tastes leaned towards the expressive passionate ballads and carefree dancing depicted in Latin music.

I remember my parents, when I was a small child in England, listening to the music of Tito Rodriguez, a man who sang romantic Latin songs on the radio, and years later I read about the popularity of dancing to Latin music in America, and how people went crazy to see couples dance in an uninhibited way that had never been seen before.

Certainly, there had been other great dancers at that time - *Palladium* legends who impacted the wildly exhilarating days of *Mambo Mania,* but

Augie and Margo Rodriguez were the ones who took the world of dance by storm. By incorporating modern dance and ballet into their own special Latin style, they turned the sedate pursuit of ballroom dancing completely upside down and changed it forever.

When it became clear to them that dancing was the only thing that mattered, that it was in their blood, Augie and Margo sacrificed all their waking moments to work, expanding and perfecting their skills. They became professional dancers in 1955, reaching heights that neither of them ever dreamed of.

From their very humble beginnings in Spanish Harlem and Brooklyn in New York City, they began dancing together in 1949 and by the middle of the 1950's they were on their way to stardom.

How privileged I had been to meet two people whose lives, it seemed to me, had been just like the characters that played the principal roles of *West Side Story, Grease* and *Saturday Night Fever* all rolled into one. The only difference was that this couple had lived it for real!

~~~~~~~~~~~

Augie and Margo have been hailed as Living Legends. The extraordinary artistry of their unique dance act has contributed far reaching effects to Latin Dance Styles in America and across the world, which exist to this day. If it is true what they say, that everyone has at least one story to tell, this amazing couple could stock an entire library.

CHAPTER ONE

"*Call Vegas and tell them to forget the actors.*" Said Gilles Ste-Croix, "*We have what we want.*"

They were a handsome couple. The man, slim and around five ten, had smiling dark golden eyes, and a tanned, fine-featured face. His head was balding, but his thinning "pepper and salt" hair curled gently on the back of his neck, and his agility and energetic demeanor belied his age.

His wife was a beauty. Short dark hair cut in a flattering bob, intense green eyes, and a slim, but strong-looking small body, which moved on the dance-floor with precise, fluid movement, and totally disciplined elegance and grace.

They were quite a find; something of a miracle, really - for both *Cirque du Soleil and* the couple. *Cirque* personnel had been seeking dancers like this for weeks, advertising, searching the web, asking around. Then one day, someone knew someone, who knew someone else, who knew . . . . . .

~~~~~~~~~~~

Several weeks went by, and they heard nothing. They were not surprised. After all, it had been a while since they had performed their dance act, and *Cirque du Soleil* had the reputation of searching the world until they found the best performers.

Augie and Margo had now slipped, albeit reluctantly, into another daily routine, described by Margo as, *"Tennis in the morning, then a snack, then television, an early dinner, then television, then bed. It's so boring,"* she said, laughing ruefully. *"Television, television, television: we watch it too much and we're not used to it!"* It was clear that both she and Augie were restless, but they had no idea where to funnel their energy.

One morning Margo was in the drug store, aimlessly wandering up and down the aisles, when suddenly the thought of the dance tapes in Montreal seized her mind. She and Augie had already given up on hearing anything, so it was unusual that her thoughts persisted. She wondered if the tapes had been seen yet and, if so, what the people at *Cirque du Soleil* had thought of them.

Musing on the length of time that had passed since she and Augie had mailed the tapes to Canada, where *Cirque* had their international headquarters, she began thinking of their dancing career.

For years they had been in great demand. From the start, celebrities had asked for them to perform in their shows - to open their acts. Would they *ever* know what *Cirque* had thought of the tapes they had sent?

The one from the *Ed Sullivan Show*, where he had announced them as the best dancers of the century, or the one where Steve Allen had put them on his television show being broadcast live from Miami, and had them dance on a platform of wood on the beach, inches away from the rolling waves and salt spray. Allen had no idea that a platform, five feet long, and thirty two-inches wide for their act, required a superhuman effort to perform on; but they did it anyway and brought the house down.

What, Margo wondered, had the choreographer at *Cirque* thought when she saw that performance? She would surely have known what a feat they had achieved. She and Augie had been damn good, Margo thought, couldn't they even get an acknowledgment that the tapes had arrived? After all, a quick phone call - a 'yes' or a 'no,' would only take a moment. Suddenly, she felt the fine hairs at the base of her scalp tingling, and a goose-bumpy shiver passed over her body.

Over the intercom in the store, a voice she had come to know almost as well as her own started to sing, and she had the strangest feeling the words were meant for her ears alone. *"It only, takes a moment..."* Sammy Davis crooned.

~~~~~~~~~~~

When she got home from the drug store, for some reason she didn't tell Augie. On reflection it had seemed a bit bizarre, and Margo is the kind of person whose feet are always firmly fixed on the ground; but the feelings stirred in her by the incident were very real - she couldn't get Sammy out of her mind.

Later that afternoon, the phone rang. It was Celine, the choreographer in Montreal, who helped select *Cirque* performers. She told Augie and Margo that their tapes were fabulous, that the one of their slow jazz/ blues routine was amazing.

Margo had laughed and said, *"Thank you so much, but you need to understand, we don't do that any more."* Years of spins and slides had taken their toll on Margo's knees, and the exacting muscle control, strength and timing required to dance the slow routine especially, made her flinch at the very thought of attempting it.

Celine was not deterred, she had been very impressed with everything she had seen, and was anxious that they should fly to Montreal for an audition, so that Gilles Ste-Croix, the Creative Director of *Cirque* should see them perform.

That night, their minds were in turmoil; excitement, disbelief, anxiety, delight, every emotion coursed through them. Though possibly the strongest feeling they had was one of satisfaction. Even if nothing came of this, the people at *Cirque* had loved their tapes, and Celine even went as far as to say she had never seen dancing like it before. It was a good feeling, a great feeling: to be recognized and complimented by such hard taskmasters as the people at *Cirque du Soleil*.

The next morning when Augie awoke, he remembered, for the first time in years, his dream. He was in a room filled with people he knew;

he saw his father, Augustin, and his older brother, Michael. Then Aurora, his mother appeared, and Sammy Davis Jr. and then he saw Max Hyman, the owner of the great *Palladium* where it had all begun: his and Margo's life together.

Everyone in his dream looked wonderful; young and happy and beautifully dressed. Sammy was right in the middle of the group, wearing one of his legendary snappy suits, with a huge smile on his face - the smile Augie had come to know so well. He looked directly into Augie's eyes and seemed to rise up a little, above the group of people. As he rose, still smiling, he lifted his arms, clenched his fists, and grinning from ear to ear he put both thumbs in the air and pointed them at Augie, moving them back and forth in a huge gesture of delight!

When Augie woke, his memories were beyond a dream, it had all seemed real: as though he had actually been with everyone the night before - before going to bed. Unlike Margo, Augie unloads his feelings immediately they occur, so he told Margo what had happened, and her usual calm demeanor showed some signs of emotional agitation. After hearing his story, she then told Augie about her experience in the drug store the day before. There was no doubt in their minds whatsoever. Sammy - or Sammy's spirit - had let them know he was still with them, and that he would be along for the ride, all the way.

"It only, takes a moment . . . To be loved a whole life long."

~~~~~~~~~~~

On the morning of March 28, 2005, the day after Easter Sunday, Augie and Margo Rodriguez prepared themselves both physically and mentally to appear and perform that night on the world famous stage of *Cirque du Soleil*.

They would be dancing in *Zumanity*, the extraordinarily successful show which is playing in the Hotel New York New York in Las Vegas. This show is very different from anything else they have performed in, but the main theme, which is that of passion, desire, and sensuality, is completely familiar to them, since those are the emotions they have consistently and brilliantly woven into, and portrayed, in their own brand of Latin dance style.

At rehearsals the day before, Augie and Margo had seen the entire show performed for the first time. They were incredibly impressed. Having seen many extremely talented dancers in their lives, they were amazed at the skilled and disciplined performers that the creators of *Zumanity* had pulled together from all over the world to perform in a show which the *Cirques du Soleil* producers themselves describe as "provocative and challenging".

The theme of the show is that of a human zoo, which is inhabited by people of many varieties. All shapes and sizes, colors and types, age and condition, they rejoice in their differences and the infinite variety of ways they can express their own sexuality. *Zumanity* is multi cultural, erotic and sensual; its acts are disciplined, but more theatrical than the acrobatic productions that *Cirque du Soleil* is usually noted for.

Risqué and quite uninhibited moments are interspersed with acts of agility, water-dance, contortion, unrestrained African dance and movement and raucous comedy, in a strong, bawdy European cabaret style, making the show much more hilarious than offensive.

At the full rehearsal, Augie and Margo had found the artists to be absolutely awe-inspiring. Their physical strength and timing were impeccable, their moves, flawless. They had to be, because those who performed the acrobatic feats did so, swimming underwater, climbing ropes and flying through the air with no safety net below them, and an audience in the closest possible proximity.

After performing their part, at the very end of the rehearsed show, Augie and Margo were deeply touched, Augie, to tears, when the other performers gave them a standing ovation. It was a reaction they had not expected, in view of their amazement over the talent of their fellow performers, and it not only delighted them, but gave them the right amount of encouragement to be happy about their decision to be in the show at all.

It had been a whirlwind agreement between them, with no time for reluctance or second thoughts. The producers of the show had been searching for months for the type of dancers they had in mind, but they were equally concerned about injuries during the performance.

Guy Laliberte, the founder of *Cirque,* had all but decided to hire actors to play the parts required. However, the lengthy investigation had turned up information on Augie and Margo Rodriguez, and they had been asked to send their resume and dance tapes to Canada, where *Cirque du Soleil* has its international headquarters, for consideration.

Augie and Margo had flown to Montreal only five weeks before Easter, but were a little disappointed when they arrived at the studios, to be told that the parts for which they were auditioning would very likely be taken on by professional actors. They didn't travel all that way, they said to each other, to just turn around and go home, and they are way too proud of their multitude of achievements to "call it a day." In a totally predictable way for them, feeling they had nothing to lose by showing their dancing ability and talent, and as a testament to their entire lives on the stage, they made a decision to pull out all the stops.

Five people watched the audition. Gilles Ste-Croix, Vice President of Creation and New project Development, three of his producers and Celine, the head choreographer. Celine introduced Augie and Margo to Ste-Croix, who turned to them and said, *"OK, show me what you can do."*

Afterwards, when they had danced the required *waltz,* and then shown what they could *really* do by following it up with a *tango* and a *mambo,* Gilles Ste-Croix turned to Celine, *"Call Vegas and tell them to forget the actors."* He said, *"We have what we want."*

~~~~~~~~~~

The three weeks of rehearsals in Montreal had been relentless and exacting. Every day they worked in the studio and then had to go to the gym to work out, but as professionals, Augie and Margo understood the necessity of getting into shape. It had been a while since they had performed on stage.

Cirque du Soleil is famous for the precision and perfection of its productions. The management team will accept nothing less, but in order to achieve the very best from the performers, they are provided with everything they need.

Augie and Margo were very impressed with the facilities and the excellent treatment they received, as well as the friendliness of everyone on staff. They felt themselves getting fitter and stronger each day, so by the time they arrived in Las Vegas, they were raring to go. It was fortunate they felt that way, because rehearsals in Vegas intensified as their first appearance on stage loomed ever nearer, in fact, it was to be only four days after arriving there.

On the day of their debut in *Zumanity*, Augie and Margo dressed at 11:30 A.M. and got ready to go for a late breakfast in a restaurant next to their hotel, a couple of blocks behind "*The Strip*". It was to be their last meal of the day. The next one would be around 1:00 A.M. the next morning, after the second show of the evening which began at 10:30 P.M., and ended at midnight. They had already slipped comfortably back into the routine of show business people, whose nights become days and mornings turn into nights,

Margo dressed in black pants and a white tee shirt, and put on her basic make-up, prior to having the obligatory *Cirque* make-up, required of all performers, expertly applied on top. She had also arranged her hair to her satisfaction, and while waiting for Augie to get his belongings together, inspect their newly-heeled and stretched dance shoes and prepare for his day, she relaxed in front of the television, feet up, in a pair of fluffy pink slippers, to watch the tennis tournament between Ferrarah and Sampras in the Nasdaq-100 Open at Daytona Beach. Tennis is her great love. She and Augie played every morning together before she injured her knee, about two months previously.

Augie spent half-an-hour going through a stack of letters which had just arrived from their home in Florida, where the mail had been piling up for almost a month. Despite the domestic scene and calm atmosphere, there was a feeling of anticipation in the air.

They had flown into Las Vegas only four days before, after the three weeks of intensive preparation in Montreal. Still jet-lagged, and physically and mentally drained from the continuing studio and gym requirements for the upcoming show, they were, nonetheless, clearly full of enthusiasm and excited about their debut that evening.

~~~~~~~~~~~

At the restaurant, Margo ate a very light breakfast; a bagel with cream cheese and a cup of coffee. She felt it would be enough to get her through the rest of the day, and she does not like dancing on a full stomach.

Augie, on the other hand, had a good appetite and wanted to keep his strength up for the final rehearsals before the show, which could go though the entire afternoon. He needed to keep his energy level high that day. Gilles Ste-Crois was in town and expected to be at the rehearsals before the show went on that night. He wanted to see for himself that his new dancers would end the show with the *pizzazz* that he was looking for.

Augie talked animatedly about the show all through breakfast, while managing to finish a full plate of eggs, bacon and hash-browns. He ate well - it was the amount of food and size of plate one only sees in Vegas! During the course of the meal, he and Margo discussed the fact that they wanted to arrive at the theater an hour before the rehearsals began, in order to speak with the costume and make-up designers. Margo had to remove a coat during their performance and she needed to get the sleeves altered, to help the coat slip off easily. She also wanted to confirm the arrangements for her hair and make-up.

The producers of the show had told her she looked too young for the part she will be playing. They want her to have graying hair - maybe they will even give her a gray wig - and they also want her to have subdued face make-up. "*Why do they want me subdued?*" Margo said later, on their way to the theater. "*I don't know how to do subdued. I've never been subdued*".

The Opening Act

They parked in the massive nine story *New York, New York Hotel* parking garage, and walked down a concrete ramp to a vast loading dock behind the building, where a private door into the backspace area was located. Immediately inside the door they were confronted by a gray, wooden sign, made to look like a board of old planks nailed together. Scrawled on the board in white paint were the words "Turn thy back on LUST", a humorous reminder of the nature of the show.

More such reminders appeared as they progressed towards the dressing rooms. A few steps on, a nude life-size rag doll hung wantonly over a chair, her limp neck hung over the arm and her hair, made from thick strands of red yarn, hung down and brushed the floor below. Later, hooked to a nail in the wall, a massive brassiere with cups the size of voluptuous melons hung by one strap, just waiting to be worn, and giving the impression that *Zumanity* was likely to be a downright unusual, if not very interesting show.

Augie laughed as he passed by the props, and recalled the clown acts in which they had been used the day before in rehearsals. He talked to Margo about some of the performers they had met. How friendly and welcoming they had been. It was clear from his voice he was starting to feel eager about the up-coming final rehearsal and seeing everyone again. His animation increased as he stepped up his pace to get to their dressing room quickly and start preparing for the show, Margo trotting behind him; cool, calm and collected.

~~~~~~~~~~~

Rooms reserved for the staff and performers, behind the theater in the Hotel New York, New York, are modern and very well equipped. Passageways leading to workshops and offices contained wheeled racks of costumes, ready to be transported to the dressing rooms, or to be altered. On the corridor walls, notice-boards announced rehearsal times for the week and the requirements for the day. There was a feeling of energetic professionalism in the air.

Along with the notice boards on the walls, a few paintings that related to the subject of the show, sensual but not crude, imparted an earthy, artistic style that oddly gave the impression that everyone *really* understood what *Zumanity* was all about. Also, strategically placed on the walls in the corridors and rooms, were several framed photographs of the dancers whom Augie and Margo were replacing. The printed message under their picture said "Farewell and we will miss you". It came over as a very genuinely good-natured thing for the staff and cast to do for them.

They were professional ballroom dancers who had come to *Zumanity* as stand-ins for a week, when a previous dancer in the spot was injured, but they had stayed on for five months while the producers decided exactly how they wanted to close the show.

It was felt that the show ended on a flat note, when the desire was that it should end on a high. The producers needed a couple of dancers with professional experience who could close the show with a spirited, sensual and exciting feeling: a feeling that would elevate and up-lift the audience, as they filed out of the theater inside the hotel, and re-entered the streets of Manhattan. The streets, as depicted by decorators and designers, in the vast interior of *the Hotel and Casino, New York New York*.

Back-stage, walking along the maze of corridors, Augie and Margo were just beginning to get familiar with the location of their dressing room. They passed by the wardrobe area, where personnel were busy in their rooms, pinning garments or working with sewing machines on costume alteration. Several technical members of staff, with headphones and wires like springs down their backs which came from a box clipped to their waistbands, were bustling in and out of various offices. The performers in the show had started to arrive and prepare for the rehearsal, which would begin at 2:00PM that day, and could possibly continue until around 5:00PM.

Sometimes, if the choreographer or general stage manager was not satisfied with one detail or another it would be rehearsed and perfected right up until make-up time. The first show that evening would be at 7:30 P.M. and the last one of the day would begin at 10:30 P.M., exactly the same as it is seven days a week.

Augie and Margo spent most of their time before the rehearsal in their dressing room, getting to know more of the staff and performers and sorting out their wardrobe requirements. They were joining a very large cast, and performing for a highly exacting organization, so the more they knew and learned the happier they would be.

~~~~~~~~~~~

Backstage and located near the dressing rooms and offices in the so-called green room, prior to final rehearsals it was just another day for everyone else in the show. Some of the performers had been in *Zumanity* for two years or more, and with fifty members in the show, most people as they arrived went straight to their dressing rooms. A few performers came from their homes less than an hour before rehearsals, and some came to eat, relax or have physical therapy before going on stage. One or two looked as though they had very little sleep the night before. Not everyone went to the green room, but for those who wanted to "chill out" or take a snooze, it was a perfect place to go.

A slim, very beautiful young girl with long chestnut hair, wearing dancers' woolen leg-warmers and a hooded jacket, was curled up like a cat on one of three overstuffed couches. Hugging a plush pillow, she was soundly asleep and completely oblivious to the noises in the room.

Lying on her back, on the floor, an extremely tall slim girl rested her head on a pillow. The lower half of her bent legs rested on a chair, and her long blond hair tied up in a loose knot on top of her head, spilled like golden ribbons onto the floor. She dozed mostly, but occasionally contributed a few comments to the different conversations drifting above her.

A bearded male small person, wearing grey sweats, also lay on the floor, but he lay on his side with one leg raised, his small foot resting on the seat of the couch above: barely reaching it.

Some people were eating take-out lunches; Chinese, Wendy's, salads, deli-style soups and sandwiches. Different aromas wafted about on the air, one dominating over another as foods were warmed up in a microwave oven, situated on a counter top against one wall. Next to the counter were a water cooler, a coffee maker and stacks of plastic cups.

Occasionally, musicians, performers and crew members just passed through the green room to check on some detail or another, or to work on one of the three computers provided for everyone. A man in his forties sat down on a couch and asked if it was OK if he turned on a wall-mounted TV, to watch a program about decorating houses - as he put it, *"Changing pits into palaces."* Everyone told him to go ahead, and a beautiful African American woman with a completely shaved head of white hair, one of the show's two singers, walked over and joined him on the couch to watch the show as well.

Within a few minutes she was distracted by a small group of female friends who came and told her what a stunningly beautiful daughter she had. Evidently the daughter had been visiting her mother and had been to see the show the night before. The singer agreed with everyone and thanked them for their compliments, adding that she was concerned about her daughter, as she was about to go and live in London on her own. She was worried that her daughter would have lots of boyfriends, fall in love over and over, sleep around, have heartache and go through all the experiences of meeting lovers on one's own terms. Then she laughed, realizing the irony that she herself was singing in a show that applauded all those very things.

CHAPTER TWO

As the time for rehearsing drew nearer, and people came and went, the green room became a kaleidoscope of interesting and unusual human beings.

Sitting in a chair across the room from the microwave, a tall, black, handsome, young man, with a very muscular body and a London accent, was telling his friend about his failed attempt at love with someone he had met in a place called *Male Erotica* the night before. *"He played hard to get for over an hour".* He said, *"And finally I said to him, 'You have to know you're in a gay bar. I really would like to get to know you better.' Well, he was friendly and chatty with me all night, and then when the bar closed we took a walk down The Strip."* The Londoner then lowered his voice and clearly went into some detail, ending loudly again on the few final words, *" . . . and then, after all that, he told me he was married and had to go back to his hotel!"*

The young friend, to whom the Londoner related his story, was lying back in a very expensive-looking massage chair. Also tall, muscular and handsome, but a Slavic-looking blonde with beautiful tanned skin, he had a look of complete euphoria on his face, while he fiddled with a remote control and made the chair do wonderful things to his back and shoulders. As he listened to the sad tale, his ayahs, aaaaah's, and sounds of sheer bliss, punctuated the details of the unrequited romance, and served to make the story appear a bit more interesting and seamy than it really was.

Another young man, an American, wearing denim jeans, a leather jacket and several earrings strode into the room and entered into their conversation. Laughing loudly at the Londoner's story, which he had probably heard similarly a hundred times before, he chipped in with a little jibe, *"It's different in the clubs in London, dear, married English gays are faaaah too polite to turn down an offer like that."* His comment was not intended to be unkind and was not taken that way. The other guys laughed and were pleased this third friend had joined in, but he didn't stay long to chat as he had a lot of preparations to make his transformation for the rehearsal.

To say the very least, he was striking in appearance. His white blonde hair was spiked and cut in a short Mohican style. He was tall, around six feet four inches, and his face had the chiseled, aesthetically beautiful look of a Greek statue. He removed his jacket as he strode across the room, and revealed a leather singlet. Every visible inch of his muscular upper body was tattooed.

At one point, everyone moved to make space for a young man heading across the room toward a closed door on the far side, which led to the backstage area. Yet another beautiful male, with a perfectly tanned muscular body, he wore the briefest pair of underwear imaginable, and was hopping quickly but rather awkwardly on one foot. Closer examination of his raised bent leg, revealed that the knee was liberally covered with long stainless steel needles, which wobbled as he moved. Acupuncture was obviously another service provided to the *Cirque du Soleil* performers.

Also teetering about rather awkwardly, only this time on 3 inches high heels, two extremely overweight sisters from Brazil came periodically out of their dressing room to greet friends as they arrived in the green room. Scantily dressed in short little silk robes, open almost to the waist, they revealed huge bouncing breasts, and thighs that should never have seen the light of day.

Their jet black hair was pulled back severely from their faces, which accentuated the large shiny cheeks, wobbling chins and tiny rosebud mouths in their half made up faces. They spoke in high pitched voices with strong Portuguese accents and punctuated every few words with loud, excited laughs. Delightfully friendly and disarming, they chatted and giggled to each person who passed them by, and gave the impression they were completely oblivious to the rather shockingly conspicuous appearance they made; as, it seemed, was everyone else in the room. Arriving a little late, just a half-hour before rehearsals, an exceptionally tall thin young man with a long, narrow face, bubbled hurriedly into the room and greeted everyone with a flamboyant kiss on the cheek. Reminiscent of a younger version of Ron Moody's Fagin in the 1968 movie "Oliver", everything about him seemed long and narrow.

He wore a large, floppy artists' beret over a mop of reddish-brown curly hair, and had a long pointed nose, a mustachioed upper lip, and a sharply tapering Renaissance-style beard. On his long narrow feet he wore pointed black shoes, and when he stood still, which was not often, his thin, lanky legs, clad in black tights seemed to be clamped together, while his toes pointed outwards in a ballet pose.

His appearance was more frail than muscular, and a feminine Spanish-accented voice added to his delicate air, but strangely enough his black sweat-shirt, black beret and beard, gave him a more masculine air than some of his muscular, more "beautiful" counterparts. He was a clearly a dancer. Seeing him on the street dressed as he was, in his "normal" attire, one could never imagine he belonged anywhere except on the stage, but in this eclectic group of interesting people he appeared completely at home and not particularly unusual.

The office of the general stage manager opened onto the green room. He appeared to spend most of the pre-rehearsal time on his computer, but every now and again he walked through the room to go backstage and check on details. A young Englishman, he was very friendly, very relaxed but completely professional; obviously popular and a much respected team member he was able to inspire the stage crew and performers alike.

At exactly ten minutes before 2:00 P.M. an announcement over the intercom let everyone know rehearsals were about to start. The choreographer walked through the green room and rallied the performers. It was clear from their response that everyone was extremely well disciplined, because they reacted to her immediately and made their way to the backstage area of the theater. Augie and Margo came from their dressing rooms looking relaxed and completely at home. They were 'on the road again' and looking forward to perfecting their performance before the first show of the evening.

~~~~~~~~~~

The final act of *Zumanity*, and the act leading up to it was the one being rehearsed. They were both part of the new ending, since the dance style and music had been completely altered to accommodate Augie and Margo, who would close the show. Because it was the finale, the entire cast of fifty was required on stage, and as Gilles Ste-Croix had come especially to see the rehearsals and work with the staff, everyone was "on their toes" and concentrating on doing their best.

The entire *Zumanity* set was custom made for the show, and specially designed to engage the audience in as much participation as possible. The main stage is circular, and protrudes into the theater for maximum audience participation. In the center and on either side of the stage, three sets of gilded steps go down to the main auditorium, to allow for even more interaction between the performers and the audience.

The center of the stage houses a brilliantly designed circular mobile section, which enables uninterrupted transformations of the set. Performers and props can either appear or disappear from the stage in an instant, or move in a circular direction, as if riding on a turntable.

Below the backdrops and connected to the circular stage, a platform about 12ft deep is large enough to hold the entire cast for the finale of the show, and high above that section, a metal "bridge" which can be raised and lowered, holds six members of the band. On either side of the bridge, a set of spiral steps coil down to the stage below. Two pianists and a violinist who perform on the main stage comprise the remaining band members.

The rehearsals began exactly on cue, everyone - performers, musicians and technical staff, had a job to do and they did it well. The choreographer and Gilles Ste-Croix, when they were not moving around and talking to individual performers or up on stage demonstrating what they wanted, sat in the back row of the first block of seats in front of the stage.

.... The Opening Act

The stage manager, an attractive young blonde woman, sat a few rows behind them, from which vantage point she could observe the entire set, and get a better impression of the complex lighting functions. She communicated with the general stage manager in a very soft voice, through a small microphone in front of her lips, which was connected to her head-phones; while he moved around in the auditorium area during the entire rehearsal with several other technicians, and directed the musicians, lighting and stage personnel.

At the beginning of their act, Augie and Margo are seated in the audience; a few rows back from the stage, and are to all intents and purposes supposed to be an ordinary couple seeing the show. They are selected from the audience by Joey Arias, the MC, who is known as "The Mistress of Seduction," an extremely likable humorously vulgar transsexual character, who comes down into the auditorium and asks them a few questions about themselves.

Drawing them into his risqué view of the world, he soon has them making unintentionally humorous comments which cause great hilarity in the audience. He persuades them at the end of the show to dance a waltz. They reluctantly agree, and nervously step up on the stage. A gentle waltz tune plays, and Augie and Margo, looking a little unsure, twirl around to the music while the audience claps encouragement.

As the dance comes to an end they kiss, thereby showing the now delighted audience that true romance and love can be long-lasting, and is available for everyone who cares to look for it. The crowd begins to call out and whistle as the kiss continues and begins to get a little heated, at which point the music changes from the slow waltz tune to a driving salsa sound.

With that, Augie tears off his jacket and throws it behind him, while Margo tosses her head back and slips out of her coat, stamps a foot, swivels her hips and faces Augie, and the two of them go into a hot routine which is intended to shock and delight the audience and cast alike. The cast all begin to move forward, in time to the infectious salsa music, and join Augie and Margo at the front of the stage, who then turn away from each other and face new partners, to show them how the dance is *really* done. Soon, everyone is dancing the salsa, and they all slowly move back to the rear of the stage to take their final bows.

As the rehearsal progressed, Augie and Margo needed to perfect a few new moves in their act, suggested by Gilles Ste-Croix. The act before theirs, known as the orgy scene, also had several changes in order to streamline the new ending of the show, so an extra hour of rehearsing was required. Everyone was told there would be a short pause, so they should rest backstage while they had the chance. Most people trooped back to the area of the green room, and others sat about in the theater to relax and close their eyes, while the people who would be affected, discussed their changes with the directors until they were ironed out. Half-an-hour later, a bell rang and they all began again.

~~~~~~~~~~

It was decided during the break that Margo's coat was too awkward to slip out of before the music changed, so a new dress was going to be designed for her when the *Cirque* costume designer came from Paris a couple of weeks hence, and the coat would no longer be worn. This change would streamline her movements in the transition required from the waltz tempo to the upbeat Latin music.

The scene before Augie and Margo's, was the culmination of the entire show, when most of the cast ended up sitting, standing or lying on the turntable in the center of the stage, while demonstrating their individual proclivities in an orgy-like portrayal as the tunable took them round and around. With the dance changes, the music, lighting and stage sets had also been re-worked, so the choreographer had everyone go through their routines several times until they became mechanical.

Over and over again, the music started up, the singers sang and the make-believe orgy participants regrouped on the turntable stage to display, inoffensively, their own particular versions of *per*versions. So despite the lighthearted image the scene projected, everyone was seriously working very hard to "get it right".

In one of the many rehearsals, when Joey had again delightedly whipped everyone into a frenzy of display with their various acts of love from the sexual smorgasbord, he leaped for the fourth or fifth time down into the auditorium to talk to Augie and Margo, and he mistakenly referred to Augie as *"Orgie"*. Everyone laughed, and a certain tension was broken.

When the hour was almost up, the technicians, musicians and performers had repeated their parts in the performance so many times that the lighting was right, the music was on cue and the dancers and singers were perfectly coordinated with everybody else. At that exact point, the choreographer was satisfied that everyone correctly knew the routine, so she called a halt to the rehearsal and announced they had two hours to relax before the show. A young male dancer leapt off the stage and hurriedly headed for the green room, muttering under his breath, *"We got it, we fucking finally got it!"*

~~~~~~~~~~~

It was ironic that one of the greatest acts of love during that rehearsal went unrehearsed and unnoticed.

Since it was required that Augie and Margo had to go up and down the steps from their place in the audience to the stage many times, it was imperceptible and not noticed at all, but although there are only three steps, they are quite steep, and every time Margo had to go *down*, Augie went first and put his hand out to help her.

During their act, each time she broke into her salsa routine, her movements had been creative and *perfect*. The mobility in her feet and the coordination of her hips and legs was unmatched by anyone else on stage. When she danced, it was clear Margo had not lost that special "something" she had captured long ago, when she had turned into motion what the music had always imparted to her.

She had never once complained about her injury from the tennis accident eight weeks previously, and she is stoic enough that she never would, but Augie knew that while walking *up* the steps was fine, walking down, over and over, would give her knee such punishment, that it could result in serious injury. He made sure each time they returned to their seats, that he went first, so he could put out his arm for Margo to lean on, as she very slowly descended the three steps to return to their seats in the auditorium.

An intuitive act of love, indeed, and just one of thousands that they had shown each other over the years, after all, they had been married since their early twenties.

The countless hours of training and dancing together had paid off. The unconscious understanding they each felt for their partner's stress or discomfort while performing had stayed with them, despite a thirty-year hiatus.

They had wowed audiences dancing together around the world. Their names had appeared in lights outside the famous *Roseland Ballroom* and *The Palladium* in Manhattan. They were friends with numerous famous artists, had danced for three Presidents and the Queen of England, and that night they were going to walk on stage in front of an audience and dance again.

During the two hours before their debut, as they put on their costumes and make-up and chatted to members of the crew and cast, their entire career, and images of numerous other debuts danced about in their minds. For over thirty years, they had *opened* shows, and nothing was going to stand in the way of their closing this one, for the world famous *Cirque du Soleil*. They were about to complete the circle.

Nothing was going to prevent them from re-living the wonderful, elated emotions they felt when performing together, and showing the artistry in dance that they, themselves, had so magically perfected. Not jet-lag, nervousness, tired limbs, or tennis injuries; and certainly not old age!

When they threw themselves into that wild *salsa,* in the final rehearsal that afternoon, *no one* would have known that Augie was 77 years old, and that two weeks from that day, Margo would turn 76!

CHAPTER THREE

A long time before Jazz was born in North America, Latin music was there. It came through an inter-mingling of cultures that evolved gradually between the indigenous people, the invading Europeans and African slaves. It also came into the country across the borders and through the ports of entry into the cities of Los Angeles, New Orleans and New York.

In the years before 1803 under the rule, at different times, of both the French and the Spanish, New Orleans had enjoyed a considerable cultural and commercial interchange with many Latin American cities, like San Juan, Caracas, Santo Domingo, Havana and Veracruz.

With the people from those regions came different 'strands' of Latin music. For example, the origins of the *son* and *merengue* are traceable back to the Dominican Republic. From Argentina came the *tango,* from Spain the *flamenco* and Puerto Rico gave birth to the *bomba* and *plena*.

Creoles from the Canary Islands, who immigrated to Cuba in the eighteenth and nineteenth centuries and intermarried with the African slaves, were at the center of the development of Afro-Cuban music, which was expressed through the *rumba*. In African music, the drum is the instrument that imitates the pulse of life and it remains a critical instrument in Afro-Cuban music. Interestingly, because the Spanish allowed slaves to have their drums and music, the purity of it remained intact; whereas American slave owners who were largely European

Christians, considered the music 'savage' and banned it. They did, however, allow the slaves to sing religious Christian songs, which resulted in the *negro spiritual* and later the *blues*, both of which intermingled with jazz and eventually developed their own very special identities.

The influence of Spanish music styles in Mexico, like the *corrido*, were coming into the country along the border between Mexico and the American Southwest at the beginning of the 1900's, and by the middle of that century, Los Angeles, with its many Mexican immigrants, had become captivated by the *mambo*. This was as a result of Band Leaders like Perez Prado coming from Mexico City and taking Los Angeles by storm with his music.

New York, as a major port of entry into the United States, welcomed thousands of immigrants from all over Europe, but at the turn of the twentieth century the city experienced a large influx of people from the Caribbean islands of Puerto Rico and Cuba. Many of these immigrants came to work in factories, or as cigar workers, and others were political activists and intellectuals who came as a result of America acquiring the islands after its war with Spain.

Many immigrants were escaping from oppressive regimes, some came to participate in the building of 'the new world' but all of them were looking for a way to improve their lives, forsaking family, friends and the land of their birth, in order to have a shot at *The American Dream*.

~~~~~~~~~~~

One such immigrant was Augustin Rodriguez, who lived in the province of Lugo in the Galicia region of Spain. In 1898, at the age of 16, he left his town of Quirogo, to join the Spanish Merchant Marines. He embarked on a career which took him across the world to the islands of the Caribbean, where he worked his way around the islands, occasionally staying on land to try different kinds of work. When the severe flu epidemic, which had killed millions of people around the world, came to Cuba, he was working there cutting sugar cane. The rampant sickness took hold in the island, so Augustin decided to leave and return to the Merchant Marine.

One of his ports of call was Santo Domingo in the Dominican Republic, and it was there that he met his future wife Aurora. The first time he saw her, he fell in love, but she was very young, just 13 years of age, and although in those days young women married very young, good sense told him to wait.

No doubt Augustin met many other beautiful young girls while he sailed around the islands from one port to another, but the image of Aurora was imprinted on his mind, and one year later when he was 20 years old, love won the battle over good sense, and he went back to Santo Domingo to marry her.

~~~~~~~~~~~

Augustin and Aurora moved to the United States of America immediately after their wedding, to begin their lives together. They chose to live in New York City and found an apartment in Manhattan, close to the Canal St. area, where several large shipping companies were located and where Augustin could find work.

He joined the Clyde Mallory Line as a Longshoreman, which had ships traveling to and from the West Indies, bringing fruit and sugar back to America. He worked for that company for 9 years, leaving home early in the morning and returning late at night, sometimes covered in black dust from loading coal into the holds of the ships which were taking it to the islands. He was determined to make a good life for himself and his new wife, and was not afraid to work hard in order to achieve it.

For Aurora though, life was proving to be very difficult. Living in a huge, strange city, with no family nearby, Aurora found it hard to settle down. Barely out of childhood herself, she became restless and lonely during the long days, missing terribly her family in Santo Domingo. Augustin tried to understand his wife's dilemma.

He was beginning to make a good living with the shipping line, so in order to make Aurora happy they moved into different apartments in new areas to, hopefully, find some people she could relate to. Augustin believed that this would give his wife the security she had felt in the islands, but try as he might, nothing seemed to work to make her satisfied.

When she became pregnant with their first child, at the age of 16, Aurora persuaded Augustin to let her return home to be with her mother and sisters when she was ready to give birth. She traveled alone to the Dominican Republic, but as he was an employee of the shipping line, Augustin was able to secure his wife a first class passage so she could travel in comfort. On December 15th 1926, Augustin and Aurora had their first child, who they named Michael.

When Aurora and Michael returned home to New York, Augustin hoped that the new baby would settle his wife down and help to bring about her contentment, but sadly for them all, she was constantly restless. They moved several times with Michael, and by Dec.1929, when they were living on Bleeker Street, Aurora gave birth to their youngest and last child, Anthony.

There were now three boys in the family. A middle son was born shortly after they moved into the Bleeker Street apartment, in 1928. He was named after his father, Augustin Rodriguez Junior, but from the very start he was always known as Augie.

~~~~~~~~~

Augie Rodriguez was a good boy who loved his brothers and did well in school. He adored his father, and to this day he remembers the many stories he was told about his father's childhood. He wanted to learn all about his paternal grandparents and the country of his ancestors, and he never tired of listening to the stories. He clearly remembers to this day what his father told him about all the different places he had visited, and he was fascinated to hear of the many cultures, languages and music of the West Indies, the Caribbean and Spain.

In 1961, when he was sixty five years old, Augie's father retired and returned to Spain, to see again the town of his birth. He decided to stay there, and did so until the day he died peacefully in his sleep, at the age of 83 years old.

Augustin deeply loved his sons. He was a good father who taught them well, spending a great deal of time with them when he was at home. He encouraged them to believe in themselves and supported their hard work and attendance in school. He tried hard to understand Aurora's dilemma, but his job was very important in enabling him to provide for his family, so in order to keep his wife happy he was willing to accede to her whims and wishes when she became restless, and let her move them all from one apartment and one neighborhood to another. Despite all his efforts to stimulate a balanced and stable environment for his children, the fact was that they were destined to have a much disrupted life and education.

~~~~~~~~~~~

In 1933, when Augie was five years old, his mother Aurora finally seriously snapped, and decided she wanted to take her children back to Santo Domingo, where she could be with her mother and sisters and the extended family she missed so much. At that time Michael, the oldest boy, was seven and Anthony, the youngest, was four.

Much against his will, and hoping that this was another phase that would pass, Augustin obtained tickets for his family's passage on the 429 ft passenger steamer *El Coamo*, and the little group of four set sail for the Dominican Republic.

Augie's memories of their first trip to Santo Domingo are clear. He remembers the excitement of boarding the ship and waving goodbye to his father between the railings of the top deck. He remembers that they all traveled first class in one cabin and that the food on the ship was wonderful. He recalls that everyone was summoned to meals in the dining room by a seaman who rang a loud bell.

The trip took about five days, and Aurora was very sick the whole time and had to stay in her cabin. This freed the boys up to explore the ship on their own, and they did so with great excitement. Wildly running and hollering all around the cabin areas and up and down the stairs to the different decks, they were excited and thrilled with the new adventure they had embarked upon.

Since their Mother was so sea-sick, most of their meals were eaten in the cabin in her presence, but on occasion they were allowed into the dining room to eat on their own. Their demeanor changed markedly when they sat down with all the other passengers to eat.

Essentially, they were very shy boys, and were somewhat in awe of the people sitting down at their tables. All dressed in fine clothing, they took their time over the elegant courses of fine food the waiters brought to them.

Augie remembers being fascinated by everyone on the ship. The passengers, who were looking forward to visiting friends and families, some from the island of Dominica and some from places he had never heard of, and the crew of the ship who all had jobs to do, taking care of the passengers or helping to make sure the ship was in good working order.

He spent many hours in the cabin with his brothers, watching everyone pass by, peering through ventilation slats that were situated above the top bunk. He was excited at the prospect of meeting his grandmother for the first time, but would equally have been very happy to just stay in that strange but fascinating world afloat, on the *El Coamo*.

~~~~~~~~~~~

When they finally docked in the town of Puerto Plata, Augie's grandmother, Emelinda De la Cruz, was there to meet them. She was thrilled to see her daughter again and to meet her second and third grand-sons. She arranged for Aurora and Michael to bring all their bags in a car, while she, Augie and Anthony walked home so she could show off her grandsons to all her friends.

Augie's strongest memory of that first day in Santo Domingo is of his grandmother, striding down the streets of the town towards her home on the outskirts, and calling out to people who were sitting on their doorsteps in the hot sun, *"Look, look,"* she cried, *"These are my grandsons! Aurora's children! Are they not beautiful?"* He felt very important and very much loved.

CHAPTER FOUR

The family stayed with Emelinda and Federico De la Cruz, Aurora's parents, and became very settled with their extended family of aunts and cousins. Augie remembers very little detail about that time, but he recalls what a strong woman his grandmother was, and how devout in her religious beliefs.

Once, when he caught Malaria and on another occasion, Typhoid Fever, while he was going in and out of delirium his grandmother always seemed to be there by his bed, with his mother and Aunt Julia, praying over him and wiping his forehead with cool absorbent pads.

As Augie recovered, Emelinda sat with him and told him stories of her native Santo Domingo, saying that at one time God had forsaken the island, when the Spanish came and killed many of its local inhabitants. Crucifixes were all over the house, and Emelinda prayed to them regularly.

She and his Aunt Julia, Augie recalled, were also extremely superstitious; believing that spirits, both good and evil were all around them. If his grandmother had a strange dream at night, or a funny feeling came over her, she would say that the spirits had 'touched her feet.'

All this supernatural belief became quite vivid for the young impressionable boys, but Augie shared a bed with his big brother, Michael, surrounded by a mosquito net, and most of the time his imagination allowed him to sleep soundly through the night. Sometimes, however, he woke. Scared and shaking he would get out of bed and walk around the house looking for the spirits, and wondering why they wanted to touch his feet.

Eventually Augustin, working back in The United States and missing them all very much, sent word that he wanted his wife and children home again.

They returned to New York almost a year after their departure, and despite the fact that Aurora complained about the cold weather and her missing relatives, she made a brave attempt again to settle down and raise her children in America.

∼∼∼∼∼∼∼∼∼∼

Augie and his brothers went to school and the family resumed their life together in the city, but when Augie was eight, three years later, Aurora, started becoming increasingly restless, so the family moved again. This time it was to an apartment on Van Dam Street in Brooklyn.

Augustin was now employed with the Standard Oil Company, and was back in the Merchant Marine on board ships again, working as a Third Officer. Augie clearly remembered an evening when his father came home covered from head to toe in black soot and was visibly shaken. He had been working on a cargo ship, and was down below in the engine room while engineers were stoking up the boiler to get the engines powered up and ready for departure.

After a while it became unbearably hot, so Augustin mounted the stairs to the above deck for some fresh air. He had just opened a door and stepped outside on deck, when there was an enormous explosion below. The boiler had overheated and the increased internal pressure caused it to literally blow up. Several fellow seamen were killed in the blast, and a much shaken Augustin came home feeling that an enormously powerful guiding hand had taken care of him that day.

∼∼∼∼∼∼∼∼∼∼

Perhaps, now her husband was going back to the islands, Aurora saw an opportunity to spend more time in the Dominican Republic and less in America, so after a constant flow, over a three-year period, of telling Augustin how dissatisfied and unhappy she was, she finally wore him down until he relented.

He agreed again to her leaving their home in New York; except that this time he understood she wanted to stay permanently, and to take the children, some furniture and some personal possessions with her.

The memory of watching his father packing up boxes and crates, and wrapping protective covers around the few items of furniture which had been selected for shipment, still saddens Augie. It seemed to him that his mother had finally won the battle to leave America for good.

Augustin assured his wife that he would send money on a regular basis, so they could live independently of her family. He told them he would come and visit as often as possible, and Aurora too, promised she would travel back and forth to New York so the boys could see their father and their friends. All this helped the parting on the quay-side when the final departure came, and the three little boys with their mother walked up the gang-plank onto the passenger steamer *San Jacinto*.

~~~~~~~~~~

This time, when they arrived in Puerto Plata, Aurora and the three boys stayed in a boarding house, close to where her parents lived. Everyone began to settle down in their new surroundings. It was a beautiful area. The town, situated on the north coast of the island, was surrounded by golden, tropical beaches and lush countryside. To the south of the town, the green and magnificent Isabel de Torres Mountain could be seen rising 800 meters into the blue sky. It was a place for the boys to grow up and be happy, with grandparents, aunts, uncles and cousins all around to watch out and care for them.

The boys went to school, and got used to being called *"Americana"* and *"Blancito" (white boy)*. It was all very good natured name-calling and not intended to hurt. People would occasionally call out to them in the street, *"Hey, Baseball Player",* because of the knee-length pants they wore, called knickers, just like the ones worn by baseball players in America. Bringing them such admiring attention, their clothing was worn proudly, almost like a badge of honor.

They enjoyed being noticed as Americans, but equally felt they belonged in the Dominican Republic, in the place where their mother had been born. If anything, the language was more familiar to them than English. They also greatly enjoyed the music of the island, which they learned from their grandmother and great-grandmother, who knew many local folk songs. Augie still remembers those songs, with their stories to tell, and their wonderful rhythms.

~~~~~~~~~~~

He also remembers when a large number of German Jewish refugees came on ships to Santo Domingo in 1938. The President and Dictator, Rafael Trujillo, welcomed them to his country, and gave them each a tiny plot of land in a place called Sosua in the region of Puerto Plata. In fact, Santo Domingo was the only nation to accept Jews at that time, and it became an important sanctuary for them during the Second World War.

It was said that Trujillo favored their arrival as a means of bringing educated Europeans to the island, which he anticipated would stimulate the economy. It was also said that he hoped, as the Jewish people intermarried with the native Dominicans, three-quarters of which were of African European heritage, that the skin-tone of the indigenous people would lighten.

He was proved to be correct in both cases, and the beautiful, prosperous village of Sosua, exists in the Dominican Republic to this day, visited by many tourists and acting as a banner for the far-sightedness of President Trujillo. He did not prove to make many other humanitarian decisions, however, in his life as President of the island. He became very unpopular in later years, and was assassinated by his own people in 1961, after several unsuccessful prior attempts.

~~~~~~~~~~~

Sosua was not far from Augie's home, and he remembers often walking there with his brothers. There was a fence around the settlement given to the Jewish people. They had arrived in the country with very little, if anything, but on every tiny plot of land allocated to each family, they had built makeshift housing of wood, metal and palm leaves - anything they could find in the countryside to provide a form of shelter.

The boys went to look through the fence out of curiosity, but when they were spotted one day by a refugee, he was equally fascinated by them. Three light-skinned children, staring wide-eyed through the fence!

The fact that the children spoke English compounded the conundrum. When the Jewish man discovered that the boys had arrived in the island from America, he offered them a home in his compound with the other refugees.

Augie thanked him, and explained that their mother was on the island with them and all her family and that they lived in a nice home; but he always remembered how kind the Jewish man had been in thinking they needed to be rescued!

~~~~~~~~~~

After a month in the boarding house, Aurora started to look for a place of her own, for herself and the boys to live. She found a small house with two acres of land, where she could grow vegetables for the family and enough left over to sell in the local market. Augie remembers how she planted rows and rows of onions with his grandmother and great-grandmother helping her; in the cool early morning, bending over the tilled soil and planting the seedlings.

The boys missed their father very much, but they had lots of love and attention from their mother's family. Many times in the evenings they would all eat supper together, sitting outside afterwards around the doorstep, to cool off while the hot days drew to a close. For Augie, one of these evenings stands out in his memory as being the first time he became really aware of his skills as a dancer.

The Opening Act

~~~~~~~~~~~

As on many other occasions after the evening meal, everyone sat outside to chat about the day's happenings and to feel the refreshing air, which came quickly when darkness fell and replaced the heat of the sun.

Augie's mother was talking intensely about something, as adults do, with his grandparents, aunts and uncles while the boys ran about with their cousins, playing around the yard and keeping themselves entertained.

Augie was twelve years old at the time. He remembers sensing that he no longer felt comfortable trying to fit into the younger children's games, which seemed stupid and boring. Sitting with his mother, on the other hand, didn't appeal to him at all. Neither ready nor old enough to get involved in the adults' conversation, he sought out the company of his older brother Michael, who often came up with some good schemes to keep occupied.

The two boys, hands in pockets, started to wander away from the family, who were still grouped around the house and engrossed in their conversation. Augie waited to see if his brother would figure out something to hold their attention, but kicking stones off the pathway to see who could kick the furthest, seemed to be the only activity available.

The problem was that it was almost dark, and in the twilight it was getting harder and harder to see where the stones landed; so as they chased after them, the adults' voices and shrieks of laughter from the children faded into the distance. When they realized how quiet it had become, they stopped, looked around and realized they had arrived at a dusty, narrow, back-road which led into town.

Something interesting at last! They thought a little exploration of the area might turn up all sorts of new discoveries, so deciding to take a chance they wouldn't be missed, their enterprising and adventurous spirits kicked into high gear, and they sprinted quickly away from familiar territory. Michael was an excellent runner, and Augie had always been athletic, so in a few short minutes they were close to town, and it was only a matter of time until they heard the music.

It came to them on the night air. Not drifting gently, but thumping with a rhythmic, intoxicating beat. It was not loud, but sounded close enough for the two boys to be able to find it, so eyeing each other, and without saying a word, they started running faster, down the still hot, dusty, palm tree-lined road, towards the sound that, arguably, set the entire course of Augie's life.

~~~~~~~~~~

As the boys drew closer to the outskirts of town the night grew darker and the music grew louder. It was not long before they traced the source of the music to a "cafe-bar," with a group of people outside. Barely visible in the shadows, they were illuminated only by a dim light emanating through the open door of the bar. Four men were playing instruments and others were sitting or standing around, watching a few dancers step and swing in time to the music.

The boys were fascinated by the scene. They were a bit shy and, in any case, were not supposed to be there, so they hid on the opposite side of the street and peeked around a corner to watch the activity.

A young man beat out a complicated rhythm on a set of bongo drums, which were gripped firmly between his knees and resting on the stool upon which he sat. He appeared oblivious to everyone around him. His dark-skinned face, eyes closed, could easily be seen in the shadowy light, glistening brightly with perspiration, his expression, completely blank. Transported, it seemed, to another world by the mesmerizing quality of his repetitive, hypnotic beat on the drums.

A second young man, shaking maracas, counter pointed the rhythm, and nodded his head in time; while an additional beat was played by a toothless, very old man, tapping with a stick on what appeared to be a hollowed-out gourd.

The fourth musician, small, plump and middle-aged, played the melody of the song with an instrument which looked a bit like a small guitar. As he played, he strutted around on his short legs between the other musicians, bowing his head toward them with the music, a wide smile on his mustachioed face.

Sitting on a stool while she watched the dancers, a very large woman clapped encouragement with the rest of the watching group, as they stood around tapping their feet to the music. The excitement mounted as the dancers spun around, and it soon became a bit like a dance competition where, at the end of each piece, everyone laughed and called out to the perceived best dancer, *"You buy the drinks!"*

The boys were not strangers to music or dancing. They had seen their aunts and mother swaying to a *tango* or *merengue*, and they knew a lot of the local music off by heart, but Augie was mesmerized. He did not know whether it was his fascination with the movement of the dancers or the beat of the music, but as he watched and listened he felt his feet and hips moving with the influence of the sound. Before long, he was lost in the rhythm, and gaining confidence he moved a little closer to the circle of dancers until, without even realizing, he found himself dancing just outside the group.

At one point he looked up and was startled to see the large woman on the stool watching him. Smiling broadly, she beckoned him to join the dancers, and to his surprise, without a second thought, Augie joined in. He must have become so lost in the music and his own interpretation of movement, that when the words *"Good moves, Americana"* broke through to his consciousness, he realized that everyone was clapping and shouting for him, and that he was now dancing alone in the center of the circle.

He began to feel proud of himself, and the cheers brought him confidence. He danced on, and as he danced he felt a soaring feeling of self-assurance that he had never experienced before. He wanted to keep on dancing when the music finally stopped, but flushed and happy, at the end of the number he realized that everyone in the group was calling to <u>him</u>, *"You buy the drinks!"* Suddenly, he felt twelve years old again.

The large lady came over to rescue him, still laughing and applauding his performance. She swept him up into her arms and took him back to her stool, where she sat down, placed him on her lap and nestled his head into her ample bosom.

It had been quite a night for Augie; first dancing with a group of adults and then being cuddled into a strange woman's cleavage. A lot of unfamiliar and confusing feelings were beginning to overwhelm him. He wasn't sure how to handle them all at once, but he *was* able to identify the strongest one. Above everything else, he knew he was very happy.

He finally understood why the spirits that haunted his dreams at night had wanted to touch his feet. He had discovered something inside that was his alone. A skill that was an intrinsic part of himself, that no one could ever take away, and he could hone and perfect it, till one day, he would be the best in the world.

CHAPTER FIVE

They had been living in Santo Domingo for two years, when Augustin came over to visit his family, and begged Aurora and the boys to go back with him to The States. It was clear that he missed them all so much; he wanted everyone back home again with him.

Augie was happy at the prospect of going home with his father, and his brothers were also pleased to be returning to America, but Aurora was uncertain. She agreed to go, but nobody could predict how long it would last.

They returned to Brooklyn, and tried to get back to their life as it had been before, but the boys were now thoroughly unsettled, and quickly came to regard their father as the only stable parent they had. It was just a matter of time, they knew, before their mother would be unhappy again, living in America.

Aurora left her husband and children again when Augie was 14, and went back again to her family in Santo Domingo. This time, the boys stayed with their father. They were all clearly distraught to lose their mother, but Augustin was determined to give them all the best opportunities he could, by maintaining their equilibrium, sending them to American schools and keeping them in one familiar home.

Losing their mother had an affect on all the boys. As many children do, they probably blamed themselves for her departure. Augie started sleepwalking again, obviously emotionally affected by Aurora's loss, and the constant turmoil around him. Likewise, his brothers were affected by the past disruption of their young lives, and found themselves getting into trouble more than once, when they tested the limits of their father's patience.

When Augie was fifteen and a half and attending New Utrecht High School, he got himself a part-time job in a local shipyard. The work was menial, but he really enjoyed his pay-check at the end of the week, so six months after starting the job, he began thinking about quitting school and earning some real money.

His older brother Michael's best friend, Pete, egged him on. Pete was already in the Merchant Marine, and he convinced Augie that it was better to be a seaman with a regular wage, than to stay in school and graduate before working full-time.

The shipping company was the *United Fruit Company*, and the *"Pomona Victory"* was the name of Augie's first ship. He was taken on as a Mess Boy, which meant that he worked in the ship's galley and fed the crew.

On his first trip, the ship had barely left the dock when he noticed the engines had stopped running. He ran up to the top deck, and the first thing he saw was the *Statue of Liberty*. They had stopped at Ellis Island.

A shipmate explained they were there to pick up German prisoners of war, and that they were taking the prisoners back to Europe where they would all be set free.

The ship was bound for Le Havre in France, and it was there that the prisoners would be allowed to leave. At the start of the voyage, they were all restricted to one area of the ship, and one of Augie's jobs was to bring food to them. He became quite friendly with several prisoners, and found them eager to talk to him, some of them explaining they had wanted no part in the War, but had no choice but to do what they were ordered. They all seemed relieved that it was now all over and that they were on their way home.

After a couple of days at sea, the prisoners were allocated jobs around the ship, and some of them were sent down to the galley where Augie worked.

Remembering how he had met the German Jews in Santo Domingo, and how kind they had been to him, Augie was more than willing to be pleasant towards these German prisoners. He became especially friendly with one man, who talked a lot about his home town and his family in Germany and was very excited to be finally going home. He gave Augie his address, and invited him to visit if he ever came to Germany.

When the ship docked in Le Havre, Augie waved goodbye to his new friend and watched him join in the long line of German prisoners, hurrying down the gang-plank to freedom, falling over each other in their excitement to be on land in Europe. Suddenly, as the deliriously happy band of men stepped onto the dock, a group of French military officers stepped up and barked orders at them to stand in line.

The crew of Augie's ship watched the process from the decks of the ship, and were stunned to see that the men were made to stand absolutely still for two hours in the burning sun. Eventually, they were allowed to sit cross-legged on the dock. Again, they were not allowed to move for several hours until eventually the French officers had them peel off into groups.

Word filtered down to Augie eventually through the ranks of seamen that the prisoners would actually not be going home for a very long time. They would be put to work for at least two years, all over France, repairing all the damage that the Nazis had done during the War.

~~~~~~~~~~~

Augustin was making a good living at this point in their lives, and he did his best to keep the boys on the straight and narrow. When they became teenagers, Augie spent a lot of time with groups of youths from his neighborhood but, unlike his brothers, he does not remember really getting into too much hot water.

When he entered his teens, Augie was still sleepwalking; a manifestation of a still emotionally insecure young man. One night he got out of bed and walked out of the house and into the street. His frightened and worried father found him early the next morning, huddled under the stoop outside the front door; still sound asleep.

After that incident, Augustin began tying a string around his son's ankle and securing it to the bedpost, to stop Augie wandering out into the street and getting knocked down by a car.

Just before working full-time at the age of sixteen, Augie remembers bringing a girl back to his home when his father was still at work. He learned years later that his father had entered the house quietly, and immediately realized that Augie was in his room with a young woman when he heard their soft voices.

Augustin went into the living room and started banging things around to give notice that he had arrived home. He waited to see what his son was going to do, probably with a smile on his face.

The only way out of the apartment and into the street was through the front door, which was beyond the living room. There was a back door in the kitchen that led outside to a small yard, but the yard was surrounded by a very high fence which was impossible to climb.

Augustin had not counted on the acrobatic ability of his son! When Augie realized that his father had returned home, he was so frightened of being discovered that he took his girl-friend and crept with her into the kitchen and out into the back yard. Quite a testament to the tight rein that Augustin kept on his sons!

Once outside, Augie took his girl to the high fence and bent down so she could climb on his shoulders, at which point he vaulted her up, and over into the street on the other side. The only problem was that the poor girl landed with a resounding crash into an area where all the trash cans for the buildings were located!

Augie innocently went back into the home to seek out his father, who was never able to figure out how the young lady did her disappearing act, until his son told him very many years later.

~~~~~~~~~~

Augie remained in the Merchant Marine for over two years, until he was eighteen and a half. By then, he had reached a point where he regretted not having graduated from school and getting his diploma, so he decided to go home and finish that part of his education. It took him a year to complete, but at the end of the studies, diploma in hand, he still did not really know what he wanted to do with the rest of his life.

He had always liked dancing, and at that time he started going about the neighborhood with two old acquaintances, Tommy Diaz and 'Cuban' Pete, who spent most of their leisure time in a ballroom at the *Manhattan Center* on West 34th Street, where all the great dance orchestras played.

Dancing was "the thing" in those days. The ballroom at the *Manhattan Center* held between 1,500 and 2,000 dancers, and people of all ages from all walks of life went there. Ballroom dancing, then, was the most popular form of entertainment.

Hotels and restaurants all over Europe often held weekly "Tea Dances," where people went in the afternoon to drink tea, listen to live musicians and take a few turns around a small dance-floor. It might be just a single violinist providing the music, or a trio, or in some cases an entire orchestra; it didn't matter, just as long as there was space available for dancing!

America was no different, and in New York, in addition to the afternoon tea dances, clubs with live music and dancing through the evening, sometimes until the early hours of the next morning, sprang up all over the city, especially in and around Harlem where many Latin immigrants lived.

Traditional dance halls around New York, and other American cities, were enormously popular amongst servicemen in the 1940's. They were places to go and relax while on leave. Places to, maybe, find a pretty girl who could help them to forget for a while the wretchedness of a war-torn Europe, and months, maybe years, of spending most of their days in male-dominated surroundings.

To help facilitate the finding of such a partner, dance hall owners hired young women to supplement the supply of females willing to dance in their establishments. They were named "Dime-a-Dance" girls. The servicemen, or any other single man for that matter, paid a dime for a dance, and in those days of high unemployment, young women found it a fun way to make a little pocket money.

Dancing *had* been a relatively sedate and formal activity up until the end of the War, but during the Depression it became an important means of escaping the misery of the times. No longer were the upper classes only, enjoying the pastime. It was everyone, from all walks of life and ethnicity. The gentle, staid and rather dull form of dancing still lived on, but it was about to be changed forever, and it was all going to happen in New York.

On one Sunday a month, the *Manhattan Center* organizers started introducing a new and increasingly more popular type of music into their ballroom. It was presented by Latin orchestras who often played extravagantly "hot" rhythms, and had vocalists who sang demonstrative, emotional songs.

The Latin orchestras held in high regard at that time, were led by musicians like Marcellino Guerra, Noro Morales and Jose Curbelo, and a little later by Tito Puente and Tito Rodriguez, but the most popular New York-style Latin orchestra by far, was led by a Cuban man named Frank Grillo, though Machito is the name he was always known by.

He had come to New York in 1937 as a vocalist in a band called *La Estrella Habanera*, but three years after arriving in America he formed his own orchestra which he named the *Afro-Cubans*. Machito's music embodied the essence of the mambo, but it also incorporated Latin jazz and had a strong hypnotic style about it, which captivated the dancers at the ballroom; especially the young dancers, who were always looking for something new and exciting.

~~~~~~~~~~

Augie had been enthusiastic about dancing since his experience in Santo Domingo. He had recently become an expert at the *lindy hop*, which was a new dance played by the conventional dance orchestras, but when Latin orchestras came to the *Manhattan Center* to play, those were the ones he went to listen to.

He found himself going back every spare moment he had, not to dance, but to watch and to listen. Some of the sounds were already in his soul, born there in his childhood, but Machito was playing a new and exciting dance called the *mambo*. It swiftly became the latest craze, and Augie was hooked. He was mesmerized by the music and by a young Puerto Rican dancer named Joe Vega.

Joe had once been a prize-fighter. He was six foot two inches tall, had a lean, muscular body and he danced the *mambo* like a pure athlete. Eventually he became a dance instructor. His style was smooth, but there was an earthy quality to it, and Augie had a feeling that more than anything else in his life, he wanted to be able to dance the same way.

He went home in the evening to practice in front of a mirror the moves he had seen that afternoon, but the problem was that one day a month just wasn't enough. Looking around the city for other places that played Latin music, he heard from a friend that *The Palladium* on 53rd Street and Broadway had a Latin orchestra playing four nights a week.

The format at *The Palladium* was to have an American orchestra playing *waltzes, fox trots* and *tangos* for the first half of the evening, and another band playing Latin music, American style, for the second half. That band was led by Ray Armando, whose musicians were mainly Americans. They played the Latin-based music well, but without the soul that it deserved.

~~~~~~~~~~~

During his eighteenth year, Augie's strongest inclinations and desires were directed toward dancing. He was beginning to feel "driven" and went four nights a week to *The Palladium*, where he couldn't get enough of the music and the new *mambo* dance, which was becoming more and more popular.

On Wednesday nights, *The Palladium* held dance contests, which the very good dancers, usually twelve to fifteen couples, participated in. Average dancers did not compete. This competition was not for the faint-hearted as, if competitors didn't really know what they were doing, the crowds of on-lookers would have booed them off the floor. After the competition, the dance instructors gave exhibition dances for the eager audience, who were keen to try all the new moves when they next hit the ballroom.

No one was more observant than Augie Rodriguez, who absorbed every detail, to the extent that very soon he was dancing with style and confidence; interpreting the music into artistic movements of fantasy, in a way which increasingly fulfilled and satisfied him. His friends, Cuban Pete and Tommy Diaz, were so good they became innovators of many mambo steps still used today; but Augie Rodriguez was destined to do much more, and go much farther than his friends, or even he, ever dreamed could be possible.

While he was watching and learning dance steps, Augie rarely asked anyone to dance with him. He told himself he wanted to feel really confident before he shared his newly-found skills with someone else; he told himself that, but in fact there was one person he would have given *anything* to dance with.

A beautiful young woman caught his attention every time he entered *The Palladium*. She had attracted him since the first time he laid his eyes on her. A dark brunette, about five feet four inches tall, with high cheek bones, voluptuous lips and long braids that she wound around into coils and pinned on either side of her face. This was the girl he really wanted to dance with. Augie had watched her on the dance floor with different partners, his eyes glued to her gyrating hips, which he remembers to this day, gave him goose-bumps. He tried approaching her between dances, but she was always surrounded by a large group of would-be suitors, and Augie could only gaze from afar. He didn't even know her name. He didn't stand a chance!

CHAPTER SIX

To say that Margo Bartolomei had always marched to the beat of her own drum would be an understatement. She was born on April 6 in 1929 in Manhattan, New York, the eldest of five girls. Her sister, Alice was born two years after her, and then there was a year between the next three girls, Olga, Gilda and Gladys.

Her maternal grandfather, Simon Madera, was a well-known composer and musician, who taught music at the University in San Juan. He had eleven children, and he taught each one of them a different musical instrument.

Margo's mother, Mencia, had learned the piano, and eventually became a concert pianist, playing in San Juan and at many famous concert halls in the region.

Her father, Santiago, was of Corsican descent. He was an accountant, and after his marriage to Mencia in 1928, between the two World Wars, like many other Puerto Ricans he made a decision to take his wife to North America, to get a better job than the one he had, and try to improve his family's circumstances.

By the end of the First World War, around 10,000 Latinos were living in East Harlem in Manhattan. The majority of them were from Puerto Rico, and they had come to America in a steady stream since 1917, when the US granted Puerto Ricans American citizenship. Many immigrants, including Margo's parents, sailed to New York on a ship named the *Marine Tiger*.

Over time, the *Marine Tiger* became quite a famous vessel. The thousands of immigrants who boarded her frequently made life-long ties with each other, as they often left family members behind and were fearful of starting over again in strange and unfamiliar surroundings. To this day, Latinos who made that momentous and traumatic trip to New York on the *Marine Tiger* so long ago look for each other through passenger lists and computer web sites, so that they can arrange re-unions with each other and search for missing relatives.

~~~~~~~~~~~

More often than not, the Puerto Ricans who came to New York worked in the tobacco industry, and settled in the areas around East Harlem, which had previously been almost entirely populated by Irish, Jewish and Italian families.

After the 1935 race riots in Harlem, which was triggered by discrimination over housing and employment, the local authorities began, in 1940, to build public housing in an effort to improve the situation in the area. This attracted many African Americans and Latinos, who up until then had found it very difficult to find reasonable accommodations.

Twenty years before that time the area was still quite rural, and many people vacationed there, but by the 1940's it was becoming part of the city suburbs. Families moved into the brownstone apartment buildings and got to know each other. They formed extended families and happy neighborhoods, and eventually brought their relatives over to settle with them. However, in the years between 1940 and 1945, most of the Irish and Jewish communities moved away in a mass exodus to other developing areas, like Queens and Brooklyn, after which the empty houses were occupied by mainly African American, and Latino families, though some Italian and Spanish families also remained. From that time on, the area was re-named Spanish Harlem, or El Barrio.

Like the thousands of their countrymen before them, Santiago and Mencia found their home in East Harlem. Margo remembers that when she was growing up, the Italian people in her neighborhood kept pretty much to the area they lived in, and the African Americans did likewise. The Hispanic people who settled in Harlem brought their values with them. They went to Church, corrected their children and made sure they went to school.

Youths formed groups of their own ethnicity, and it was very rare and unusual for anyone to "cross over" and make friends with another group. Later on, these groups formed gangs, which caused huge problems for the area, but at that time it was more of a cultural familiarity that kept people somewhat isolated from the others in their neighborhood.

For the following generation it would prove to be an on-going struggle, when bringing up their children became a day to day battle for parents, with street gangs and all types of crime having to be contended with. In the 1940's and 1950's, drugs, gangs and weapons were certainly a part of the youth scene, but had not yet overwhelmed the society, as it did for a decade in later years.

~~~~~~~~~~~~

Margo's father, Santiago, worked at an accounting firm on Wall Street and he was very successful, eventually ending up as a manager of the company and able to support his family well.

Margo was born on April 26, 1929 in New York. Santiago had set his heart on his first-born child being a son. He was quite disappointed to be told that a girl was born, but when he saw her, he was so delighted with his daughter that he swallowed his displeasure, and decided to teach her all the things that he would have taught a male child. This resulted in Santiago having a very powerful and positive effect on his daughter Margo, the consequences of which stayed with her all her life.

That is not to say that her mother was not also a strong influence, as indeed she was. When Margo was a little girl of four or five years old, she remembers that after listening to Mencia play a piece of music, she would then sit down at the piano and play the same piece by ear.

She loved playing the music that way, until at the age of six her mother tried to teach her to read the notes. Suddenly, the enjoyment dwindled and it began to feel like hard work. The more her mother encouraged her to practice and read the music, the less Margo liked it, so because Mencia felt her daughter was really gifted she found her a good music teacher.

Margo kept on playing for three years with the teacher, and became quite accomplished, but actually becoming a professional pianist like her mother and grandfather did not appeal to her. In later years she was really glad her mother had persisted that she took lessons. Playing the piano gives her great pleasure to this day, and she had no idea at the time that being able to read, play and understand music, would prove to be an invaluable asset in her professional life, many years later.

Another member of the family who had a lasting impression on Margo was her Uncle Ralph, Santiago's younger brother, who lived nearby. He was an actor in the Spanish theater, and to Margo he seemed to live quite an exciting and bohemian life. She looked forward to Ralph's visits to her home, because he always spent time playing with her, showing her how to dance and present herself, just as he did on the stage.

She was about seven or eight years old when he introduced her to *Brujeria*, or voodoo/witchcraft style music, which originated in Haiti from the African slaves, brought there by the Spanish. He taught her how to move her shoulders and perform dance steps to it, and Margo loved the lessons.

Shaking and stamping to the unrelenting drumming sounds of the music, she clearly showed a natural talent for dance and rhythm at that young age, and her uncle noticed it; so when she was older, he took her to the *Gloria Palace* in Germantown, where he taught her proper dance steps.

Latin bands played at the *Gloria Palace,* and at that time the rumba craze was in full-swing. The music had been played by many Latin and American bands in North America since the 1930's, but most of it was only a version or interpretation of the original music. Cubans said that the really authentic *rumba* music only came from the poor people: the ones who lived in the tenements of Havana.

~~~~~~~~~~~

Margo had a special bond with her father. He loved all his daughters but, perhaps because she was the child most like him in personality, and four other daughters were born after her, he continued to treat her a lot like the boy he never had. Margo had always been independent and not easily influenced, and her father recognized it enough to want to teach her his beloved game of baseball, since he thought she would do very well at the game. As soon as she was old enough to throw and catch a ball, he took her out and taught her to play like a boy.

She remembers him teaching her how to be brave, and not cry when the game didn't go her way, how to persevere and how to be independent and trust her own instincts. Her baseball skills were short-lived, but the rest of the training her father gave her lasted a lifetime. By the time she reached her teens, Margo wouldn't allow anyone to push her around, and her newly found inner strength would prove to be invaluable to her; not only when she was bullied constantly by older African American youths in the neighborhood, but over the years, when there was always someone around, trying to persuade her into something she didn't want to do.

The first test at being brave came sooner than she would have liked. One day, an unexpected turn of events disrupted the entire family, to the point that it would never be the same again. Mencia discovered that her husband "had an eye for the ladies," and after struggling with it for a while, feeling her own values were being compromised, she decided she could tolerate the situation no longer.

Margo was fifteen at the time, and she remembers well the day she waited outside, and watched out for her father who walked home from his office, just as she did on any other day; except that this day was different. Suddenly, she saw her mother open an upstairs window, throw all her husbands' clothes out into the street, and then cry out to him to never come home again!

Loving her father a lot, and having the very strong bond with him, it was especially upsetting for Margo to see him leave. Her mother was a very determined woman who could not be persuaded if she disapproved of something, but Margo was always able to twist her father around her little finger.

She saw him often after her parents' separation and eventual divorce, and she always maintained a good relationship with him. He continued to be good to her, and spoiled her, by giving her money for clothing items or shoes that she wanted badly but couldn't afford.

Eventually, Santiago met a woman with whom he lived for twenty five years, but he never married her. Mencia, also, never remarried. She was too busy taking care of her five daughters, and barely even found the time to play her piano for pleasure at home, let alone professionally, again.

Her relationship with her father and the life lessons he taught her, helped Margo handle the tough times she would have to handle in later years. She became a woman of great courage, unaffected by emotional influences and able to stay focused and strong in the face of adversity. She was a person who a partner could trust, and lean on; a woman who could equally trust that partner to carry her.

~~~~~~~~~~~

Margo stayed in Mabel Dean Bacon High School until she was eighteen, very unsure about what she wanted to do as a career. She liked History and English, but had no desire to teach, and though she enjoyed playing the piano she did not want to become a professional pianist like her mother.

Mencia worried about her daughter. Her other girls were starting to settle down and marry, but Margo seemed to be always looking for something more in her life. She showed no interest in a special career or in taking her life seriously. When Margo asked her mother if she could get her ears pierced, the answer was no, which did not help her relationship with her rebellious daughter.

Mencia decided to consult her friend and neighbor, a Cuban woman who was known as a fortune teller and spiritualist. The woman took one look at Margo's palm and told Mencia to worry no more. Peering at the fine lines, she said that Margo was going to marry a man with blue eyes. Quite a revelation for a Latin girl! It was also clear to Mencia's friend that Margo would have one son and that she would travel. She explained that Margo was an artist and that she would find her own way in life. Mencia must have been very relieved, because after that, she trusted her daughter to make her own decisions and allowed her to look after herself!

During her last three years in high school, Margo decided to take a diploma course in hair and make-up, so she could get work in a beauty salon as a beautician if no better ideas came to her. The problem was, that from the age of sixteen she and her best friend, Lucy, had only one important thing in their lives, and it seemed to overwhelm everything else; it was music.

It was also in the lives of her friends who studied serious music, friends who went to the *Metropolitan Opera* and *Carnegie Hall*, and it was in the lives of all her friends in school, but it was not the kind of music Margo's mother played and had taught her.

It was a different kind of music, and it had affected her deeply from the first time she heard it, in the very early days of her teens. It was a type of jazz with a new pulsating sound, beaten out on bongos and conga drums. It was a thrilling kind of music, with a rhythm that could sound hypnotic, infectious, instantly arresting and sometimes primitive and wild.

She and her friends sat together in the high school cafeteria, beating out the new rhythms on the tables with their notebooks, captivated by the staccato sounds and the new culture that reached out to them every day over the air waves.

By the time she was seventeen, Margo had become completely infected by "the beat." She went out to buy the sheet music so she could understand and play it at home, and she listened religiously when programs playing the music were on the radio. As a child, she had become familiar with dances like the *rumba,* the *tango,* the g*uaracha* and the me*rengue,* but the new dance beat was different. The music had African origins and it came out of Cuba. It was called the *mambo,* and it was infecting everybody she knew.

CHAPTER SEVEN

In her last year in high school, Margo learned about a ballroom on Thirty Fourth Street and Eighth Avenue, called *The Manhattan Center*, which played Latin music on one Sunday every month. She started going there with her friend Lucy, but if Lucy couldn't make it, she went on her own. It was the one day in the month she looked forward to, when she would dress up to the nines and become part of the great mass of people going to the ballroom to get lost in the music of the *mambo*.

In those days, a single girl in a dance hall scenario was perfectly acceptable. She could arrive at the ballroom alone, dance with complete strangers and leave alone. It was no different than going ice skating or playing tennis. Latin orchestras, usually two or three of them in each session, began playing at 1:00 P.M. and finished at 8:00 P.M., when the American bands began playing traditional dance music like *waltzes* and *fox trots*.

The Manhattan Center ballroom held between 1,500 and 2,000 people, and whether they arrived there alone or in a group, by the time the music started it was just a question of getting onto the floor to strut their stuff! The men and women tended to stand around in groups. All of them dressed to kill!

The men groomed their hair into slicked back styles. They sported jackets, narrow ties, sharply creased trousers and highly polished pointed toe shoes. The women wore body-hugging sheath dresses or full-skirted ones with a tight waistline. Their shoes had very high heels and their make-up was all heavily lined eyes, mascaraed lashes and bright red lips.

The girls stood around with their friends, or alone, tapping their feet to the music as it started up, pouting their lips and looking under their lashes; impatiently waiting to see a pair of pointed shoes stop next to them, and to hear a deep voice saying *"Bailamos?"*

~~~~~~~~~~

At around the age of sixteen, Margo became friendly with a young man, Victor, a senior from her school. He was five years older than she, but after graduating he kept in touch with Margo. They drifted into a loose kind of boyfriend girlfriend relationship over the three-year period before Margo graduated, by which time there was an unspoken agreement between them that they would eventually get married.

When she graduated, Margo became employed as a beautician for a prestigious Beauty Salon on Park Avenue. She really enjoyed the work, and had several well-known Manhattan socialite clients, including Claire Kahn, wife of the prominent banker, and the wives and daughters of the founders of both the Ford Motor Car Company and CBS. She could also tell her friends that she had twice held the hands of the scandalous Wallace Simpson, the Duchess of Windsor. Admittedly, it was while manicuring them, but what a great story!

Now she was earning money, and had the independence to buy new outfits to go dancing, Margo gave little thought to her "serious" relationship with Victor. He was employed as a waiter and worked long hours, so Margo began meeting lots of new friends when she went dancing, and she went whenever she could. Sometimes with her sister, sometimes with friends and occasionally with Victor, but if they, on certain days were not able to go, it didn't matter to her, she went alone.

As she gained confidence and enjoyed dancing more and more, going occasionally was not enough for Margo. She found herself only looking forward to that one day in the month. That Sunday, once every four weeks, when she could thrill and move to the sound of the new music, as it was blared out on trumpets, beaten out on bongos and conga drums, extemporized on a piano and vocalized by a romantic-voiced baritone shaking maracas.

She asked a friend one day at the *Manhattan Center* if anywhere else in town played Latin dance music and he told her to go to *The Palladium*, a dance club on West 53rd Street and Broadway. *"The Palladium"* her friend said, *"has Latin dance music four nights a week."*

Margo was ecstatic. She now felt inspired; it was as if her life had suddenly found a purpose. Since she regards it as being a main turning point in her life, she

remembers vividly the first time she walked into *The Palladium* ballroom.

~~~~~~~~~~~

It was the fall of 1948. The dance club was located on the second floor of the building and was reached by a narrow flight of stairs. At the top of the stairs, an elderly man took the tickets and directed people towards the ballroom, which was very large and very gloomy.

From the ceiling center, above the huge dance floor, dark maroon velvet draperies stretched out in pleats, and fanned out to the tops of the walls, giving an effect of being in a huge Arabic tent. Straight ahead of the entrance, in the center of the back wall, a low bandstand, large enough to accommodate a fifteen-piece orchestra was located, with a triple arch of lights over the entire platform, which not only illuminated the musicians but could flash on and off to suit the mood of the music.

To the left of the entrance was a long bar with a huge mirror behind it, which enabled young women sitting on the high bar stools to see, under their heavily mascaraed eyelashes, which prospective partners were "homing in" on them without actually having to stare them in the face.

About twenty-five tables and chairs on the left-hand side of the ballroom, close to the band, were provided for the VIP's; the "fashionable set;" the well dressed and well-to-do. On the right side of the ballroom, which was strictly for the stags, two benches were the only seats available. Six wooden columns supporting the ceiling were spaced around the dance floor. The columns had lights around them, which were an important part of the decorations, for if they turned from their passively attractive illumination of the dance floor to fast-flashing red, it meant there was trouble on the premises!

From the mid-40's, the club has been described in different ways. An Irish dance ballroom, an Anglo dance hall and a *lindy hop* joint, to name a few. The truth is though, however the place was perceived, when the owners, Frank and Tommy Martin, saw how well the clubs playing Latin music were patronized, they began to re-think their ideas about attracting people to their own place, and decided to include a second band with a Latin sound every weekday evening.

The format was to have an American orchestra playing traditional dance music first; *fox-trots, waltzes, pea-body, lindy hop*, and so on, and a second band playing Latin music. The Latin band was led by a man named Armando, and consisted mainly of American musicians. They played Latin music, but in an American style.

By that time, people like Arthur Murray were beginning to take an interest in Latin music, and were teaching a watered down sedate type of *rhumba,* which was included in the traditional ballroom dance repertoire. This encouraged the traditional dance clubs to provide the bands, but both the music and the dance moves were devoid of ethnicity, and greatly stylized to appeal to the mainly Anglo-European patrons.

~~~~~~~~~~

Just before Margo started going to *The Palladium*, several significant things happened. Frank and Tommy Martin took on a partner, Maxwell Hyman, and equally important, a young musician named Tito Puente, who played at that time with a band called *The Piccadilly Boys,* started playing Sunday afternoon matinees there.

Suddenly, the ballroom became packed with dancers on Sundays, and as Armando and his band became more influenced by the Latin music and improved their style, the Martin brothers began to notice on week nights that the American dance music was becoming less and less popular. People stood around waiting for the traditional dance music to stop so they could dance to the Latin sounds.

The person who had persuaded the Martin brothers, in the mid-1940's, to play Armando's session of Latin music each evening at *The Palladium*, which was then called the *Alma Dance Studios,* was a dance promoter called Federico Pagani. He had dubbed the evenings "Latin Nights," and once he realized a dwindling number of people were going to the ballroom to dance to American music, Pagani began to look for an opportunity to promote some of the other Latin bands he represented. Most of these were, at that time, playing in clubs in Spanish Harlem and other ethnic communities around the city, but Federico Pagani had big plans to promote them into more lucrative venues.

He found his chance when Max Hyman bought out his partners and became the sole owner of the studios. Pagani had a very close relationship with two leading exponents of Latin music at that time, Frank Grillo, a band leader known as Machito, and his brother-in-law, Mario Bauza, who played trumpet in Machito's band and was his musical director. When Machito and Bauza formed the band, known as the *Afro-Cubans,* in 1941, swing music was the most popular, but jazz was a close second. Because of a long-time friendship with Dizzy Gillespie, Machito started to put jazz inflections into his Latin music, thereby attracting jazz fans, as well as a large Latin crowd.

There were plenty of clubs in Harlem where he played to packed audiences, and also in the *Park Plaza Ballroom* at 110th Street and Fifth Avenue, but Harlem at that time was considered unsafe for whites, so very few of them had heard his music. Ethnic nightclubs around the city were also familiar with Machito, but he had never brought his music downtown.

One day Pagani boasted to Max Hyman that he could easily fill his club on any given off-night if he would book Machito to play there. He promised that the Latin band would attract large numbers of people.

This was not as simple as it may sound. Segregation was still openly practiced in some areas of Manhattan, and though the city was more progressive by far than other parts of the country, there were still numerous un-spoken, but widely accepted barriers. Several years would pass before black people could openly and legally integrate in all levels of society, and it went without saying that if ethnic bands were going to play at the *Alma Dance Studios*, ethnic people would come to listen to them.

Max Hymen thought about the proposition, and pointed out to Pagani that to some extent, if he allowed the really ethnic bands to play in his club, he would be going out on a limb. The popular wisdom is that in reply, Pagani said to Max Hyman, *"Well, the only thing is then, Max, I guess it all boils down to whether you prefer the color black over the color green."*

Max Hyman thought no more! He had a huge place to maintain and a staff to pay for running the place, not to mention two bands a night. Coupled with the fact that admission into the club was only one dollar, he needed as much help as he could get. Besides which, he had a very soft spot for the romantic and emotional sounds of Latin music.

He threw himself wholeheartedly into his new project and never looked back, and the first thing he did was to tear down the name *Alma Dance Studios* on the outside of the building. He then erected another sign, brightly lit and much larger, proudly displaying the club's new name: *The Palladium*.

CHAPTER EIGHT

(THE PALLADIUM)

Maxwell Hyman was a very interesting man. He started life in New York as a penniless immigrant, having escaped from a concentration camp and fleeing to America during WW2. Starting out as a lowly tailor in Manhattan, he made a rapid transition into the fur trade, becoming a store owner and furrier, and a highly successful one at that.

He was quite a small man, with horn-rimmed glasses, and grey, thinning hair. Though his disposition was somewhat tense and excitable, he had a very kind heart and an emotional soul. People liked Maxwell Hyman because, on the whole, he liked them, and it showed.

Once his financial situation was secure, he began mixing in the higher echelons of Manhattan society, and it was in those circles he met the woman who was to become his wife, an heiress to the Otis Elevator Company fortune. He was now able to do what he really wanted with his life, and after all the suffering he had endured, he wanted to bring the world a little happiness.

Having made the decision to commit himself to the new format of his dance club, *The Palladium*, he did it wholeheartedly and with no reservations. He booked Machito's band to debut on a Wednesday night, and having agreed to give Federico Pagani a small percentage of the "take" if the evening proved to be successful, he sat back and waited for the results.

Pagani and Machito were elated! They went to work distributing flyers all over the Latin communities in the city, and the word spread like wildfire. Max Hyman, good businessman that he was, anticipated that Machito's band would attract a large group of people to *The Palladium,* but even he never imagined the upheaval that particular Wednesday night would bring to his dance club, indeed, to the entire city of Manhattan as well!

People started lining up outside *The Palladium* for their tickets in the morning, and by 3:30 P.M. the line had doubled and stretched all along Broadway. By early evening, the crowds were so great that the police had to close down Seventh Avenue and Broadway, both of which were jammed with two lines of excited people; all hoping that night to get into *The Palladium.*

And what a night it was! People of many nationalities, Italians, Jews, Asians, Spanish, African Americans, Cubans, Puerto Ricans, Anglo Europeans; everyone who had been seduced by the music lined up together and flooded to hear it played that night. All ethnic and social barriers were permanently penetrated on the day of Machito's debut at *The Palladium,* and after his performance the ambience of New York City's nightlife was changed forever.

~~~~~~~~~~

From that day onwards New York, a city divided by day, met by night to dance the *mambo. The Palladium* was now the place to be; a multi-cultural gathering place where it was perfectly acceptable for people with a variety of nationalities to rub shoulders together. It was a phenomenon because they all had one thing in common - they were there to dig the music and dance.

Everyone came dressed to the nines; the men in suits and wing-tipped shoes and the women, teetering along in three inch high heeled

The Opening Act

shoes and body-hugging sheath dresses or short flounced skirts, cinched at the waist with wide belts. Many came on the subway, and as the train approached the station, it went one block past *The Palladium* where the music could be heard from the train. The rhythmic beat set everyone off, and when the train stopped at the station, hundreds of people could be seen dancing down onto the platform and then dancing the block's walk to the club. All the time they waited in line to get their entrance tickets, they were dancing, and they continued to dance their way up the long flight of stairs to the ballroom.

Once inside, it was like stepping into another world; a world of action, anticipation and excitement. Many people have written that as they walked into the ballroom from outside, the magic would begin. It just hit them!

A purple-blue haze of smoke hung below the velvet draped ceiling, and every night the place would be packed with people, often as many as a thousand. Most nights, people were turned away. Machito's band had a huge following, so before very long Max Hyman eliminated the American band, which had been the main one of the evening, and kept Armando's band as the House Orchestra.

People were excited and inspired by the music, which included everything from erotic Afro-Cuban rhythms to African American jazz and big band swing. All of it played in rich, complex styles, on trumpet, sax, flute, timbales, bongos, congas and maracas.

Machito was the head-liner, but it cannot be overstated enough that his musical director brother-in-law, Mario Bauza, was the musical genius powering the band's music. Another important asset to the band was Graciela Grillo, Machito's sister. Born in Cuba, she began singing as a teenager in Havana, but when her brother Machito was drafted into the U.S. Army in 1942, she came to New York to co-lead the band with Bauza, whom she eventually married.

Machito sustained an injury in 1943 and was discharged, but his sister remained the band's singer and her powerful renditions of Latin songs subsequently earned her the title of "The First Lady of Latin Jazz." As a central figure in the birth and development of Latin Jazz, Machito was known for his music style, which was described as Latin funk or Afro-Cuban.

Having collaborated with Mario Bauza for many years, he was the first bandleader to fuse the sounds of Afro-Cuban music and American jazz, which incorporated several rhythmic styles - the original Cuban *rhumba*, known as the most tantalizing dance since the birth of rhythm, *guaracha, mambo, jazz-swing and Cuban bolero*, he now devoted his band to serious big band jazz arrangements.

Machito's popularity was already legendary among the Latinos in New York; long before he came to *The Palladium*, but over time, because he kept his music very authentic and close to the roots of its Afro-Cuban beginnings, he became widely accepted throughout the entire international music community, and was eventually acknowledged to be the "Father of Afro-Cuban Jazz."

The most famous piece of music he produced with Mario Bauza was known as the *Afro-Cuban Jazz Suite,* which effectively became the blueprint for Latin jazz. The second was *Tanga,* a powerful, hypnotic piece, also written by Bauza that embodied the spirit of *mambo*, and quickly became the theme song for the band. Machito's fans came in their thousands to *The Palladium,* to hear the Cuban rhythms and the blended jazz swings, loaded with hyperactive bongos and congas, mahogany clave sticks and razor-edged, riffing brass. Mainly though, they came to dance.

When the intense rhythms and beats of frenetic mambo sounds had brought the dancers to near-exhaustion, Machito would slow everything down by playing a *Cuban bolero,* or "Dance of Love." Graciela Grillo would sing to the emotional dramatic lyrics, and the dancers were able to regain their energy by dancing slowly for a while to the sultry romantic sounds.

Named after its Spanish counterpart, the *Cuban bolero* is the same in name only, and bears no resemblance to the *Spanish bolero,* whose roots originated in the *Flamenco*. The first *Cuban bolero* can be traced back to 1883 and exists in the form of a slow, romantic song named "Tristezas," written by Hose Pepe Sanchez.

It is said that *Cuban bolero* is the first major vocal combination of both the African and Spanish elements of music, which comes from the same Afro-Cuban roots as the *rumba*, but is danced in a slower 4/4 time. The dance is the slowest of the rhythm dances, and is characterized by long, sweeping side steps, which create a smoothness that makes it dramatic and unique. Originally, the lyrics were famous love poems, but by the 1930's when *Cuban bolero* was becoming popular in North America, people were writing their own lyrics.

In Cuba the saying goes, *"There is no love without a Bolero,"* and certainly after more than a century of popularity it looks as though boleros will be around as long as love is around. It is so much an integral part of the Cuban music scene that native Cubans refer to it as *"A Ballad with rice and beans on the side!"*

~~~~~~~~~~~

In 1948, Max Hyman hired another hugely popular Latin band, led by Tito Puente, who had played there with his earlier band, *The Piccadilly Boys,* on Sunday matinees. Puente had played percussion with Machito's band in the early 1940's, and soon realized the powerful combination of jazz and Latin music that Machito was creating. To add more polish to his own arrangements, he expanded the size of his band and was now playing a hard-driving brand of Latin jazz, as well as showing his own amazing skills when he accompanied his band on the timbales.

Shortly after Puente, Hyman hired a third band, much admired by the Latin music fans. It was led by vocalist, percussionist and composer, Tito Rodriguez, who knew Puente as a teenager when they lived on the same block of 110th Street in East Harlem, and had played baseball together. Later, in 1946, they had played music together in the band of Cuban composer and pianist, Jose Curbelo.

Rodriguez went on to form his own band, called the *Mambo Devils,* in 1948, and immediately recorded eight tunes, four of which were arranged by Tito Puente. His tunes were so successful that Rodriguez expanded his band and signed up with Tico Records, who objected to the name *Mambo Devils,* so he re-named them *Mambo Wolves.*

After the two Titos left Curbelo's band, they both scored chart-topping hits, which turned them into musical competitors. The *Mambo Wolves* band had become much bigger by then, and was thereafter known as the *Tito Rodriguez Orchestra.* Tito Rodriguez, who has been described as 'The Frank Sinatra of Latin music' was an extremely talented vocalist who touched the dancers with his romantic, sentimental songs. His style was highly disciplined and controlled, but he knew exactly how to bring the passion and fire out of the dancers, and he never failed to get their emotions running high on the dance floor. Coupled with the fact that his band was very popular, Rodriguez was as great a crowd-puller as his rival, Tito Puente, and his friend Machito.

Puente also played romantic tunes, but in his music he always used the disciplined approach of imagining the choreography represented in the piece, and how it would be danced to. His maxim was that people danced to the beat of the music, not to the lyrics; which could have been a dig at his rival Rodriguez, but Puente stuck faithfully to his principle, and never wrote or played a piece without running the dance through his mind first. This influenced his music so much, that the impulsive and complex rhythms he played at *The Palladium* were the beginnings of what was to become the pulse of Latin Jazz in the future, and he became the sweetheart of hundreds of thousands of ardent dancers.

Puente was the first bandleader to put the timbales at the front of the band and make them the main feature. He assumed the title of "Puente and his magic timbales," since it was said there was no way a person within their sound could stand still!

By the time Puente and Rodriguez were hired to play with *Machito* at *The Palladium* the tenuous competitive connection they had, bubbled over into a fierce rivalry. People flocked there to dance and listen to the energetic, boisterous and hard-charging new sounds.

All three bands had huge followings, and their leaders were multi-faceted musicians, so before long they became competitive with each other, and everyone came on a Wednesday night to hear what became known as "The Battle of the Bands." The air around *The Palladium* became heavy with the competition of the three 'Mambo Masters' and the fans lapped it up, creating a dance phenomenon at *The Palladium* that has never been seen since.

~~~~~~~~~~

As Latin bands were now the main attraction at *The Palladium,* a group of exceptional dancers from around the city came too. They were the innovators of the new dance, the *mambo,* and because so many people wanted to learn the complicated steps, some of them had become teachers.

The Palladium had an unwritten rule which was always observed. The better dressed people, the celebrities and the dance teachers always sat where the tables and chairs were, on the left side of the ballroom near the band. Since no liquor was served, if you wanted to drink it you brought your own - usually disguised in coca-cola bottles or in hip-flasks in ladies handbags.

The right side of the ballroom, the stag side, was for people who only came to dance but did not have a partner, and it became known as the side for the 'street people'. It was as if an invisible line was drawn between the two sides and, quite mysteriously, no one ever crossed it deliberately. If they sometimes did by error and stayed for a while, which occasionally happened, the feeling was so uncomfortable they soon went back to where they 'belonged.' To cross over to the left side was possible, but one had to earn the privilege, and that meant one had to be as good a dancer as the teachers.

There were a couple of other rules. If you were banned from *The Palladium,* no matter what the reason, it was a life sentence. A couple of exceptions have been recounted, like the time a young man's priest went to Mr. Hyman and begged him to allow his parishioner back, on the understanding that the young man would never misbehave again! The second rule was that no one, except servicemen in uniform and friends of the club bouncers, could stand in front of the bandstand and just enjoy the music. People were there to *dance,* not just listen!

Max Hyman was delighted with the atmosphere he had created, but at the same time he realized that right under his nose a remarkable new era was being born. Thousands of people from all over the city now came to his club, and some of them were unconventional. The new enthusiasm for Latin dancing was enormous, and Hyman was willing and happy to host it, but certain standards needed to be observed.

It was rarely blatant, but drugs were an ever-growing part of the culture, and they were commonly brought into the dance and night clubs, and filtered down through all levels of society. The drugs of choice were cocaine and marijuana. In *The Palladium*, cocaine was known to be there, but few people used it, usually keeping their habit discreetly hidden by snorting it in the bathrooms. Others smoked marijuana, and that was done more openly, the evidence of which could be seen in the purple smoke suspended in the air over the dance floor.

Interestingly, the drug culture was most evident on the 'stag' side of the ballroom, and the drinking was done mostly on the side frequented by the wealthy and the famous. Hyman was prepared, and smart enough, to go with the flow, but he determined the only way to keep people in line was to make sure his basic house rules were enforced.

To do that, he hired three bouncers. They were tough, they were huge, and they were brothers. Their names were Tony, Vic and 'Yumpy'. Tony, the slightly more aggressive one of the three, took his job very seriously and to add a little weight to his credibility, he always wore a fedora; much like Elliott Ness, but on the opposite side of the law! Vic was huge, like a great bear. His massive size was all he needed as an aid to wielding his authority at the *Palladium* when things got out of hand. Yumpy was not as large as Vic, but was also a big man. To some extent, his nature was gentler than his two brothers, but he was not averse to punching a trouble-maker's lights out if his brothers ordered him to do so!

Even between the three of them, the amount of grey matter was somewhat limited, but since they were hired to do one thing only, they accomplished their task very well indeed. Of course, the fact that they had "connections" gave them a huge advantage! Another pair of bouncers, named Tony and Pete, were taken on at *The Palladium* some time later when the crowd became too large for three men to control. They were also brothers with "connections," and were extremely tough, known by the Manhattan police as the two most famous blonde Latinos in New York!

No night at *The Palladium* was exclusively for anyone, but a pattern began to establish itself that Wednesday nights were favored by the Jewish and Italian patrons, Friday nights were very popular with the 'hip' Puerto Ricans and Saturdays were for the 'squares,' or *jibaros*. Occasionally, a disagreement bubbled up between the latter two groups.

It was a rare occurrence, but if anyone stepped out of line and started causing real trouble, the lights on the wooden columns around the dance floor flashed red, and one or all of the bouncers went to find the perpetrators. If the conflict was a serious one, the troublemaker would be unceremoniously hurled, or rolled, down a long narrow flight of stairs to the back entrance on the ground floor, and if it was really bad, one of the brothers would follow him down and bloody him up some; he was then barred for life, never to be seen in *The Palladium* again!

~~~~~~~~~~~

At that time, to be caught possessing drugs of any kind meant a mandatory jail sentence, so clubs packed to the hilt with hordes of people were subjected to unannounced police raids. *The Palladium* was no exception. Every once in a while the police came to check up on the activities of its patrons, but they came with sirens blaring and much hullabaloo, so everyone had fair warning to secrete their illegal possessions.

Margo remembers one occasion when she was dancing with a guy who called himself Dynamite. Quite possibly, he chose that name because he thought he was a dynamite dancer, but whatever the reason was, he sweated profusely when he danced and always carried a handkerchief to wipe the perspiration off his face.

Suddenly, during their dance, they heard the words *"La Jara - cops,"* being yelled around the room, and in an instant absolute bedlam broke loose! As the police came running into the ballroom, joints were immediately dumped on the floor, and other people broke away from their places and ran to the restrooms to flush their more serious evidence down the toilets.

Dynamite, on seeing the cops, thrust his handkerchief into Margo's hand, but her intuition told her there was something illegal in it and she gave it right back to him. She could tell from his expression he was quite shocked when she did that. Realization quickly dawned that Margo was not going to take the fall for him, or anyone else, whereon he fled, and was not seen again that night! In the midst of the melee, the band played on, louder and louder, and it didn't stop until everything calmed down and was back to normal!

On another occasion, in the middle of the usual noise and exhilaration, all the lights went out. This of course stopped the music for a while, and during the short silence all that could be heard was the sound of guns and knives thudding and clattering to the floor. When everything was impounded, everyone had to give their names as they exited the building, before anyone was allowed to leave. On the whole, though, this sort of thing created an air of terror and excitement at the same time, and seemed only to serve as yet another enticing facet to making people frequent the place!

CHAPTER NINE

When Margo first stepped into *The Palladium* in the fall of 1948, she thought she had died and gone to heaven! Nothing had stopped the growing passion she felt for dancing, and the more she went, the happier she became. In her own words, she just couldn't get enough.

Every day, she dreamed about the way she felt when she heard the exciting, pulsating music of the Latin bands. It was a feeling, almost like being woken up and brought to life. She cherished a secret fantasy that one day she might be good enough to do a fantastic ten-minute dance routine in a Broadway show. Ten minutes; that was all she wanted.

One dancer excited her enormously. He was a Puerto Rican called Pedro Aguilar, who grew up in *El Barrio*. He was an untrained dancer, but had a natural talent for choreography, and an ability to create what seemed like one new step after another. Aguilar's gift lay in the fact that he was able to dance exactly on, or off, the clave beat, which is the basis of all Cuban music and the space into which every element of improvisation and arrangement has to fit.

Based on an offbeat 3/2 or 2/3 rhythmic pattern spread out over two bars, it is the most difficult aspect of truly mastering the *mambo*. With his fast and fancy footwork and coordinated arm movements, Aguilar had won so many dance competitions at *The Palladium* that in 1949 the MC dubbed him "Cuban Pete," which is what everyone called him forever after.

It was while watching him cut up the dance floor one day that Margo had her epiphany. At that moment, she knew what she was going to do with the rest of her life. She *had* to learn to dance like that, and then learn even more. At the time, she thought it would come easily!

One aspect which helped her practice was the fact that she was never at a loss for partners. For one thing she was a beautiful girl. About five feet three inches tall, with piercing blue eyes and long dark braided hair; she had the look of a young **Audrey Hepburn**, though her body was healthy and athletic as opposed to Hepburn's fragile, willowy one.

Having a gift for interpreting the music and a talent for feeling the sensual, provocative movements of the dance, Margo caught on quickly to the complex new beat of the *mambo*. She watched the dance teachers and the demonstrations they gave, and practiced every move until she *felt* the movement in the music. Once her feet began to move naturally to the mysterious, syncopated rhythms, they became hers forever, and in a short time she started expanding and perfecting her maneuvers.

She shook her shoulders, and quivered and bounced her breasts to the steamy beat, which in turn rolled her hips and gave her buttocks a life of their own. Her movements appeared at times to be enticing, even provocative, but she concentrated completely on the rhythm of the music and her dancing was never vulgar or inappropriate.

~~~~~~~~~~

This cannot be said for all the dancers. The pulsating excitement created by the extraordinarily rich music arrangements, especially Machito's *Tanga,* which, roughly translated means wild, savage woman, whipped everyone into a state of excitement that was mesmerizing to observe. It was like a frenzy; a seizure that kept everyone in its embrace and took them to another world. Many girls lost their reputations dancing to the *Tanga*! As they wiggled and spun around their partners, their short tight skirts and bulging cleavages often gave everyone a pretty uninhibited view of the next weeks' laundry!

The band leaders were also caught up in the Afro-Cuban hysteria, created quite deliberately by all three of them! There were huge disagreements about 'top billing' which also meant top pay, and no matter what Max Hyman did to make it fair for them they were never satisfied.

In 1951, Puente and Rodriguez became 'house bands,' and every night, they played at *The Palladium* with one guest band, such as Noro Morales, Villos Caracas, Benny More or Prado. These guests had to be good enough to compliment the two Titos: If they could not play as well, it was simple - they just couldn't play there.

Machito, Puente and Rodriguez were first-rate artists in competition with each other to 'bring the house down,' and sometimes it nearly happened! On the ground floor underneath the ballroom there was a drug store, and one day Margo was inside it when a particularly wild number was being played. With hundreds of people uninhibitedly stomping to the pulsating rhythm of the music, she literally thought that the ceiling would cave in and come crashing down around everyone in the store!

The owner of the store didn't seem too perturbed when his ceiling started shifting. *"It always moves like that,"* he said, and went on calmly serving his customers! Many people think the fact it never did happen is a miracle.

The band leaders were all pros who knew precisely what they were doing - playing the audience and their reactions as finely as they played their own music; each one of them trying to prove beyond a shadow of a doubt that they were the best!

The reputation of the fabulous music and dancing at *The Palladium* spread like wild-fire, and people came in droves to experience the extravaganza for themselves. Even passers by and tourists thronged to see what was going on, curious to find the source of the exciting music and enthusiastic shouts of the people they heard, while walking on the sidewalk below.

The Palladium had an official capacity of five hundred people, but once the *mambo* fever took hold of New York, a thousand occupants would more often than not be crammed into the ballroom, and very often as many as two thousand would try to pack themselves in. It was enough to make a Fire Marshall turn in his grave, but at that time regulations were somewhat loose!

It was well known that all over New York on Wednesday nights it was impossible to get a baby sitter! Everyone was dancing at *The Palladium*! The dancers were insatiable: all of them driven into an electrical storm of excitement by the weekly "Battle of the Bands," and the overwhelming, provocative and sensual styles of the *mambo*.

~~~~~~~~~~~

Margo's sister, Olga, was already married by then. She and her husband, Tommy Diaz, were part of a group of friends who were also bitten by the *mambo* bug. Some of the group had become so skillful at the dance they were good enough to enter competitions. Tommy was extremely talented. He was a natural dancer, able to interpret the beat of the music and add his own innovative steps to it, many of which people tried to emulate. Sometimes jumping high in the air and sometimes spinning like a top; with formal training he could easily have become a professional dancer, but sadly his background didn't provide him with the right kind of self discipline that was required.

In and out of reform schools as a child, and then caught stealing and sent to jail, he found himself on a fast track to self-destruction that ended up with a drug habit. They started out as 'light' ones, which quickly spiraled out of his control until the hard ones took their place. Sadly, when still very young, he died from an overdose of heroin and was found dumped into a garbage can one Christmas Day. In the better times though, when Tommy and Olga were first married, they loved to go dancing and compete for the prize money, which could often be well worth winning.

One day, Olga called Margo to ask her a favor. She was looking for someone to fill in for one of Tommy's dance friends, who needed a partner in order to enter a dance contest the next day in Long Island, at Lido Beach.

Margo's reaction to the request was wary, to say the least. For one thing, she had never entered a dance contest, and what was even more important to her she did not consider herself a good dancer. Her nature was not impulsive. As a person who liked to weigh things up before making a decision, she wasn't about to put herself into a position that made her feel uncomfortable.

When she voiced her reluctance, Olga told her not to worry. She explained that Tommy's friend would do all the dancing and that all Margo had to do was follow. Margo was still not sold on the deal, but Olga persisted; so on the condition that everyone arrived at her sister's house earlier than the time of departure for the contest, Margo agreed to go. This way, she could spend a little time rehearsing with her partner and trying out some steps together before leaving for Long Island.

The next evening, Margo arrived at her sister's house to find Olga and Tommy just getting out of bed. She was not too surprised. Their lifestyle was not exactly the kind she had envisioned for herself, but she was not judgmental. Her attitude was if that was the way they wanted to spend their days, good luck to them.

Her sister made coffee, and when they sat down to drink it, both she and Tommy lit up a joint and offered one to Margo. When she declined it, they shrugged and went on smoking. As far as they were concerned, Margo was a tiresome person who always went her own way, in other words, she was a drag and they didn't care one way or another, *what* she did.

When the first of the friends eventually arrived, Margo opened the door to let them in. Cuban Pete entered with his partner, Millie, and as soon as they sat down, they lit up a pipe with marijuana and proceeded to get stoned with Tommy and Olga.

The last group to turn up was Jackie Danois, her partner Little Georgie and Augie Rodriguez.

~~~~~~~~~~~~

Augie was stunned when the door opened and he saw Margo! *This* was the girl, the object of his longing gaze across the dance floor, at least a hundred times, at *The Palladium!* His shock turned into delight. The girl of his dreams had fallen right into his arms, so to speak. He now knew it was going to be a great evening; with one dream coming true, he was going to fulfill another one that night and win the dance contest. He couldn't have been happier!

Margo was oblivious to the turmoil going on in the head of the strikingly good-looking young man she was introduced to as being her partner for the evening. All she could think of was that when her sister had persuaded her to come and join her friends for the dance contest, she had failed to mention that the group would consist of some of the best dancers at *The Palladium!* However, it was too late now to back out, and once Margo made a decision she stuck to it; so she said nothing, let the three guys into the house and brought them through to the others. Little Georgie took in the scene, immediately lit up a joint and got stoned like the rest, but Jackie and Augie were not interested.

Margo looked at Augie anew. Here was a handsome boy; she looked again, a *very* handsome boy who, like her, was not into the drug scene. Her curiosity about him was piqued, and in that moment she decided she wanted to know him better. Her desire to rehearse for the contest, though, jolted her mind back to the issue at hand, so she led Augie into another room where the phonograph was located.

When they started to move to the music, Margo realized immediately that Augie was a terrific dancer. She felt she wasn't even half as good as he, but he led her well, and with her natural ability and the skills she had recently acquired on her own, she was able to follow him.

That night at *The Lido*, fifteen eager talented young couples entered the dance contest; but Augie Rodriguez had a dream to realize and nothing was going to stop him. Not now he had found his girl. They danced up a storm that night, and perhaps Augie was the sole person in the group of friends, after they had all danced their hearts out, who was *not* surprised when he and Margo walked away with the First Prize!

∼∼∼∼∼∼∼∼∼∼

After their success, Augie and Margo started going to *The Palladium* with each other, and despite the fact that some of the best dancers in the city were to be found there, they began to dance so well together that they thought they would soon be good enough to enter the Wednesday night dance contests.

The person considered to be the *crème de la crème* of the dance instructors was a man named Joe Piro, who, because of his amazing skills on the dance floor, was known as Killer Joe. He was given the name in his teenage years, when he frequented the *Savoy Ballroom* in Harlem, where he was known to be a fanatical dancer. However, winning dance contests of all kinds, was only one thing he became famous for; it was the amazingly fast pace he kept up for hours at a time, exhausting partner after partner, that earned him the name Killer Joe.

He won a national jitterbug contest in 1942 at the famous *Harvest Moon Ball*, while serving in the Navy during WW2. Soon after that he was transferred to the *Stage Door Canteen* on Broadway, where he had the opportunity to dance with many stars from the shows.

After the War, he was offered the job of MC at *The Palladium* and he stayed there until it closed in 1962. Joe was a small man with a fabulous personality. He gave mass dance lessons at *The Palladium,* offering instruction in just about any dance that existed, and challenging people who thought they were better than he.

When he brought the amateur dance acts out onto the floor on Wednesday nights, his farcical smile and loud vocal delivery drove the crowd wild, as he boomed out over the sound of the band the word for which he became famous. *"Via"* he would roar, *"Via, go, go, go, cha, cha, cha."* Everyone started stomping to the music, and the Americans in the crowd shouted the phrase, *"Shave, hair-cut, shampoo,"* to imitate the beat, until their words became synonymous with the Latino's *"Go, go, go."*

When the excitement of the crowd was at fever pitch, everyone entering the contest, usually eight to twelve couples, were brought out by Joe onto the dance floor, where the entire ballroom would be vibrating with excited anticipation.

The teams danced together for a while, giving the audience a chance to see which couple they admired the most. The band played to its hilt, the audience yelled and screamed encouragement, and the louder and wilder they got, the less inhibited the dancers became. Twisting and twirling, gyrating and jumping, the whole scene made the movie *Dirty Dancing* look like a Vicarage tea party!

As the band sounded less and less restrained, blaring forth its harmonic syncopated sounds and beating out its hypnotic rhythms, the dancers were driven to do anything to get more audience members on their side. They grew even more frenzied, improvising their choreography and trying out moves they had never previously attempted, for at the end of the contest, it was the audience who voted for the winners.

After about five minutes the teams danced solo, to compete with each other and demonstrate their own particular talent. Each couple had their own individualistic style, and it was a matter of pride that no one would dream of imitating anyone else. When everyone had 'strutted their stuff' and the audience had stomped, screamed and yelled loud enough to determine the undisputed winners, a hugely grinning Killer Joe presented them with their reward.

It doesn't seem like too much today, but at that time, the prize money was well worth having. The first prize was fifteen dollars, the second, ten and the third, five. After the contest, the dance instructors did exhibition dancing, which everyone clamored to see, so they could try and practice any new steps that might be demonstrated. The mambo was still an evolving dance at that time, and The Palladium didn't earn its reputation as *The Mecca of New York's Most Progressive Dancers* for nothing!

~~~~~~~~~~~

Augie and Margo continued dancing together, and felt that if they kept practicing they would soon be good enough to enter the Wednesday night contests. Despite the fact that they had won first prize in *The Lido* contest, which, by the way, was a huge $100 which they had split between them, neither of them had reached a level of confidence that they could go on and win prizes at *The Palladium*.

Not only were their own dance heroes there: the tall dark and handsome Puerto Rican, Joe Vega, and his partner Tybee Afra, a Jewish girl from Monticello, a town in the Catskill mountains of New York, who danced Latin like a dream; and Cuban Pete, with his Italian girlfriend Millie Donay - another great dancer; but many other titans. Larry Selden, an immaculate stylish guy, with an exceptional dance ability, Mike Terrace, a handsome topnotch ballroom dancer who was amazingly popular with the ladies, Little Georgie, all five feet two inches of him, with an incredible ability to put acrobatic movements, like flips and splits, into his dancing style, and a group of three boys called *The Mambo Aces*, who were so smooth and compact, they were able to dance as a team, while retaining the rhythmic authenticity of the *mambo*, and make it look as though they were one-person.

In the face of all that talent, Augie and Margo felt somewhat inadequate. As young people from relatively humble backgrounds, they had a hard time imagining that they could ever be good enough to be accepted on the left side of the ballroom, which was always dubbed as the side for the people of a higher echelon. By definition, this meant one had to be very rich, well dressed, famous, powerful or a dance titan.

Outside *The Palladium*, they occasionally met and discussed their passion for dancing, but Augie was impatient to tell Margo about his other passion. The one he had for her. He didn't want to rush things and scare her off, but she was quickly becoming more important to him than anything else in his life, and he was anxious to tell her so.

Margo also had a problem. She was beginning to have feelings for Augie. It could have been a perfect situation, but she had never mentioned anything to him about her boyfriend, Victor, and the fact that she was supposed to be marrying him.

The pressure on her to marry at that time was greater than she knew how to deal with. Mainly, because Latin girls married young at that time, and as the eldest of the five girls in her family, she and her baby sister, Gladys, were the only unwed daughters. This fact gave her an inadequate, albeit unnatural, feeling of guilt, so she decided it would be best to let Augie know about Victor before their friendship grew into something more serious.

Victor had been perfectly OK with her going dancing before the contest in Long Island, but suddenly he was taking more time off work than he had in ages. He started going with her every time she went to

The Palladium, hanging around the perimeter of the dance floor, and never taking his eyes off her while she was doing the *mambo* with other, more expert dancers. It was as if he sensed she was drawing away from him, and he was beginning to get jealous and possessive.

The situation was just getting too complicated for Margo to deal with, so one day, something happened that brought everything to a head, and Margo had no choice but to lay all her cards on the table.

She had been dancing with Augie and trying out some new steps. It was going so well, she had the feeling that they were really beginning get somewhere. A couple of dancers near them stopped to watch what they were doing and then tentatively tried the steps for themselves. It was a good feeling, seeing that people wanted to emulate them, and it gave her a surge of confidence about her own ability.

Feeling so strongly that she and Augie were becoming like a real dance team on the floor, they must have looked like one too, because Margo suddenly saw Victor's eyes boring into hers from his position at the edge of the dance floor. They were truly the color of green!

That evening she told Augie everything. How her relationship with Victor had more or less drifted to the spot where it was, but that he expected her to marry him; so in order to keep Victor happy, she felt that dancing with Augie would no longer be possible.

Augie was devastated. So much so, that to this day he cannot talk about it without getting visibly upset. It is as though he went through the entire period in a haze, remembering nothing after Margo gave him the news that they had to break up.

Margo also remembers nothing, but her loss of memory is quite different, for when she talked about this stage of her life she didn't even remember that Victor existed, and had to think very long and hard to even remember his name!

The period of time that followed for both of them, though, was clearly not a happy one. Margo continued working in the beauty salon and dated Victor for a while, but ended the relationship after a few months when she realized she was not in love with him and never would be.

When she went dancing, it wasn't the same as before. The special feeling of camaraderie and mutual interest that she had experienced with Augie had gone, and was replaced by an empty, lonely feeling, despite the fact that she was always surrounded by family, friends and would-be suitors.

Augie worked on in the Merchant Marine, and he continued dancing when he came home to New York, but he was not satisfied with his life; it had felt disjointed and unpredictable since he was sixteen when his brother Michael, who had joined the army, brought his best friend Pete home.

Pete had turned out to be quite an influence on the Rodriguez family. Not only did he talk Augie into quitting school and joining the Merchant Marines, he had an even stronger sense of persuasion on Augie's mother Aurora, who was there at the time, on one of her visits to New York.

She and Pete soon began a relationship which resulted in his mother and father getting divorced and his mother marrying Pete!

The fresh turmoil didn't help Augie's insecurities, and his sleepwalking continued. Meeting and connecting with Margo had been a bright shining moment in his life, and now it was over. When he came home from work, he hung out with his friends and dated a few Jewish girls from his neighborhood, but the girl of his dreams was missing, and no one came close to replacing her.

CHAPTER TEN

Several months passed before they got together again. The fact that Margo's brother-in-law, Tommy, knew most of Augie's friends helped a great deal in bringing their reunion about. One evening, they found themselves together in the same group, and realized immediately how much they had missed each other. From that day on, they never looked back.

Dancing as partners again came easily to them. Neither one of them had forgotten each other's moves, or the ease with which they slipped into each other's arms. It felt comfortable, almost like a law of nature, when they united again on the dance floor.

From that moment on, every spare minute available to them was filled with dancing, and before long they were even better than they had been before. When they moved together it was as if they were a single entity. Their natural ability to 'feel' the beat of the music and their passion for the dance, fused their partnership on the floor, and gave them a special quality of movement.

Now the audience at the ballroom formed circles around them when they danced, clapping and shouting encouragement, so much so, that they felt enough confidence to start entering the Wednesday night dance contests. To their delight, within a short time they were walking away with prize money, which they shared.

They both knew by this time that dancing was what they wanted to do professionally. Apart from a few, who also wanted to be professional dancers, the majority of their friends seemed to be happy living their lives with day jobs and going dancing at night, but Augie and Margo wanted more. Having both found exactly the creative outlet they had been seeking, they wanted to take it much further, so deciding to take the next step and make a serious commitment was not a difficult decision for them to make.

They applied for a scholarship to the Katherine Dunham School of Dance and Theater, on West 43rd Street in Manhattan. Katherine Dunham was an anthropologist, choreographer and dancer, whose academic studies on the dances of the Caribbean had made her a world authority on the subject. Having lectured and demonstrated for many years, and appeared in numerous shows around the world, she now ran one of the most prestigious dance schools in the country, teaching ethnic and modern dance and theater.

Doris Duke, the tobacco heiress and philanthropist, was a significant patron of the school, and for a time was also one of its dance students. Other notable performers who studied under Katherine Dunham were Marlon Brando, Shelley Winters, Ava Gardner, James Dean and Jose Ferrer.

Augie and Margo were both accepted at the school, and realized immediately they were about to make the first major turning point of their lives. Some of their dance class contemporaries were Chita Rivera, Harry Belafonte's wife Julie Robinson, the great choreographer Dee Dee Wood, Peter Gennaro and Shirley MacLaine. They remember, ironically, Shirley being sent to the back of the class because she could never get her steps in time to the music, and therefore had a tendency to put the other dancers off!

~~~~~~~~~~~

The new techniques Augie and Margo began learning in school, soon started to show in the Wednesday night *Palladium* dance contests. Not only did they win more prizes, the prizes were always firsts, but to their great dismay the contestants started to complain about the frequency with which they won.

That was the *bad* part of getting better, but the good part was that suddenly the dance instructors and really good dancers started complimenting them on their style. They wanted to know where Augie and Margo were from, and where they had learned to dance so well. Quite unexpectedly, people from the *elite* side of the dance floor, were anxious to be their friends!

To be honored by all this recognition was wonderful, especially since it meant that as soon as it happened, Augie and Margo were invited over to join them on the left side of the ballroom. They were thrilled! It wasn't so much a snob thing that made them happy, but the fact that they now understood they had a status among the good dancers. They never crossed back to the other side of the ballroom, and regarded it almost like foreign territory ever after!

They continued winning the dance contests, and had a huge following of fans that came to see them on Wednesday nights; but the problem of the audience always voting them in as winners persisted with the other contestants.

To keep everyone happy, Max Hyman came up with a plan. He was very fond of Augie and Margo; after all, they brought in a lot of business, so he checked with them first before implementing his idea. He explained to them that the other contestants also needed to have some winning success in order to keep things fair; that all the others had friends and supporters coming to *The Palladium* as well, and that pretty soon, if Augie and Margo always walked away with first prize, everyone would think the contest was rigged and stop coming. As Max Hyman probably knew they would, Augie and Margo understood completely, a typical reaction for people of their generous character, so Hyman immediately put his plan into action.

He decided to have a number pinned on the backs of the male dancers, and to ask four people from the audience to judge the contests. As each team finished their competition piece, the judges wrote a score between one and ten, scoring from high to low. As the judges were escorted from their seats in front of the band, back to their places at the tables, Max Hyman would take the cards and shuffle the numbers around, so everyone had a chance to be a winner!

The judges were usually celebrities, either famous or infamous! People like Arthur and Kathryn Murray, the artist Jackson Pollock, Harry Belafonte, the notorious gangster Joe Costello or Carol Channing, all regulars at *The Palladium*.

Sometimes it was so obvious who the best dancers were that the judges would be amazed at the results, wondering aloud why their choices didn't win, but in the tumult of getting them back to their seats, and Max Hyman thanking them for a great job and greeting their friends, they either forgot, or were distracted from taking the final decision any further.

After the contest, Killer Joe danced solo for the entertainment of all present. His performance was often the climax of the evening, as he demonstrated his incredible stamina and creative style to the extreme; parodying the mambo with rubbery, gyrating limbs and exaggerated, gravity-defying moves.

Just before his routine came to an end, he beckoned the dance contestants back onto the floor, to come and join him. They walked on, to roars of approval and waves of applause, and danced the mambo until everyone was excited to fever pitch, at which time they broke away from their partners and went into the audience to randomly select someone to bring onto the dance floor. Within moments, the whole floor was jammed with dancers, good, bad or indifferent. Nobody cared!

Occasionally, bursts of comic antics interspersed with the standard dance steps, got the audience hysterical with screams of laughter. These were usually attempted by the real dance pros, who knew they could get away with it, or by the completely inadequate dancers, who had nothing at all to lose. They would attempt the splits or prance around with legs crossed and try to spin like tops, delighting everyone when they ended up sliding across the dance floor on their knees.

~~~~~~~~~~

The undisputed King of the knee-slide, though, was *The Palladium's* resident photographer, Harry Fine; a heavy set man with horn-rimmed glasses and a wide, comical grin, who was actually a fabulous dancer. He and his wife were mambo crazy and often won prizes in the Wednesday night contests. He was much loved by the audience, and responded to them by taking endless photographs in a hilariously amusing way.

If he saw a female dancing with particularly sexy and enticing moves, he would knee-slide all the way across the ballroom to get close to her, charging between the dancers as he slid, to snap the one hip-shake she made where her panties would be showing. Time after time, Harry broke up the audience with his antics, snapping the image of a move, or an expression on the face of a dancer that he thought was either comic or tragic, and he was always there for the amazing steps and moves of the pro's in the dance teams.

A couple of the dance teams were clean-cut looking Americans, who wore traditional dance dresses and suits. They looked completely different from the other contestants, who tended to be from Spanish Harlem, and wore updated zoot suits, short or tight skirts and low cut, ruffled blouses, in an array of riotous colors.

The American dancers may have loved the mambo, but they had a hard time looking ethnic when they danced. To the Latinos it looked more like mimicry - an absurd imitation, and their moves never failed to bring farcical applause and screams of hysterical laughter from the audience. They were great material for Harry Fine!

As the band blasted harmonic mambo sounds, and the Americans gyrated and twirled, he compounded the whole situation, driving everyone into a frenzy of delight as he popped off one snap after another, as and when he determined the dancers were looking their least inspiring. Harry was hysterical, but always, always, good-natured; and everyone adored him.

One of the great things about *The Palladium* was that, despite the occasional raid or fight, there was a kind of innocence about the place; everyone was there to have fun. They were all participating in a vast ballroom extravaganza, and were in their own fantasy land. For a few hours they were lost there; everyday woes and ills were forgotten, at least for a while, in that magic place on Broadway called *The Palladium*.

~~~~~~~~~~~

Now that Augie and Margo were 'on the other side', they felt they needed to look the part, so Augie saved his money and bought a suit which he wore only when he went dancing. Margo was still working as a beautician, so she could afford to buy new clothes every once in a while. She was working very hard now, at the beauty shop during the day, studying dancing at the Katherine Dunham School at night and going to *The Palladium* on Wednesdays.

Before very long, she and Augie were given the position of exhibition dancers there. Even with all the card shuffling Max Hyman did with the judge's scores, it was obvious they were too good to be regarded as mere amateurs. In the new job they actually earned a salary! Twenty-five dollars every Wednesday! The entrance fee at *The Palladium* had also gone up. When the club opened, it had started at a dollar, but had been raised incrementally over the past months to a dollar seventy five. The new fee was accepted without a quibble. How could anyone complain about such a relatively small amount, Hyman thought, when all that great music and dancing were available; arguably, the best to be had in the entire country. The teachers and exhibition dancers got in for nothing though, an added little perk for the people 'on the left side'.

Once they started exhibition dancing, Augie and Margo began to feel they were really a part of the show business scene - that they had 'arrived'. *The Palladium* was becoming even more, *the* place to go, and they were seeing and meeting many famous people. People they never dreamed they would meet. Rolls Royce's and long black limousines could be seen outside the building every night, their chauffeurs sitting patiently inside, waiting for stars like Marlon Brando, or Yul Brynner, or the directors and producers from one or another Broadway show.

George Abbot, the famous writer and director loved Latin music and dance, and was a regular there, as was Dizzy Gillespie, whose club, *Birdland,* was a short walk away. Between breaks from his own appearances, he would often go to *The Palladium* and sit in with his friend, Machito's, band.

Singers and dancers from Broadway shows came to watch and dance, after their own performances for the night were over, and even dance schools around the city began sending their pupils to watch and learn the new *mambo* steps and the techniques of the exhibition dancers.

Mixed in with the fancy crowd were also a few notorious characters. Since the 1920's when prohibition was in full swing, New York had become a city full of law breakers and money makers. Private clubs began to spring up, and mobsters moved in to supply the owners with alcohol and 'protection', and the club scene still attracted them like flies, especially the successful clubs.

The Palladium was no exception. Some of the gang bosses from around the city, or drug king pins paid visits there, and were even acquainted with a few celebrities. Vic, Tony and Yumpy, the *Palladium* bouncers, were Angelettes, members of the most notorious family in Harlem, and it didn't hurt Max Hyman to have them on his side! They took care of any trouble that cropped up and were careful to guard the dancers.

~~~~~~~~~~~

Augie and Margo were making friends with all kinds of people once they became a couple. Not only regulars in the club, but the teachers and exhibition dancers. Mike Terrace had married a beautiful girl called Nilda, and the two of them were noted as being the most handsome couple in the dance club, both of them tall and fair-skinned with black hair. Whenever they danced together, they created great excitement.

Mike later divorced and married another beautiful girl. A red-head named Elita, and she and Mike are still very close with Augie and Margo to this day. Joe Vega's girlfriend, Tybee, was madly in love with him, but her parents didn't approve of her relationship with a non-Jewish boy, so instead of marrying she chose a dancing career instead. Cuban Pete married his partner Millie Donay, who went on to dance in a fabulous dance duo called *Marilyn Waters and Millie Donay*. It was the first all woman dance team at *The Palladium*, They, also, were later divorced.

With the individualism they were learning to put into their dance style at the Katherine Dunham School, Augie and Margo were beginning to 'overtake' all *The Palladium's* resident dance pro's, at least in the eyes of hundreds of their fans who frequented the club, and Max Hyman himself, who decided to put them into the elevated spot of closing the show.

It had taken them almost a year to get to this point, and by that time they both knew without a doubt that they wanted to be married. There was only one problem, they had no money saved; but a little detail like that was not going to stop them once they had made their minds up, so they put their heads together and figured out a plan of action.

The annual dance contest at *The Lido* in Long Island was coming up, and the first prize was again one hundred dollars! They decided to enter and, if they won, get married right away.

The same contestants as the previous year also competed, but this time Margo was feeling a lot more confident. With the hard training of the past months behind her, she was not overly nervous, and she had every confidence in Augie and the valuable schooling they had both experienced. It justly proved to have been worthwhile, because once again, she and Augie walked away with the contest and the hundred dollar prize!

On September 2nd, 1950, one year exactly to their first meeting at her sister's house, Margo Bartolomei married Augie Rodriguez in the City Hall in Brooklyn New York. She wore a black and silver dress for the occasion, and he bought a new suit. They spent an absolute fortune. The dress cost a whopping twenty five dollars and the suit was fourteen dollars and ninety five cents!

After the ceremony, which was attended only by Margo's best friend, Lucy, who was Maid-of-Honor, Mencia gave a big dinner party for all the family. Augie's mother was not at either occasion as she was in Santo Domingo at the time, but some months later, when she returned to New York, she persuaded Augie and Margo to go through the whole ceremony again, but this time in a church!

CHAPTER ELEVEN

All the exhibition dancers at *The Palladium* were starting to become celebrities by the time Augie and Margo Rodriguez were married. They were getting booked to work what were known as the 'champagne' hours at various clubs and hotels in the city, or at popular Jewish venues in The Catskills, like *Corey's*, a beautiful hotel near White Roe Lake. It was worth their while, as the pay could be anything from twenty-five to thirty-five dollars a show.

They really began to feel they were 'on the road', when a friend and dancer at the Dunham school, Ralph Alfaro, asked them one day if they would like a job in Uruguay, with the *Enrique Madriguera Orchestra*. Madriguera was a well-known Latin band leader who had played with some of the greats, like Tito Rodriguez and Bandleader Xavier Cugat, and the chance to perform with his band was a great opportunity.

As a dancer himself, Alfaro was going to join up with Augie and Margo to make a trio. They needed to work up three dance routines for the show, which was fine, but there was a slight problem remaining. They had to front the band.

It was a twelve-week contract, and the pay was four hundred and fifty dollars a week for the three of them - too much to let a little item like having to learn to play musical instruments get in the way! With her piano training and ability to read music, it was not hard for Margo to figure out how to play claves, and with their intuitive talent for rhythm, the same was true for Ralph, who ended up playing maracas, and Augie who played the conga drums.

The tour proved to be a great success. Adding the instruments to their performance gave another dimension to their act, and they had been able to perfect it, away from a highly critical, perhaps, New York Audience. It also played a role as a stepping stone to the next booking for the three of them, with Xavier Cugat and his singer wife, Abbey Lane, at *The Waldorf Astoria,* but this time they ended up criticizing themselves.

They worked up a program together of Latin, island-style dancing, similar to their act in Uruguay, and are embarrassed to talk about it now, as they thought the routine would be better if they performed barefoot! When they realized what an elegant place they were in, it was as much as they could do to continue with their act.

Despite their new exposure to travel and the night club circuit, Augie and Margo still felt naive, inexperienced and largely unsophisticated in the ultra-stylish community. They were happy and comfortable in the familiar environment of *The Palladium,* but they were learning that to be a successful professional performer, studying dancing alone was not going to be enough. They had to observe popular taste trends in the stamping grounds of the "upper echelon" in society - the likes and dislikes of the elite - and they needed to work them into their routine and make them their own.

An innate intuition and knowledge of their dance routines told Augie and Margo they should not have performed such an ethnic dance at the *Waldorf,* but from the point of view of the person who booked the trio to appear there, they were great Latin dancers; so he promptly put their names down to play a couple of shows a week at the club *Havana-Madrid* in Manhattan!

They were often double-billed now, with other *Palladium* dancers, like Mike and Nilda Terrace or the *Mambo Aces*, each of whom had their own individual styles, but in their efforts to constantly hone and polish their own skills, Augie and Margo continued with their dancing lessons.

Quite unusually, at the same time they attended class, several ballet dancers had started coming to the *Katherine Dunham School*. At first, the new students appeared awkward, stiff and somewhat clumsy, but after about three weeks of classes, Augie and Margo noticed that they had completely dominated the Dunham technique, and were looking better than anyone else in the class.

Watching this phenomenon week after week, proved to be too fascinating to ignore, so one day Augie asked their dance teacher why, after all the hours of practice and dance study he and Margo had done, they did not look as light and limber as the ballet students.

The answer came when Syvilla Fort, the school's Headmistress called them into her office. Much to their surprise, she told them to consider studying ballet. She seemed convinced they had the ability for it, but instead of giving them a long explanation, she handed them two tickets for the *Saddlers Wells,* Britain's top Ballet Company, who at that time were performing in New York. Syvilla Fort wisely thought it best that her students saw for themselves the high level of poise and perfection that could be attained; if they cared to reach for the skies.

Augie and Margo had never before been to the Ballet. Their seats were right in front of the stage, and they sat on the edge of them throughout the entire performance, completely captivated by the scene unfolding before their eyes. When they saw how the dancers flew through the air, spun on their toes and leaped as lightly as cotton-balls across the stage, they were completely in awe.

They realized immediately that the strength and suppleness of the ballet dancers' bodies clearly played a major role in their capabilities to perform such feats. They further imagined what that type of training would contribute to their own style of dancing, and it blew them away! At the end of the show, when everyone had left the theater, they were still sitting in their seats. Augie broke the silence when he turned to Margo with wide eyes and said, *"Margo, we've GOT to study this ballett!"*

~~~~~~~~~~~

It was the next major commitment. They barely second-guessed their decision, even though they were both quite old to be starting ballet training. They knew that if they wanted to take their capacity to dance to an even higher level, it had to be done with intense training.

Almost immediately, with the help of their teachers at Katherine Dunham, they applied for positions to study at the *American Ballet Theater School* on West 57th Street, and were accepted. To reach that point, it was not necessary to audition. They simply had to be present at a class, which may or may not have had other applicants in attendance. Various teachers then came in to observe the students, and according to their level of skills and potential they were selected to be in one class or another.

Augie and Margo were assigned to the 11:30 A.M. class, which was a mighty compliment to their ability; their teacher could not have been more prestigious. She was Valentina Pereyaslavec, the internationally renowned Ukrainian prima donna, choreographer and greatly esteemed teacher of ballet. In fact, she is hailed as one of the top five ballet teachers in the world.

A small, squat woman, with impeccable deportment; her head and neck always held proudly, Pereyaslavec was a remarkable woman, totally possessed by her love and devotion to dance. Her 11:30 class was like a page out of *Who's Who* in the world of ballet. Dancers including Svetlana Beriosova, Oleg Briansky, Rosella Hightower and Anton Dolin studied under her tutelage.

Whenever the *Royal Ballet* from London or other foreign ballet companies were on tour in The States, ballet luminaries like Rudolf Nureyev, Merle Park, Lynn Sermour and Margot Fonteyn came to the school and were regulars at the 11:30 class. Fonteyn was even known to frequently make a special stop over in New York, in order to attend the class when she was on her way to Australia or Panama.

It was into this atmosphere that Augie and Margo entered, to begin the next phase of their training. Pereyaslavec was the kind of teacher who let the steps do the teaching. She was demanding and exacting, using her body and her voice as constant suppliers of concentration and energy to all the students all the time. She missed nothing: keeping the discipline in the class unusually high, she was an always-vigilant observer and a relentless corrector.

As she called out commands to the students, her voice ranged from hoarse barks to a singing contralto, and her movements, which could all be seen through her baggy pants and blouse, seemed to be willing them into dancers through her own proud carriage, and arms and shoulders which were in constant play. She understood her world completely, knowing full-well the constant struggle, dedication and superhuman effort required in becoming a dancer, but her vibrancy and positive attitude every day was a huge inspiration to her students, and her influence over them lasted a lifetime.

Augie and Margo were no exceptions. Pereyaslavec treated them with the same discipline as she did her ballet students. She was a stickler for maintaining progression, and could be quite excessively concerned if, for example, a student at the barre lifted her leg too high in degage. In her strongly accented English she would say, "*Now, in first time we do this, must be low - later, higher.*"

Margo experienced this type of gentle admonition quite often. Although small, she was a strong dancer with good knees, and she could jump as high as the boys in the class; perhaps a talent she acquired while jumping for balls during the hours and hours she spent playing baseball with her father. Because of this talent she, and three other girls who were also good jumpers, a Russian, a dancer from China and one from Cuba, were put in with the boys' class to exercise.

At the barre, Margo stood behind the Russian girl, who was tall, so she could exactly copy the girl's jump and try to go higher, but each time she succeeded, she heard Mme. Pereyaslavec's voice call to her, "*What you do Margo? What you do? We are no in competition!*"

~~~~~~~~~~~~

Suddenly, Augie and Margo were bitten by the learning bug! They decided to enroll in two more classes, and both of them turned out to be highly beneficial in more ways than one. The first class was taught by Walter Nicks, who had begun his career as the youngest member of the *Katherine Dunham Company,* and went on to form his own, specializing in modern dance techniques.

Nicks had, and still has, a sparkling career as a choreographer, and was once named, by *Dance Magazine* as "The Teachers' Teacher." Having his direction in modern dance proved to be invaluable for Augie and Margo. He gave them huge encouragement by telling them they had a wonderful natural talent, and when they developed routines he helped them stylize their performance. One in particular they remember was a number called *Jubilation,* which they became so proud of they used it for many years, and were always grateful for Walter's advice and direction when the applause came.

Ballet became such an important facet of their training that Augie and Margo decided to take a second class. They joined the *Ballet Arts Ballet School* at Carnegie Hall in Manhattan, where they were taught by Master ballet teacher Vladimir Dokoudovsky who taught beginner and intermediate students. Dokoudovsky was an amazing teacher who had danced with, and was then working for, Olga Preobrajenska, St. Petersburg's best loved ballerina, who had been great friends with Dokoudovsky's grandmother. He is said to have taught over 3,000 students, so was supremely qualified to open the *New York Conservatory of Dance* in 1971, with Patricia Heyes.

Within two years, Augie was leading the class, but although he was good, he and Margo sometimes saw a dancer who completely stunned them. One day they were entering the class when they saw through the half open door, what looked like a young man flying across the room. *"My God!"* Augie exclaimed, *"He looks just like a bird."* The young man was not flying, he was jumping, and the sight was enough to take one's breath away.

His name was Edward Vilella, and he Margo and Augie became fast friends, and still are to this day, spending time in each others' company whenever they can find the time. Vilella went on to have a stellar career, and was destined to be a ballet legend; he studied under Balanchine, one of the Founders of American ballet, and a leading choreographer, and was the only American to dance in Moscow and receive numerous curtain calls. Named as one of the greatest classical American dancers of the Twentieth Century, today he still works very hard for the highly renowned and successful *Miami Ballet,* a Company of which he is the founder.

~~~~~~~~~~

It didn't take too long for Augie and Margo to dominate the ballet technique, and with that powerful training supporting their style, they began to incorporate the moves into their Latin dance base, putting in pirouettes, finger turns, slides, beats and double tours.

When they demonstrated their dancing now at *The Palladium,* the crowd went wild. They loved it, and responded with shouts for *"More! More! More!"* Such a positive reaction only served to strengthen Augie and Margo's belief that they were on the right track, but their modified style of *mambo* dancing began to upset some of the other *Palladium* dancers.

A few 'purists' felt that ballet had no business being in Latin dancing; especially Joe Vega, who never actually said anything to their faces but was quite scathing behind their backs. His girlfriend and dance partner, Tybee, was in awe when she saw what Augie and Margo were achieving with their dancing, and began to study ballet herself. It was a source of great amazement to her friends that she managed to do so, because Joe was so much against it.

Mike Terrace now married to his second wife, Elita, were serious dancers, and they had also realized the benefits of studying ballet when observing Augie and Margo's technical improvement, so they started ballet training as well. It was clear to the few at *The Palladium* who intended to make a professional career out of dancing, that all kinds of schooling and dance influences were necessary to study, in order to achieve their goal.

The impression their Latin friends had with ballet, especially amongst the men, was that all male ballet dancers were gay, and that only gay people liked ballet. Clearly a chauvinistic point of view, but at that time it was widely accepted. The fact that to be a male ballet dancer meant one had to have the incredible strength and agility of a football player, had not yet crossed the average male's mind, let alone a Latino male!

Augie and Margo were not bothered by a little 'behind the hands' criticism. They had complete faith in their decisions, and no amount of gossip and innuendo was going to stop them! They continued diligently to study and train, not only ballet, but also modern dance, jazz and flamenco, and as a result they had a distinctive, unique flavor that none of the other dancers could compete with. They were becoming a 'dance act,' developing strong, seamless performances and empowering their authentic expression of Latin *mambo* - the dance they loved.

~~~~~~~~~~~

In between shows at the *Havana-Madrid,* they, still did their exhibition dance on Wednesdays at *The Palladium*, so within that area of a few blocks in Manhattan where they danced, they were becoming quite the celebrities. It's hard to know exactly what it was like for them then, because they are both very modest people, but although they set extraordinarily high standards for themselves, and probably did not see themselves as anywhere near fantastic, it's clear that by then many other people thought they were.

Max Hyman for one, had put them in the top spot at his dance club, and he did it because hundreds of people clamored to get in every Wednesday night to see them perform. For him they were "The geese that laid the golden eggs", and he did all he could to keep them happy.

The three bodyguards, Vic, Tony and Yumpy, also took care of them. They were always around to make sure no one bothered Augie and Margo in *The Palladium,* and watched the invisible line between the 'street' people and the elites in the ballroom like guard dogs - just willing anyone to cross over so they could be snapped and snarled back again.

Everything seemed quite perfect to Augie and Margo: they had wonderful new friends, dancers all, and they were moving ahead with their careers; until one day an incident happened that made them realize the kind of world they were getting into.

Half a block from the *Havana-Madrid* was a club called the *China Doll,* where a very successful dance act was being performed. Augie and Margo wanted to see it and maybe pick up a few pointers, so they decided to go and check it out one day with all their friends from *The Palladium*, when they had time between shows at the *Havana -Madrid*.

They were having a drink at the bar, minding their own business, so to speak, and watching the show, when a man slid up to Margo and started making passes at her. She saw immediately that he was stoned, but rebuffed him and told him she was married. He chose not to believe her, and persisted with his inebriated attentions to the point that Augie had to step in.

Augie is not a big man, and in many ways he is quite shy, but when he feels angry or scared, it ruffles his feathers and he immediately becomes a bird of prey. He will "pounce" - or react - without any thought for the consequences! The unwanted attentions of the stoned guy made him very angry, so he stepped between Margo and her aggressor, and told him to move off and leave his wife alone. Still the guy was not convinced, and he started pushing Augie out of his way. Pushing led to shoving and shoving led to yelling and some blows, and before they knew it, all hell broke loose in a massive free-for-all!

Three of the guy's friends came over to join in, and started hitting and punching Augie, which made Margo more hysterical than she had been when it all started! She picked up a lamp and started cracking skulls, but she was no match for the four men, who soon had Augie on the floor and were all straddled over him, getting ready to beat him to a mushy pulp.

Augie managed to yell at Margo to go and get Ralph, their dance partner at the *Havana,* and she sped out of the door, but the guy who started the whole thing was in hot pursuit of her. He didn't reckon on the speed with which Margo could run, though, even in high heels, (another reason to be glad of the baseball training with her Dad), so when she reached the *Havana-Madrid* and found Ralph, she had no idea that anyone had been following her.

~~~~~~~~~~~

By the time Margo and Ralph got back to the *China Doll* the fight had been broken up. Augie seemed to be none the worse for wear, but was checking some sore spots when Margo saw him. They looked nervously around the club in case the four guys were around, but instead were shocked to see all their friends still sitting there. It was a hard realization to come to, but no-one had come to their aid!

The Opening Act

They didn't have too much time to think about it then, as they had another show to do. Augie's side was beginning to hurt before the three of them went on stage; the sore spots seemed to be growing and spreading, but he had no time to inspect the damage then, and "the show must go on".

When it was time to go home, they called the police to escort them to the subway station. It was a long way to Brooklyn where they lived and they wanted to be sure there was no-one lurking around a dark corner, waiting to pounce on them and attend to some unfinished business!

Next day, Augie's side was so painful he went to see the Doctor. It got worse before it got better, for the Doctor had to extract lots of glass splinters, which had dug in deep. Augie must have rolled over onto the broken glass of the lamp Margo used as a weapon when he was on the floor! Fortunately, nothing serious had occurred. A cracked rib would have stopped all dancing in its tracks, and caused a serious hold-up to their career.

That night, he was very sore but well enough to dance, so he Ralph and Margo went to the *Havana-Madrid* as usual. When it was time to do their routines, they stepped out on stage and there, right in front, ringside, were the four men Augie had been fighting!

It was no way to begin an act. Their stomachs did a flip and their mouths went dry. Concentrating on their moves was virtually impossible, but somehow they managed to get through their numbers without any mishaps. At the end of their performance they hurried to their dressing rooms to evade any confrontations that might occur, and were just about to enter when someone, very softly, called out Augie's name; and they froze.

Slowly turning around to see who it was they froze again. George Angelette, the head of one of the toughest gangs in Harlem, was standing right in front of them and he wanted to talk to Augie. Margo was beginning to feel like a basket case; to be in trouble with this man, or any of his relatives, for any reason at all, was to court genuine disaster.

Angelette spoke slowly in a low, quiet voice, and explained that he had been in the *China Doll* the night before and saw what had happened. He went further, and said that 'his boy' had been way out of line with Augie and his wife, and that he was now sorry for what he did and wanted to apologize to them.

With that, the guy who made the moves on Margo appeared; at least she thought it was him. He looked a lot different than he had the day before. His face was extremely swollen and he had a cut on his very fat lip. Augie took one look at the guy and wanted to run! He turned toward the dressing room and safety, but Angelette stood his ground. To speed up his departure, Augie told him to forget it, it was all right; he was OK and the guy didn't have to apologize, but Angelette was insistent. His boy *must* do it.

So under his boss's watchful eye, a very nervous guy apologized to another very nervous guy; whereupon they shook hands and agreed to let bygones be bygones. Margo was shaking like a leaf when they finally closed the dressing room door behind them; she chalked it up as one of the most stressful experiences she had ever had!

~~~~~~~~~~

Later, a man known as Cockeyed Nino came to look for Augie and Margo at the *Havana-Madrid*, wanting to make sure they were all right. He was a regular patron from *The Palladium* who knew very well a few of the people concerned; he filled in the gaps about the incident, of which Augie and Margo were both unaware.

Cockeyed Nino explained that he, too, had been in the *Havana Madrid*, and when he saw the troublemaker run out into the street after Margo, he chased after him and tackled him down to the ground - presumably with the blessing of George Angelette. Then he went back into the club to help break up the fracas.

Suddenly, for Augie and Margo, a clear understanding dawned as to why their friends had not immediately rushed to assist. They had been going to *The Palladium*, like Cockeyed Nino, a lot longer than Augie and Margo, and, they all knew *exactly* who the people were in the fight, and were too scared to get involved; a highly understandable situation.

Fortunately for Augie and Margo, George Angelette's wife, Yolanda, loved watching them dance, and was a huge fan. Indeed, she liked them so much that she eventually became their friend and followed their careers. It didn't hurt to have these people on their side!

George Angelette was one of seven brothers who ran Spanish Harlem; he eventually went to prison for twenty years for dealing drugs, but at that time he and his family was not to be tangled with! Not only did they rule Harlem with an iron fist, they also made sure that things ran smoothly in other parts of town, including *The Palladium!* It was certainly useful to have low friends in high places.

After his release from prison, George turned up one night to see Augie and Margo performing at the New York *Latin Quarters*. After the show, he went back-stage to see them and give them his stamp of approval. It was rather a bizarre situation, almost as if he had a need to touch base with people from his past who had not been harmed by him. He told them he was incredibly proud of them and their accomplishments!

Yolanda kept in touch with Augie and Margo all down the years, and is still occasionally doing so.

CHAPTER TWELVE

The determination to succeed was fierce for both Augie and Margo, but as fate would have it, their resolute attitude was about to be pushed to the limit. Within a few short months of starting ballet classes, Margo became pregnant. She kept going for a while, but eventually had to stop the rigorous training before giving birth to their son, Richard, who was born on June 29, 1952. A year would pass before she was able to return.

Now, more than ever, they knew they had to achieve their dream. A child had arrived to bless their union, and they wanted to give him a strong family life. The money-paying jobs they had before were still there, but not a lot was coming in, just Wednesday nights at *The Palladium* and occasional champagne hours at various clubs.

Augie took a few odd jobs here and there to supplement their income, but for him, studying ballet was the most important thing he felt he could do to help them achieve dancing perfection, and in order to do that he needed to continue his classes. This of course required an income, so Margo, with the help of her mother, decided to return to work as a beautician, to help Augie achieve his goal.

The plan was that as soon as he was accomplished enough, he could audition for a Broadway show, which would bring in some good money, and then Margo could quit her job and return to ballet training full time. At the moment she was only able to go twice a week, as her job, the baby, Wednesday nights and champagne hours left her exhausted and with little time to do any more.

~~~~~~~~~~~

Augie started scanning the pages of *Variety*, a paper he describes as "The Bible of Show Biz," the one that all entertainers read to find work, to look for auditions. He found and went to a few, but had no success. While having every confidence when dancing with his partner Margo, on his own and trying to put over a different style made him feel green and inexperienced.

He kept looking though, and one day he read in *Variety*, that a Rogers and Hammerstein Musical, *Me and Juliet*, was about to debut on Broadway, and choreographer Robert Alton was auditioning dancers and singers for the chorus. The show was to be directed by the great George Abbott, who was assisted by his daughter, Judith.

Augie went along to the audition and was thrilled this time to be hired as one of the dancing ensemble, along with Shirley MacLaine. As the first Broadway role for both of them, it forged a bond which continues to this day. The show opened on May 28th, 1953 at the *Majestic Theater,* and it ran for eleven months. Not long, to be sure, but it paid Augie ninety dollars a week, a grand sum, which meant that Margo could now give up her job and go back to ballet training. With the help of her mother, Mencia, who took care of Richard, and for which Augie and Margo are still eternally grateful, Margo returned to Mme. Pereyaslavec's class.

The next few months were full of hard but very creative work for the two of them. With the incomes from *Me and Juliet,* Wednesday nights at *The Palladium* and occasional champagne hours in clubs, they were able to relax a little and concentrate on their dance routines. Then one day, Augie came home and said he had been fired!

He told Margo he got hot-headed and over-reacted to an issue with the cast. He doesn't really remember what it was all about, but puts it down to his 'Spanish temperament!' Probably, someone ruffled his feathers about something and his bird of prey reaction kicked in!

It was quite a blow to their income, but Augie was convinced he could get another job, so again started checking *Variety*. He knew he needed more dance training, but Margo had to stay in school, and if something came up he was going to try out for it.

Auditions didn't come along every day though, and pretty soon he started to get worried. The competition to get work of that kind was fierce, and he was beginning to kick himself over the loss of his last job. Things were going really well at *The Palladium*, however; he and Margo got rave reviews every Wednesday and all the top producers and stars in town went there. Surely, he thought, he could swing that success into another arena where dancers were needed.

One day he heard that a musical comedy called *Carnival in Flanders* was coming up, and the choreographer was looking for dancers. He jumped at the chance immediately to try out for it, but went along with a lot of unease about past failed auditions and the fact that he was fired from *"Me and Juliet;"* however, he was beginning to feel desperate and impatient for work, so he had no choice but to go.

It seemed to him that no matter how early he arrived for an audition, there were always about fifty people standing ahead of him, and this time was no exception. Augie got into line to wait his turn, but suddenly he saw someone he knew standing at the head of the line, and this person was calling the people in to audition! It was Jerome Robbins, a producer, director and choreographer, and although Augie didn't know him personally, he had seen him at *The Palladium*.

'This is a big shot', Augie thought, and immediately his bird personality flew into action. He wasn't angry this time, though, he was scared. Scared he may not get the job and scared that he had a wife and child to take care of, and very little income. Probably, without even knowing what he was going to say, he ran to the front of the line and pulled Jerry Robbins aside. *"Mr. Robbins,"* he said, *"I'm Augustin Rodriguez, and I'm one of the demonstration dancers at The Palladium, I'd like to show you my mambo."* The reply was, *"I don't care who you are, or what you want to show me. You get back in line like everyone else!"*

It was a bit devastating, but Augie learned a lesson that day: not to push in!

~~~~~~~~~~

As it happens, Jerome Robbins did remember him when it finally came to Augie's turn to dance. He liked his dancing at the audition, to the extent that most of the other applicants were rejected and Augie joyfully discovered he was amongst a final group of eight. They asked for his phone number, to call him when he was needed for the elimination test, but as a poor, young just-married guy, he had to explain he had no telephone!

Joy turned to dejection; he thought 'that was it,' he had lost the opportunity, but the next day he got a telegram - *Please show up at 10:00 a.m.*

Again, hope sprang in Augie's heart, but he knew that the kind of dancer they were looking for was not exactly a *mambo* dancer, and he was concerned that he didn't quite understand the dance style needed for the show. Augie is nothing, if not impulsive! Next day he turned up *really* early, so he could sneak into the theater and watch who he thought was Jerry Robbins's assistant choreographer dancing; then, he figured, once he knew the types of moves required, he could practice a little what he had seen before going into the audition.

Everything worked out fine, until he started to try out the steps he had watched being danced by the lady "assistant," but unfortunately they were quite complicated, and Augie still felt he didn't entirely understand the routine. What was worse, he knew it showed when he did his second audition. Feeling pretty badly about the try-out, and in one last desperate attempt to succeed, Augie asked Jerry Robbins if he could show him what he could do with the *mambo*. Mr. Robbins clearly saw a lot of talent when he agreed to watch, and after the demonstration he asked Augie to go and see the choreographer, Helen Tamiris, to see what she thought.

Augie pulled out all the stops and demonstrated everything he knew for her, but although she told him she was impressed with his style, she turned him down for the show, and advised him to go and take more ballet training.

That, of course, was exactly what he knew he needed to do, and what Margo was in the process of doing. Having this kind of confirmation from two highly experienced choreographers, who actually hired dancers, only served to make Augie more determined to study ballet until he was the best he could be.

It was a lesson he profited from a lot more than if he had been hired for the show. *Carnival in Flanders* opened at the *New Century Theater* on September 8th, 1953 and it closed four days later on September 12th! In the Broadway archives, there is no mention of Jerome Robbins having had anything to do with the show, so the chances are that he was helping out his friend, Helen Tamiris, who is credited as having staged the ballet scenes. No other type of dancing is mentioned, so clearly Ms. Tamiris was looking for seasoned ballet dancers only!

It was quite a blow to lose the audition, but Augie Rodriguez is the kind of person to immediately bounce back. Deep down he knew he needed more formal training, so he re-doubled his efforts. As well as continuing ballet lessons, he also enrolled at the *John Gregory School*, to study jazz dance, and it was there that Karma stepped in; at least, it was the result of this last action which affected his future fate.

A man named Bob Fosse stopped by the studio one day to watch everyone dance. Fosse was a writer, director and choreographer, who went on to direct many famous Broadway productions, including *Chicago*, which he wrote and directed, and which still, under new producers, enjoys a successful run on Broadway to this day. After watching the students' dance session, he asked some of them to come and audition for a show he was choreographing. The group included Augie Rodriguez and Shirley MacLaine, who also attended the John Gregory School.

They both landed jobs dancing with the original cast, in the Richard Adler - Jerry Ross musical *Pajama Game*, which went on to receive the Tony Award for best musical in 1955. This was a musical Augie really liked, and he was delighted to be there, dancing with Shirley MacLaine on opening night. This time, though, Shirley also played understudy for the role of Gladys. It was the show that shot her to stardom.

Carol Haney, the star who played Gladys in the leading role, broke her ankle, and Shirley had to take over at the last minute. She was an immediate success, winning unscripted laughs from the audience by charmingly bungling several scenes: such as failing to catch a hat which landed in the orchestra pit.

One of the people laughing in the audience was Hal Wallis, the film producer, who immediately offered her a film contract. The rest, as they say, is history.....

~~~~~~~~~~~

Fosse was a highly innovative choreographer. The type of dance he became famous for was jazz dance, but he developed it to the point that his style became instantly recognizable. His dance sequences were intense and demanding, requiring considerable stamina; they also exuded stylized, cynical sexuality, and had distinctive characteristics. Many Fosse routines utilized signature props like chairs, canes, fishnet stockings and bowler hats, as seen to great effect in *Cabaret,* one of his musical masterpieces.

Once again, with another income, Augie and Margo could continue their ballet training together. They both loved the *mambo*, but after the strong influences of Katherine Dunham, where they had studied modern dance, jazz and flamenco, and then the *American Ballet Theater*, they now knew there was a lot more to dancing than just concentrating on one form.

With both of them now studying ballet again, despite the extra income, finances were tight. Things were going very well, but they needed a break in the form of a little extra work and extra money, when suddenly it came along! A friend of theirs, Olga, who ran a dance school with her husband Pedro, asked them if they would like to do an exhibition dance at the *Roseland Ballroom* one Tuesday night.

Roseland was another large ballroom on West 51st Street, a short walk from *The Palladium*. It was a little more conventional than *The Palladium* in that it mainly catered to the traditional style of ballroom dancer, but it was very large and had the capacity to hold three thousand five hundred people. When dances were held, it was standing room only, which gave it less of a club-like feeling than that of *The Palladium*; nevertheless, it was immensely popular with city residents, tourists and servicemen alike.

The owner of *Roseland*, Louis Brecker, was beginning to introduce Latin bands on slower evenings, and he needed an excellent dance team to demonstrate how exciting the *mambo* could be. Brecker was willing to pay fifty dollars for the exhibition dance, so Augie and Margo didn't need a second invitation!

When they arrived on the appointed Tuesday night, it was not exactly crowded. The majorities of regulars were still into *waltzing, jitterbug* and *lindy hop*, and were not entirely convinced that *mambo* was their cup of tea. Most of the evening was slow, but it picked up a little towards the time of the exhibition when Augie and Margo came on.

After their performance, the crowd may have been small, but the reaction to them was huge! They were invited to come back the following week and the same thing happened; only that time a few more people were there to watch them. Again, they were asked back. They spoke to Louis Brecker about hiring Mike and Nilda and *The Mambo Aces* who, they suggested, could really 'round out' the entertainment. He took their word for it and hired them too.

The following week, in Margo's own words: *"Bingo! The place was jumping!"*

Little by little all the exhibition dancers from *The Palladium* came to perform at *Roseland* on Tuesday nights. It was perfect. Now Augie and Margo had Tuesdays at *Roseland* and Wednesdays at *The Palladium*, plus the salary Augie was getting for *Pajama Game*.

~~~~~~~~~

Louis Brecker was delighted. He had never had a Tuesday night as busy as the ones he was now getting: ever. He started to advertise in the newspapers and called the Tuesday night show "Mamborama," illuminating the name over the entrance to *Roseland*. The business it drew was phenomenal!

Things could have been perfect for a long time to come but, as the saying goes, all good things come to an end. Maxwell Hyman decided to drop by *Roseland* one Tuesday night to see what all the fuss was about, and when he arrived the place was jammed to the rafters.

He was astounded to see a ballroom audience crammed with many of his own staff and patrons, and 'his' top dancers at another venue in town, arguably his competition; all there to see Augie and Margo Rodriguez dance. He let them know that night that he was furious with them, and next day he called them into his office and accused them of being the ones who started the mass exodus from his club.

They explained to him that going to *Roseland* was, for them, just being at another place to make money, adding that *Roseland* was paying them twice as much as they were getting at *The Palladium*. They also said that the clientele was very different in each place, and that they didn't feel they were robbing people from *The Palladium* at all.

Maxwell Hyman vehemently disagreed, for on the night he was at *Roseland* he told them he saw plenty of his own regulars there. He told Augie and Margo he would raise their salary to fifty dollars, but that they must on no account let the other dancers know. He had already spoken to them, and talked them into leaving *Roseland* and returning to *The Palladium* for their original salary.

That night everyone danced at *The Palladium* as before, but when Augie and Margo went to Mr. Brecker at *Roseland* next day to explain to him what had taken place, he was very upset. He especially wanted Augie and Margo to continue working for him, as he explained to them he had plans to put them as an act in the next *Harvest Moon Ball*.

For amateur dancers looking for exposure, this was huge! The *Harvest Moon Ball* was the biggest dance event of the year. It was held at no less a place than *Madison Square Garden*, and that year Ed Sullivan was to be the host.

Augie and Margo were at a loss as to what they should do. They had very strong loyalties for Mr. Hyman and *The Palladium*, but this was their career and their dream, and to turn down such a proposition, which was perhaps a once-in-a-lifetime opportunity, could hardly be contemplated.

They had become very close friends with Mike and Nilda Terrace, so shared their dilemma with them. Mike and Nilda didn't hesitate. They advised Augie and Margo to 'go for it': to stick with *Roseland* for a little longer, and take the opportunity of *The Harvest Moon Ball*. It was only a few weeks away, and Max Hyman would never know. Augie agreed: they didn't dance at *The Palladium* on Tuesdays anyway, so he and Margo decided to take their friends' advice - and the risk!

The following Tuesday they returned to *Roseland* with Mike and Nilda, who came with them to offer support, and also to dance. Their plan was short-lived: next day, when the four arrived at *The Palladium*, they were stopped at the door by a red-faced and furious Mr. Hyman, who read them the riot act, and yelled his ultimate punishment at them. They were banned from ever setting foot in the place again. As he put it, several times, they were *"Barred for life!"*

This turn of events was a real shocker! They realized it had been foolish and naive to have imagined they could get away with it. Their notion that Hyman would never find out, and that they could perform at *Roseland* for a few more weeks before appearing at the *Harvest Moon Ball*, was a crazy thing to have hoped for, but they realized too late. Margo remembers that the saying "You can't have your cake and eat it too" sprung into her mind, and for the first time in her life she *really* understood what it meant.

~~~~~~~~~~

Much as they all loved Max Hyman, they had no choice now but to make the best of the situation, and do the very best they could at *Roseland*, so every Tuesday night they danced their hearts out and tried to erase the memory of the happy times they had spent around the corner at *The Palladium*.

Each week the crowds grew bigger, and they included more and more people from *The Palladium*, who came just to watch them. It took a little while, but life began to feel good again, especially when *Roseland's* roaring success was attributed, in no small part, to Augie and Margo's input there.

They were responding well to the new routine when, one evening at *Roseland*, Augie received a message that someone wanted to see him in the lobby. When he arrived there, he found three people waiting to see him: Vic, Tony and Yumpy, the bouncers from *The Palladium*. They had a message from Mr. Hyman. It was simple and direct - just as the last message had been, but much more menacing. *Stop dancing at Roseland, or Vic, Tony and Yumpy have orders to break your legs!*

Augie was astounded! The three bouncers had always been kind to him and Margo, and they all had a genuine fondness for each other. He explained to them about the tremendously promising project they had coming up, with the *Harvest Moon Ball*, and tried to emphasize what a wonderful career break it could mean for them.

The three big guys mumbled their sympathies. It was obvious to Augie they were genuinely unhappy with the message they had been ordered to relate, especially when they looked around and then bent their heads toward him and whispered, *"Go for it, but for God's sake don't tell Mr. Hyman we encouraged you to do this. If you tell, we'll all lose our jobs!"*

When Augie told Margo what had transpired she was, of course, horrified, but memories of the incident at the *China Doll* were fresh enough to make her certain she didn't want to go up against what appeared to be a very nasty situation indeed. They were trapped in a miserable dilemma, but it would only get worse if they didn't try to obtain help. After talking it over with Augie, she was greatly relieved when they made the decision to go and tell Mr. Brecker what had taken place.

Louis Brecker calmed them down. After hearing the story, he patted their shoulders and told them not to worry, that he would handle the situation.

He was as good as his word - a few days later, Maxwell Hyman called Augie and Margo and asked them to come and meet him in his office. At the best of times, Hyman was what could be described as a highly-strung individual, but when Augie and Margo entered his office and saw him under stress, they were shocked at his appearance. He was a complete emotional wreck! *"How could you say that I threatened you?"* He started screaming at them in a broken, high-pitched voice, *"I love you. I would never do such a thing. Who told you such lies? Who?"*

The situation had completely turned around. Someone had been lying, but who was it? Augie and Margo, wisely, did not delve into the complexities of the issue; rather, they told Maxwell Hyman about their chance to appear in the *Harvest Moon Ball*, and how vitally important it was to them. Hyman was now all for it, and advised them to absolutely pursue the opportunity. Hearing him say that was all Augie and Margo needed.

Later, they discovered what had happened. The District Attorney was a good friend of Louis Brecker. After being told the story, he put in a call to Maxwell Hyman and, like a miracle, the situation was immediately smoothed over! Augie and Margo learned again that it was good to have friends, but this time, high friends in low places!

CHAPTER THIRTEEN

The *Harvest Moon Ball* held on September 8, 1954 at *Madison Square Garden* was a Twentieth Anniversary event. The fields of Finalists were selected beforehand at several dance venues in the city, which included the *Savoy Ballroom* and *Roseland*, in a series of dance contests in their own particular category. Three judges selected winners at the prelims, and five ruled on the winners of the *Harvest Moon Ball*, which not only had a winning team in each category, but also an 'All Round Champion.'

Six different divisions were included every year, but they were not always the same. As new dance styles became popular they were sometimes included in the competition while others were removed. In 1954, dancers competed in the *Jitterbug, Rumba, Foxtrot, Tango, Waltz* and *Polka*.

Prizes were highly coveted, for the winners collected hundreds of dollars in prize money and group contracts worth thousands, with opportunities to appear in television shows like *The Dorsey Brothers Show*, and other prestigious engagements which gave them unprecedented exposure.

The tradition of the *Harvest Moon Ball* began in 1935 and it was held every year for forty-five years, ending in 1980. Sponsored by the News Welfare Association, Inc., it became the most famous dance contest in the world for amateurs, the only dancers allowed to enter.

It was no wonder, then, that Augie and Margo were anxious to participate. Clearly, Louis Brecker had seen dance contestants come and go over the years at *Roseland,* but in the Rodriguez's he saw a talent which was way above the norm. Giving them an opportunity to appear as part of the entertainment at such a venue, was the highest compliment he could pay them, and as much as they could possibly dare to dream.

~~~~~~~~~~~

When the day came, they were feeling both excited and terrified, but had no opportunity to rehearse or spend any time nail-biting, as Augie was dancing in *Pajama Game* that afternoon. After the matinee, he had to run to the *Garden* to appear with Margo, and immediately after, run back to the theater for the last show.

They were listed with a group of outstanding entertainers, which included Eartha Kitt, the tap dancing *Clark Brothers,* singer Mindy Carson, Eddie Fisher and Noro Morales and his orchestra, who played the song *"Shine on Harvest Moon,"* the official song for the event, when the competition started. This was a very popular moment, when the entire audience joined the orchestra to sing the song at the tops of their voices, which hyped up the excitement and enthusiasm everyone felt before the dancers came out to compete.

The entertainment acts, which came on during intermissions, were all received with great enthusiasm from the spectators. Mindy Carlson captured everyone when she began singing *"Steam Heat"* the immensely popular song from *Pajama Game,* which had become a hit musical since Augie's first night, and went on to win the Tony Award for best musical the following year.

Eartha Kitt came on wearing a skin-tight beaded black dress, wound herself around the mike and began to purr something about *"Mink, Shmink,"* delighting the audience with her *"Grrrrrrrrrs"* and *"Meeeowwws."*

Eddie Fisher, the current "King of Sing," got through three songs and then promptly forgot the words for his fourth number. It was perfectly OK with the crowd though, because, rather sheepishly, he admitted to them all, *"I think I'm in love."* No doubt a reference to his passionate affair with Elizabeth Taylor. His comment brought the house down, and fortunately he managed to remember the words when the cheers of the forgiving audience faded to silence.

Augie and Margo had a twelve minute spot in which to demonstrate the results of all their hard work and study. This was it! Their chance to show themselves to the world; and it seemed like the whole world when they walked on stage, for eighteen thousand two hundred and sixty-one dance-happy fans were packed into *Madison Square Garden* on that day!

They came on, to a glowing introduction from Ed Sullivan, and began to dance their first *mambo*. As the applause died down, the audience became completely silent, almost dumbstruck, while they watched astounding routines they had never seen before. The blending of all the influences which were developing Augie and Margo's unique style, were showcased that night for the massive crowd of dance fans, and when their performance was over the people, in unison, roared their appreciation.

The second and final dance received, if it was possible, even more applause, and calls for *"more,"* but much as they were enjoying the audience's reaction, Augie had to sprint back to *Pajama Game,* so everyone had to be satisfied with the amazing but relatively short performance they had seen.

Their success, actually, was faster than overnight. It was instantaneous. As they were walking off stage, (Augie practically running), Ed Sullivan invited them to appear on his television show.

That night, after the Ball, their mood was pure elation, and it became even more elated when they read the reviews in the newspapers next day. Josephine Di Lorenzo, a writer for the New York Times, said that when the entertainers sprinkled their stardust over *Madison Square Garden,* *"The crowd roared their approval."*

She went on to say, *"While all the acts nearly tore down the house, the most surprising and heart-warming success belonged to the dance team of Augie and Margo. The young couple, married and parents of a 2-year-old boy, were making their big-time debut as a team. Augie Rodriguez, a dancer in the hit musical, "Pajama Game", rushed to the Garden to appear with his lovely wife. They did two mambos and with yells for "more," Augie found it difficult to rush back to the theater."*

~~~~~~~~~~

They are too modest to say so, but many articles written on the history of *The Palladium*, by musicians, club members and people who became professional dancers themselves, say that watching Augie and Margo Rodriguez dance was an amazing experience. Audiences just couldn't get enough. The acrobatic single-handed lifts they performed were totally awe inspiring, and Augie was the first dancer ever, to perform a move with Margo where he spun her round incredibly fast while she was crouched down and balancing on her heels; exactly as ice-skaters "corkscrew" - but without the convenience of the ice!

They have been called 'outstanding', 'sensational', 'thrilling', 'show stealers', 'exciting', 'brilliant', the list goes on, but nobody who was fortunate enough to see them dancing at *Roseland* and *The Palladium* at the start of their career, when they were fresh out of high school and developing their act, has ever forgotten the way Augie and Margo ignited an audience, and became the idols of them all.

It is fair to say that every one of *The Palladium* dancers, who taught and demonstrated, had now polished their acts to a fine degree; they stood head and shoulders above the average people who came in to dance from the street. Although occasionally a terrific mover would stand out in the crowd, the more elite and accomplished dancers were capable of intricate steps and actions that very few could imitate. They moved like silk, elegantly and with a style of controlled informality, leaving observers almost breathless with excitement.

To watch them dance was an unspeakable thrill, and many young people who subsequently became famous dancers and performers, got their first taste of 'how it should *really* be done' when they came to *The Palladium* and saw this select few, who were dubbed "The Kings and Queens of *mambo*." Augie and Margo, Michael Terrace and Elita,

"Killer" Joe Piro, Joe Vega, Larry Seldon, Little Georgie, Cuban Pete and Millie Donay, *The Mambo Aces,* Tybee Afra and several others. They danced every spare moment and were worthy of the title they were given. They were loved and worshiped, and they deserved the adoration.

It was all work now, all the time, but for the Rodriguez family things were looking up. They had bought a car and were talking about fixing up their apartment. When they were not dancing in classes, on the stage, at *The Palladium,* or looking after baby Richard, they were sleeping.

One day Augie decided he and Margo needed a little time for themselves, so he called in sick one evening to the management of *Pajama Game.* They did not believe him, and were convinced that he was doing a one-night-stand dance performance with Margo. Next day when he went in to work he was fired on the spot.

In fact, he had gone with Margo to see the movie *Waterfront*! It was a fair cop! He could have been really upset, but he had been in *Pajama Game* for over a year by then and was getting a little tired of the routine. Also, things were beginning to go really well for them both.

Augie and Margo's intuition to make sure they performed at the *Harvest Moon Ball* had been absolutely correct. It proved to be the spark that ignited the engine which sky-rocketed them to fame! Their appearance on the *Ed Sullivan Show* was the first view they had of the earth - from the moon, but it took a while longer before they felt confident enough to officially turn professional.

In the meantime, Louis Brecker and Maxwell Hyman were delighted to still have them around, doing their exhibition dancing and making history at both *Roseland* and *The Palladium.* For one thing, they were getting top billing with the bands. Brecker was spending a fortune, advertising their weekly appearances in all the New York papers, and including photographs of them dancing in the ads.

They also had their names up in lights outside *The Palladium and Roseland* - an unheard-of event for dancers until then - and famous people were coming there now to watch *them* dance!

In the entertainment columns of newspapers where they were starting to get mentioned, Earl Wilson in his "It Happened Last Night" article wrote, *"Marlon Brando started a stampede at The Palladium last night when he came in to see Tito Rodriguez and mamboists Augie and Margo. After they'd danced for him, the crowd asked Brando to dance for them. He declined . . . His worshippers swarmed down on him . . . And bouncers helped him get out."*

Not only famous, but important people also were starting to notice them. George Abbott, the writer and director, who had actually written *Pajama Game*, loved to watch the *mambo*, and had gotten to know Augie and Margo through his visits to *Roseland*.

~~~~~~~~~~

Ten months after *The Harvest Moon Ball*, a man called David Baumgarten, head of variety acts at *Music Corporation of America*, or *MCA*, went to *Roseland* one night to watch Augie and Margo dance. He was more than impressed. So much so, that next time he went he took Merriel Abbott, the well-known booking agent, to see them too.

Her reaction was immediate. While Augie and Margo were dancing, she turned to Baumgarten, *"Get them out of here, Dave!"* She said. *"Make an act for them."*

She then told Margo to lose ten pounds, fast! She had an assignment in mind for them, and wanted them streamlined and perfect for it.

Margo knew Miss Abbott meant business. She began dieting immediately, and before the month was up she doubled the demand and lost twenty pounds! David Baumgarten agreed with Merriel Abbott's idea on the assignment, which was in one of New York's plushier nightclubs. He told Augie and Margo, *"There's no need to begin your career in some crummy joint and then work your way to the top. Start at the top, and then try and stay there."*

Suddenly, out of the blue, just as things were beginning to look hopeful for them as a pair, Bob Fosse contacted Augie and told him he was staging the dances and musical numbers for a new show, *Damn Yankees*. He wanted Augie to dance in it with Gwen Verdon, a dancer, whom Fosse actually married in 1960.

It was a very difficult decision for Augie and Margo to make. They knew all too well that nothing in the entertainment business is guaranteed for ever. Even big stars had to be given contracts, and many really talented people needed to sometimes wait for months while their Agents scouted around to find them work.

Augie discussed his situation with Fosse, telling him about the opportunity that had arisen with David Baumgarten and MCA, but Fosse was very persuasive. He even brought his ex-wife and dancing partner, Mary Ann Niles, into the discussion. She agreed with Fosse and advised Augie to stay on Broadway and not "do the circuit", where many talented people had come to grief.

With a job in a musical, so long as it was popular, there was a good chance of several months, if not years, of regular pay-checks, and having a child in the family now to support, gambling with an opportunity such as the one he had been given, seemed like a foolish venture. Despite the fact that, above all, Augie really wanted a joint career with Margo, where they could dance as a team.

The correct answer to his dilemma truly eluded him, so one evening at *Roseland,* when he saw George Abbott in the audience, he went over to ask his advice. By that time, Abbot had seen Augie and Margo perform several times at *The Palladium* and *Roseland,* and to a certain extent was following their career. Without hesitation, when Augie told him about *Damn Yankees,* and what Fosse and Niles had advised, Abbott said, *"Forget it! Stick with MCA and Margo, and take your chances as professionals. You are both good enough to make it, and I believe you have a tremendous future ahead of you both."* Words like these from a Broadway icon sunk in, and Augie took his advice!

~~~~~~~~~~~

Their first appearance as professional dancers was on July 6, 1955, when they were booked to dance in the *Starlight Roof* of the *Waldorf Astoria*. This time they *really* knew where they were going! This time there would be no bare feet! The *Starlight Roof* was one of New York

City's most elegant night clubs. They were to open the late-night supper show for Harry Belafonte, and the assignment supported quite a historic event, for it marked the first time a black entertainer had ever performed at that hotel.

Felicia Sanders was presented as the singing star of the earlier dinner show that evening. She had gained popularity for her recording of *"Song from Moulin Rouge"* and several other records, but recognized at that time as a 'café singer,' she was by no means as well known as Belafonte.

He, at that time, was starring in the Broadway show *3 For Tonight*, at the *Plymouth Theater*, and was also achieving success as a singer on the cabaret and nightclub circuit, having already recorded three albums. The last of the three, *"Calypso"*, which he recorded that year, went on to sell over one million copies and was the first record ever to have sold that many. This accomplishment paved the way for the "Grammy's," the annual award given to performers for their best musical achievements, which started four years later in 1959.

In view of his unprecedented appearance at *The Waldorf*, Belafonte drew a furor of media attention. Members of the Press were 'all over' the *Starlight Roof* that first night, and the fact that he had become an entertainer of stature with a huge following of fans, ensured the nightclub was packed for his performance. Also, many stars and famous people, including Belafonte's friends, were all there to support him.

To say Augie and Margo were nervous, is putting it mildly. Augie remembers them as being *"Two tense, terrified kids."* He even recalls that he had eye twitches! They had 'crossed over' into a different world. A world of professionals and top-flight artists, who always had to satisfy the demands and desires of an extremely fickle public; if they didn't make it now they would sink down into obscurity, like a stone in a pond, and their dream would be shattered.

Fortunately, it was a resounding success. Critical appraisals in New York papers the next day could not have been more complimentary. In one review the show was described as *"One of those nightclub experiences that linger in memory."* Even the snobby and pretentious critics had a difficult time finding something negative to say.

In one rather lengthy tongue-in-cheek review by Robert W. Dana, Belafonte's performance was barely mentioned. He described Belafonte as being *"Rated as a top folk singer in the country,"* and then just went on to list the songs he sang that night, while unknowns, Augie and Margo, in the same review had a much longer opinion on their performance, which included: *"They have fiery footwork, both are small. Margo is the sultry type and Augie with a flamenco dancer's build. Quite a mambo they do, but they'd shine more in a more appropriate setting for their wares."*

~~~~~~~~~~~

Dana's entire review of the new format at the *Waldorf,* made it very clear throughout he did not approve of the hotel - in his mind one of the last bastions of couth in the city - being overrun by anyone other than stick-in-the-mud, traditional performers, preferably white. The title of his piece said it all; "Starlight Roof Offers Miss Sanders, Belafonte", and then rather scathingly in one comment, *"The Waldorf wants everybody to know this is 1955, but they want to be different."* He then goes on to describe the type of entertainer being *"offered"*.

That particular review is, out of hundreds, the least pleasing one Augie and Margo would ever get in their entire career; which is amazing since it was their first appearance as professionals, and the whole show was a highly controversial landmark for the *Waldorf Astoria,* in any event.

Another much more typical review of that night started out, *"If their first* (professional) *nightclub appearance is anything to go by, this young dance team shapes as one of the brightest and most promising hoofing combos to come along in a long while. Young, imaginative and resourceful, they bowl Waldorf-Astoria (Starlight Roof) ringsiders over."* It continues . . . *"Act shows the couple's affinity for classical ballet. It's a knockout visually and as an exercise in interpretive dancing. Numbers are well chosen for contrast and hold a lot of excitement. Couple is beautifully coordinated and achieves a high degree of fluidity. . ."*

Review after review made similar highly complimentary remarks. Augie and Margo Rodriguez had definitely made it! It was the beginning of the rest of their lives. For the first time, after all the studying, practicing and sticking to their plan, no matter who had made fun and criticized, they began to feel it had all been worth it. Now, they felt, they were good enough to perform with the best.

Their professional career was about to begin!

CHAPTER FOURTEEN

After the great reviews from their *Waldorf Astoria* appearance, Miss Abbott threw the magic switch! She booked Augie and Margo into the *Beverly Hilton* in Hollywood, a brand-new hotel which was just opening its doors, and then in late October, only fourteen weeks after their first night at *The Waldorf,* they were whisked off to Chicago.

Their success in Hollywood had been so great, that they were now booked to perform in an eight-week revue put on by the Hilton chain, called "Boast of the Town." It was held in *The Empire Room* of Chicago's most elegant hotel, *The Palmer House*, and Augie and Margo alternated every two weeks with the same performance which was, again, at the new *Beverly Hilton* in Los Angeles.

Ever since prohibition, large hotels in cities around the country had begun to feel a growing competition from nightclubs, where entertainment and illicit liquor could always be found; so in order to counteract this, many of them instituted a policy of food and entertainment in their larger reception rooms. It proved to be such a successful course of action that it continues to this day.

When the hotels began this custom in the early 1940's, it provided an invaluable support to both entertainers and musicians, who until then had only clubs and theaters to rely on for work. By the time Augie and Margo were performing more than a decade later, hotels across the country were often in competition to attract the 'big name' performers to their doors, and they were happy to pay large amounts for them, since the idle rich were more than willing to fly across the country to wine, dine and be entertained. Agents were also paid well to find and book the acts, and eventually the entire reputation of a hotel could depend upon the type and quality of performers who were there to amuse their guests.

It was a compliment, therefore, that having very successfully opened for Harry Belafonte at *The Waldorf,* **in that hotel's controversial revue, Augie and Margo, had been slated to actually 'open' the brand new** *Beverly Hilton* **hotel in Hollywood, and then go on to perform in a long contract at the Hilton chain's most elegant hotel, frequented by the crème de la crème, in Chicago.**

At the *Beverly Hilton*, they appeared with Stanley Melba's band, which had played in all the best venues in the country, and they opened for Gilbert Becaud, the featured artist. He was an immensely popular French singer, who was enjoying the golden era of 'French Chanson,' with other notables like Maurice Chevalier, Jacques Brel and Charles Aznavour. He was discovered in Paris by Aznavour and Edith Piaf, who saw him playing piano in a nightclub. They immediately spotted his talent and helped launch his career, which included advising him to change his name, which was then Francois Silly!

During his career, Becaud wrote four hundred songs, one of which was *Et Maintenant* or *What Now My Love?* which was recorded one hundred and fifty times. The long list of singers who recorded it includes Elvis Presley, Shirley Bassey and a duet, with Frank Sinatra and Aretha Franklin. Another song he wrote with Jacques Pills, who became Edith Piaf's husband, was *Let It Be Me*, later recorded by the Everly Brothers, Tom Jones, Elvis Presley and Bob Dylan. This song was written with Pills during his tour of The United States, which lasted over a year.

When Becaud made his first appearance in Paris, at the *Olympia Music Hall*, he sent the crowd into a hysterical frenzy and, because of his electrifying performance, he earned the name "Mr. 100,000 Volts." The young women in the audience became so hysterical and excited by him during his performance, that they started breaking arms off the chairs!

He was quite an act to live up to, but Augie and Margo opened for him brilliantly, though when asked to describe him, they say that they still felt like, to quote Augie, *"A pair of dumb kids, totally in awe of such a big celebrity."* They remember him as being a delightfully charming man, and were not aware of his reputation for having a fearsome temper! Becaud died from cancer on December 18, 2001 at the age of seventy-four, and was mourned by all of France, including President Jacques Chirac who led the tributes.

Chicago's *Palmer House* show in the *Empire Room*, featured Will Jordan, a brilliant impersonator, who was launched to success by Ed Sullivan when he appeared on his television show. Jordan did a particularly good impersonation of Sullivan, who liked him so much that he invited him back on his show again. It was quite a compliment to be asked back to *The Ed Sullivan Show* - he didn't issue invitations lightly!

Jordan maintained that the secret to doing his great impressions was to "feel" like the person he was doing. It was apparently quite a jolt to see him "physically" change from Jack Benny to Bing Crosby to Bob Hope!

~~~~~~~~~~~

Another performer in the *Palmer House* show was Billy DeWolfe, a character and film actor. As well as being a master of diction, he was known for his impeccable dress, fastidious nature and masculine elegance. His dark hair, and pencil thin mustache, caused women to find him extremely handsome, so it was surprising that his most popular act was that of a middle-aged woman, whom he named Mrs. Murgatroyd, "doing lunch" after a shopping spree!

In his impersonation, he wore a hat bedecked with flowers, steel-rimmed glasses and his mustache! His campy deportment in the routine was hilarious and so popular that he went on to make dozens of appearances with Johnny Carson on his *Tonight* show, and to make several films.

The critical reviews for the *Palmer House* described the show it as being *"Razor-edged"* and the comments about Augie and Margo were that *"Boast of the Town can boast also of having the most exciting young dance team since Veloz and Yolanda electrified the Empire Room. They are Augie and Margo, who dance with passion, precision and that added spark that ignites an audience."*

It is worth noting that Veloz and Yolanda were possibly the most successful ballroom dance team in the 1920's and 1930's. As a matter of fact, in 1929 when they were still very young, they purchased the *Palmer House,* opened it up and operated it, going later into films and eventually selling the hotel to the Hilton chain. As ballroom exhibition dancers, their popularity lasted for years, and they ended up with a long-running television show and had many movies to their credit, including several Disney movies. Disney's Snow White was actually modeled on Yolanda.

A lot of good publicity must have been given the producers of the *Boast of the Town* show by MCA because, new as they were, Augie and Margo were featured on the front cover of the *Palmer House* program. The photograph of them is interesting, because the manager, who had the last 'say' in the arrangements for the show, would not allow Margo to wear pants, which she preferred to wear for her performances, since the unrestrained movements in their act made pants more practical. The *Palmer House,* clearly, was far too upscale for such scandalous attire!

The clothing for both Margo and Augie had actually been the topic of some more well-heeded advice from George Abbot. *"Never, ever, wear shirts and skirts covered with frills!"* He said. *"Your image must be more sophisticated and elegant."*

It was quite common then, for Latin musicians and male dancers to wear shirts with ruffles down the front and covering the sleeves, and for female performers to dress in a somewhat predictable style, with long or short frilly skirts in a multitude of bright, sometimes garish colors, ultra-deep cleavages and even flowers in their hair, but the effect was beginning to look extremely unsophisticated.

Augie and Margo trusted Abbott's word. Unless they had to wear an actual costume, the clothes they wore from then on were always elegant and striking. Sometimes, also, incredibly sexy; Margo occasionally wore clinging, almost transparent, or gilded body suits, which only served to enhance the sensual or passionate dance routines they performed. Many very interesting reviews have been written about Margo's 'steamy' outfits - all of them complementary!

The curious thing is, though, despite the clothing, these people could probably be described as the most modest famous performers of their time. They had no idea then how popular they would become, how many people would love them and how many icons of entertainment they would 'open' for in the coming decades.

~~~~~~~~~~~

The first one came quite quickly. Bob Hope saw Augie and Margo at the *Palmer House*, and shortly afterwards he called them personally to be in one of his shows. It was a large variety show, held in Seattle's *Amphitheater*.

Cited by the *Guinness Book of Records* as the most honored entertainer in the world, Bob Hope's achievements are legendary, and Augie and Margo performed on his shows many times after that first occasion. Mainly, they responded to benefits and charity events when Bob called them, and always felt privileged to appear with him, though they say that Bob called them a lot!

Sometimes they were unable to attend due to their busy schedule, but all entertainers' Agents expect their clients to appear at least three times a year at charity events and Augie and Margo did more than their fair share.

In September 1956, they were invited back to appear again at the *Harvest Moon Ball*, and although they had a two-week engagement date out of town they cancelled it immediately because it was more important for them to thank everyone for their big break.

The memories flooded back as they stepped on the stage to cheers and applause; all their fans were there, and Augie and Margo knew it! It was an emotional and exhilarating evening for them. They owed so much to Louis Brecker and the *Harvest Moon* management for giving them the opportunity to be 'discovered.'

They were now established on a wild and magical ride; not an idle moment or an open date had been on their schedule in the two years since their first appearance at the Ball two years previously. The sky was the limit for them now, and of course they weren't going to miss an opportunity to say *"Thank you!"*

A couple of lines written about them in the Miami Herald summed it up very nicely. *"In the opening spot were Margo and Augie, a sharply groomed and smartly routined dance combo which will wake up one morning and find they have become too good to be an opening act."*

~~~~~~~~~~

From the *Palmer House*, Augie and Margo went for a long booking to the *Eden Roc Hotel* in Miami, which opened in early 1956. Stars like Elizabeth Taylor, Lucille Ball, Desi Arnaz and Lena Horne were soon to be seen on the guest list, and the biggest names in show business would perform in the hotel's *Café Pompeii*, but Augie and Margo were there when the *Eden Roc* opened its doors for the first time!

Once again, they performed at a hotel's grand opening, and again they would be appearing with Harry Belafonte. They were a huge hit! Critical reviews were excellent, and Augie and Margo were delighted; obviously MCA considered they were good enough to handle events that might be quite tricky.

First shows in brand new hotels, could possibly make or break the reputation of the hotel's entertainment presentations; especially as the opening was accompanied by so much fanfare and publicity. So far, MCA trusted their intuition about Augie and Margo. Since they began, the favorable reaction of audiences and critics alike had been phenomenal!

Two years later, they performed at the *Eden Roc* with Belafonte again. Ed Sullivan happened to be there and he flipped over one of their routines; a slow blues number. He loved it so much that he invited them to appear again on his television show. That in itself was an honor he did not bestow on many of his guests, but his admiration of Augie and Margo really shone through when he introduced them as being two of the best dancers of the century! He put his money where his mouth was - over the years that followed he had them on his show nine more times!

~~~~~~~~~~~~

Their next booking was in South Boston at *Blinstrub's*, an eight hundred and fifty-seat restaurant and night club, which was reputed at the time to be the largest and most exciting club in the country.

Many famous stars entertained there, and when Augie and Margo went, they performed on a bill with Patti Page, who had been the first big star to open the newly re-modeled club in early 1952. At that time, many people had regarded the club as being Blinstrub's Folly, and named it so. The owner, Stanley Blinstrub, had been extremely successful as a restaurateur and night club owner since 1937, but going into the business of hiring "big name" entertainers, which he decided to do, was considered risky as the investment was very high.

Fortunately for Blinstrub, the nay-sayers were wrong, and from the first night that Patti Page entertained his guests, the night club became such an overwhelming success, that famous celebrities clamored to work there.

Five years later, when the club was enjoying its hey-day, Patti Page and several other entertainers were invited back for a sentimental anniversary celebration. A young female drummer, escorted by her very domineering mother was also on the bill, along with a comedian and the incomparable Augie and Margo Rodriguez!

The young drummer had been slated to perform before Patti Page came on, but Stanley Blinstrub had done his homework on Augie and Margo, and he wanted them to open for her, so he changed the order of appearance for everyone, putting the drummer first, much to her mother's annoyance, and the comedian next.

Augie and Margo, still very new in the business, were to perform ahead of a singing star who was the most popular and best-selling female artist of the decade. Her recording of *Tennessee Waltz* sold ten million copies, and remains the biggest selling single by a female singer. Patti Page's list of achievements is legendary, and until now, she holds the title of the female recording artist who has sold more records than any other in history, with over one hundred million to her credit! She was known as "The Singing Rage," but little did she know that a couple of young dancers from New York would steal some of her thunder that night.

Blinstrub's was packed with Patti Page fans, and next day, George Clarke from *The Boston Herald* wrote a column headed *"Patti Page Overwhelms Night Audience."* Clarke's review of the entire show was that it was fabulous. Of Augie and Margo, he says, *"The whole show was superb, especially Augie and Margo, young dancers who recently appeared at the Waldorf Astoria in new York, and who came into the audience afterwards to greet Billy DeWolfe, Quinzee's own, with whom they had appeared at the Palmer House in Chicago."*

What actually happened behind the scenes was a little disturbing. In the future Augie and Margo would occasionally have to contend with similar situations, but usually with stars whose egos were bigger than their talent, and rather than pleasing them, it came as a great surprise.

After their performance, the mother of the young drummer was hysterical that her daughter had been "pushed aside" for a pair of relatively unknown dancers. She told everyone, including Stanley Blinstrub that her daughter was a great performer, indeed, a star, who had played at important venues all over the country. The poor young girl let her mother rant, she knew her mother thought she was a star, but mother hadn't heard the *real* star of the show back in the dressing room, as she had! After the show Patti Page was upset, *very* upset.

Before coming on stage to sing, she had to wait in the wings for the audience to stop applauding Augie and Margo's performance. She waited . . . and waited . . . and waited. Finally, the announcer introduced her and she walked on, but the crowd was still applauding Augie and Margo, which angered her no end.

A person from the audience that night remembers well what happened when Pattie started her act. *"She began her first two songs off-key,"* he said, *"something that a real pro like that should <u>never</u> do!"* The leader of the band apologized to her afterwards, but she admitted to him that she was the one to blame, not him.

As is happened, and as the newspaper review said the next day, Patti Page *'overwhelmed the audience with her performance,'* so she really had no need to be so resentful of the two young dancers who had also wowed the audience that night, with their totally different act.

Christine Hamer-Hodges

The Opening Act

The Opening Act

Christine Hamer-Hodges

.... The Opening Act

135

Christine Hamer-Hodges

The Opening Act

Christine Hamer-Hodges

CHAPTER FIFTEEN

In the audience at *Blinstrub's* that day, was William Rosenberg, the founder of *Dunkin' Donuts*. He was there with his wife Bertha, and best friends, Harold and Ruth Homestock. As a resident of Boston, Bill Rosenberg had already made a name for himself.

At the age of fourteen, during the depression, he left school to help his family, by driving an ice-cream truck, but it was while working as a young man in the Boston shipyards during World War II, that Rosenberg noticed the workers had no opportunity to get food and drink 'on the job.'

He knew how much profit could be made selling food if the customer base was there; so taking a great leap of faith, he borrowed enough money to buy some old telephone company vehicles, and had them insulated like the ice-cream truck he had driven as a teenager.

He drove his aluminum-sided mobile canteens around to factories and construction sites, and after four years had over two hundred vehicles servicing workers in Massachusetts. Rosenberg soon noticed that the items bringing in most revenue were coffee and donuts, so remembering his favorite sweet treat as a child, which was a jelly donut from a stall in Quincy Market, he decided to open a coffee and donut shop, offering fifty-two varieties of donuts - one for every week of the year.

By 1955, *Dunkin' Donuts* shops were all over the Northeast, and Bill Rosenberg was getting ready to franchise his idea and open up in markets across the country. In 1960, he actually founded the IFA, or International Franchise Association, which now has over 30,000 members worldwide.

Rosenberg was the kind of man who threw himself wholeheartedly into things that interested him, and besides being a highly successful businessman he was also a great fan of Latin music. His friend, Harold Homestock, was also a fan who, after seeing Augie and Margo perform for the first time in Blinstrub's, described himself as being *"crazy about their dancing,"* As a result of their enthusiasm, Bill Rosenberg and Harold Homestock, and their wives, became, perhaps, the most dedicated followers Augie and Margo would ever have.

~~~~~~~~~~

Over the ensuing years, wherever they were booked to dance, it became commonplace for Augie and Margo to see Bill Rosenberg, Harold Homestock or both of them in their audience. Even when they were performing overseas, Harold and Ruth often went to see them. It was not so easy for Bill Rosenberg to travel long distances, because as time went on, his business commitments grew ever larger, and even included the ownership of a stable, breeding horses for harness racing, and establishing a Professorship in Medicine at Harvard Medical Schools Dana-Farber Cancer Institute. His time was somewhat limited, but if he could get to see a performance in the United States, he would go!

For Harold, following Augie and Margo around was a great adventure. He and his wife, Ruth, took great pleasure in visiting the places they went, as much as they enjoyed the thrill of watching Augie and Margo dance. Though on one occasion, in one of the most beautiful places on earth, they found they were the only members in the audience, and watching a dance routine that would have been better suited to the slapstick acts of Lucille Ball and Dezi Arnaz!

It was in Campione; a small Italian enclave in Switzerland, which is separated from the rest of Italy by the amazingly beautiful Lake Lugano and the snow-capped Alps in the Ticino canton of Switzerland.

The Opening Act

The advantage Campione had over its neighbors at the beginning of the 1900's was that it could be a little more "flexible" with its laws, so in 1917 a beautiful gambling casino and theater was built in the city, providing gambling, entertainment and beautiful girls, and it was specifically constructed for a very interesting reason.

At that time, during the First World War, it was built primarily, as an enticement for all the wealthy and powerful politicos and bureaucrats in the region to go and relax and be entertained, while experts in matters of espionage took official note of their political views when their visitor's guard was down!

By 1930, the city officially recognized the casino as being a state-registered asset, and in order to encourage more revenues to Campione, they continued the practice of making the casino a destination with the best of everything, including entertainment.

Government officials in charge of booking acts, who were assigned to the theater part of the casino, searched all over the world in order to find the best entertainers, and when contracts were written it was clear they were willing to pay very highly. Two of the performers they hired were Augie and Margo, who were not only pleased to be earning such good money, but were delighted that it was to be in such breathtaking surroundings.

It was, indeed, a beautiful place. So stunning, in fact, that Margo told Augie she would like to be buried there! They stayed in a charming little bed and breakfast *Pensione* near the casino, and were joined several days after their arrival by Harold and Ruth Homestock who came to meet up with them for a short vacation and to, naturally, go and see their show.

Despite the gorgeous surroundings, after their arrival and several days of being alone, Augie and Margo were pleased to see familiar faces. Their time in Campione so far had been somewhat isolated, insofar as during the week days, very few people came to the casino. It had not yet evolved into the year-round resort that it became in later years, and it was renowned to be an expensive place to stay, so the average hard-working Swiss tended to visit only on their day off, which was Sunday.

Italians, also, had a hard time getting there during the working week, as access was only possible over the mountains or by boat; so the enormous casino and theater, together in the same room, was only really packed with people on Sundays!

The city officials of Campione needed to ensure that patrons at the casino were properly entertained, so no matter how few of them there were, 'the show still went on', and the city laws reflected that rule. The casino was, and still is, the only one in Europe with no limit on the stakes, so as far as the City Fathers were concerned it only took one very wealthy gambler to lose his shirt on any given day to help keep the casino revenues high.

Augie and Margo were booked to do two shows a night, so when they met the Homestocks, they warned them that, since they had arrived on a week-night, the audience might be small. Augie also told them he was worried about the band. A new one had arrived a day or two earlier, and they had not been quick to learn the sheet music Augie and Margo had brought with them.

The Homestocks were in no way perturbed. They were there, after all, to enjoy the beautiful surroundings and to see their favorite dancers perform; so making a decision to have dinner early on their first day, they decided to go to Augie and Margo's second show that evening.

When they arrived, the vast area was desolate! A few solitary gamblers were dotted about the casino playing the tables, but the audience in front of the stage consisted of Harold and Ruth Homestock and two or three booking agents for the theater, who probably had nothing better to do. It could have worked out fine, except that the musicians were probably as bored as the bookers!

That is not to infer that their state of mind had anything to do with the entertainment, but rather that the permanent set of circumstances during the week, was one with virtually no audience. It followed that after months, even years, of this situation, a natural lethargy was almost inevitably going to settle in. Musicians, after all appreciate a positive reaction to their efforts.

Augie and Margo had already experienced a bit of a run-in with the band when they arrived in Campione on their first night. It was a four-piece house band of Italian musicians, which rotated with a second band every couple of weeks, and they were perfectly competent, but the routines Augie and Margo danced were quite complicated, which required that they travel with their own music, specially written for them.

The problem with the band was communication. Augie and Margo spoke fluent Spanish, but very little Italian, so when an important break in the beat, for instance, came in a certain spot, it was important to co-ordinate the break with the dance routine. The drama and beat of the music was what Augie and Margo interpreted into steps, so too many false notes or bad timing could mess up the entire routine and have everyone, including the musicians, struggling to figure out where they were.

Augie explained over and over to the leader of the quartet during rehearsals what he and Margo wanted, using lots of gesticulations and a few familiar-sounding words like *pronto*, (the Spanish word for soon) which sounded a bit like *presto*, (the Italian one) or *pare aqui*, (stop here) for the Italian *fermare qui*, which was vaguely similar to the Spanish equivalent, and at least gave Augie the feeling he was warning the conductor of the band when he should change tempo, or anticipate a dramatic move in their routine. The first piece to be played was a number called *Jubilation*, which had difficult music, and the second piece was a *mambo*.

Nodding his head, and smiling in agreement, the conductor certainly gave the impression he had understood, but from the first time they performed on stage, there were problems; either the timing was a bit off, or the emphasis was either completely wrong or left out altogether, which was annoying for Augie and Margo, but not quite bad enough that they were unable to "catch up" with their correct sequence of moves.

~~~~~~~~~~~

The night that the Homestocks arrived to watch the show, it was particularly quiet. The first performance that evening had been displayed before a nonexistent audience, and so at least during the second show, the theater bookers and the scattering of gamblers around the casino were there to keep company with them.

The problem that occurred, however, was that during the hour between the two performances the band all went off to the bar, quite possibly a common practice for them, but the biggest problem was that most of the drinking was done by the band leader! When the time came for the second performance of the evening, immediately the foursome stepped up on stage and began to play, Augie and Margo felt a shift in the atmosphere.

They started dancing their routine, but as it developed, their sense of anxiety increased. Unlike the past few days, when they had been able to compensate for the lack of one or two beats, the music now began to take on a new and unfamiliar sound. They realized suddenly that two pages of music had been turned, and that their entire routine had been sabotaged. *"Uh oh,"* Margo hissed to Augie, *"they fucked up!"*

"Well, fuck 'em!" Augie quipped back, and trying to keep the melody in his head, he kept on turning. The dance continued and Margo, starting to anticipate an up-coming lift, realized with dismay that the music was in no way leading up to it.

At this point it's worth mentioning the 'lifts' in a little more detail. Although both dancers made it look effortless, it took enormous skill for Augie to get Margo up into the air and hold her there on one hand, and it took an equal amount of dexterity to get up, and stay there! Although Margo was fearless when she made the leap, and poised motionless above her husband's head, the music, which was the signal for their timing, was critically important.

On one of her close-contact moves with Augie, she asked him, *"Sea que demonios pasar?"* Which roughly translated means, what the hell's going on? But on the next pass, Augie didn't have time to reply, as he was focused on the band leader and hissing at him above the music in a loud stage-whisper, *"Andare! Andare!"* Go! Go!

The command only served to put a look of bewilderment on the face of the Italian, who understood the word all right, since it was in his own language, but he appeared to have forgotten what it actually meant! For Augie and Margo though, realization dawned instantly! The next time they were close enough to each other to speak, they said the same thing in unison, *"El es bebido!"* He's drunk!

After that, it just went from bad to worse. What started out as an amazing dance act, became a bumbling parody. Music, the like of which had never before been heard, was stumblingly played by a thoroughly bewildered trio of musicians, who might just as well have thrown the sheet music away, since their leader had no clue where he was in the proceedings.

Augie and Margo took it all in stride, so to speak. They knew it was impossible to regain control of their act; that it was totally beyond redemption; so doing the best they could for a while, they went with the flow. By now, all the musicians could be heard jabbering in Italian, *"Sbagliata musica!"* Wrong music! Then suddenly: Bam! Everything stopped!

Harold and Ruth Homestock, seated in front of the stage, had been mystified for a while, thinking at the start that it was all part of a new act, but their perplexity was short-lived. The fact that something had seriously gone awry was confirmed to them when, right in the middle of the dance routine, when a boat-full of tourists on the lake sailed by the windows of the casino and waved, Augie and Margo waved back!

The Homestocks watched the rest of the dance in anticipation tinged with horror, to a spot where the routine became very slow. Suddenly, out of nowhere, the drummer hit a symbol and the musicians again abruptly ended their routine, whereupon Augie picked Margo up and holding her aloft yelled to Harold and Ruth, *"Harold, what did I tell you?"*

It was downhill all the way after that! Augie walked over to the front of the stage and stood with his hands on his hips. He looked at the confused and bewildered musicians for a moment, who were trying valiantly to start up again, and turning toward the Homestocks, he shouted again above the cacophony of sound, *"Sorry about all this, Harold, but we did warn you the band sucked! I might just as well be standing up here and picking my nose!"*

Next day, and forever after while Augie and Margo remained in Campione, they learned a few new words in Italian; every time they saw the band leader, he showered the words at them, over and over. *"Per favore scusarme. Scusarme, il Signore e la Signora! Scusarme!"*

~~~~~~~~~~~

Over the years, Augie and Margo became great friends with both the Rosenberg and the Homestock families. After knowing them for ten years or so, Bill Rosenberg was concerned that they might have nothing to rely on in their future. He owned a piece of property located on a major crossroad in Southern Connecticut - a premier position for a *Dunkin' Donuts* business - and he offered to give it to them if they wanted to have it. They were, of course, very grateful for the extremely generous gesture, but turned it down. They were simply unable to imagine doing anything other than dance for the rest of their lives.

Harold and Ruth Homestock had no children, and were fortunate enough to have a business that allowed them to travel. After World War II, they started a business in Boston selling yarn and knitted garments. Ruth was a brilliant knitter, and her skills developed into knitting fine ribbon yarn, turning it into exquisite jackets and dresses, which were in great demand by the ladies of Boston Society, and even by First Lady, Lady Bird Johnson.

They both loved dancing, and were willing to travel wherever it took, to see the best. Several weeks after seeing Augie and Margo at Blinstrub's, Harold and Ruth went to one of their favorite resorts, *Grossinger's*, in the Catskill mountains of New York State, and to their surprise and delight, the young couple were performing there.

After the show, they went over to greet Harold and Ruth, who invited them to sit at their table. During the course of their conversation, Augie mentioned that he and Margo would be back in the Boston area again later that year, so Harold said, *"Well. We're in the phone book, give us a call when you arrive and I'll come and meet you both."* Augie took Harold at his word, and in the car on their way to Harold and Ruth's home, they discussed what they might do together that day.

The Opening Act

After a while, Augie turned to Harold and said, *"Do you have cream cheese back at your place?"* Harold though for a moment, then, *"Yes,"* he said. *"Do you have black bread?" "Yes." "Do you have lox?" "Sure,"* said Harold, catching on, *"we'll invite a few people over and have a party!"*

And that is exactly what happened. Harold invited his friends Bill and Bertha Rosenberg, and a couple of other friends, and they all spent the whole day getting along like a house on fire!

Over the years, the Homestocks went so often to see Margo and Augie perform, that they began referring to Harold as their manager, and it took very little to persuade him to go wherever the young couple were headed. For example, as Harold explained - he always went to his business early in the morning to get things started for the day. He and Ruth had a staff of several people, and a very busy company, so he liked to organize the daily schedule before Ruth arrived. One morning around 8:00 A.M. the telephone in the store rang. Harold picked up the receiver and heard Augie's voice. *"Hi Harold, you've got a gig in Puerto Rico!"*

Harold says that to this day he knows every note of music that Augie and Margo danced to, and he knows every step of their routines. After seeing them at *Blinstrub's*, Harold freely admits, he was hooked. He says he has never seen anything like the moves they made, probably because no one had ever done them before.

"Sometimes," he says, *"I would sit in the audience and feel myself sweating, because I knew what moves were coming up. How difficult some of them were, and how easy they made it appear. One dance especially,"* he went on, *"would get me writhing in my seat. When Margo would raise her leg and twist it around at the same time. Then she would hold Augie's finger - one finger, mind you - and she would spin down like a top, faster than any skater, until she was spinning on her knee. Poor Margo, she really beat up her right knee, and she paid for it later, but she was amazing. No one else ever dared to do what Margo did. She was fearless."*

~~~~~~~~~~

Augie and Margo's friendship with Bill Rosenberg lasted a lifetime. When he died at the age of 86 in September 2002, they attended his funeral in Cape Cod. As for Harold Homestock, his beloved wife Ruth has passed away, but Harold continues to follow their career, and he surely deserves an award for being their most loyal fan in the country. Now, a little older, somewhat house-bound, but with a memory like a steel trap, at the age of 93, he remains a dear friend, who telephones Augie and Margo every week; and no one is more delighted, or less surprised, than he, that his dance idols are still wowing audiences and kicking up a storm.

Only, now, it's in front of twelve hundred people twice a night, and not at all like that night when he and Ruthie were the only ones in the audience, laughing until their sides split so much, they could hardly get up from their seats at the end of the show, (when Augie and Margo finally gave up and called a halt to it). All those years ago, in a place that was like heaven on earth - in Campione.

CHAPTER SIXTEEN

Ed Sullivan's show, which aired on Sunday nights at 8:00 P.M., was the longest running television variety show ever. CBS opened the show in 1948, and it closed twenty five years later in 1971. Sullivan started out with a vaudeville type format, and many vaudevillians appeared on the show, but as entertainers they were accustomed to performing a single, highly polished act. This more or less eliminated their chances of appearing again on television, since after being exposed to literally millions of viewers at once, the demand to see them again was unlikely.

Sullivan did invite, however, virtually every type of entertainer imaginable to perform, including clowns and opera singers. His two most famous shows were the ones with Elvis Presley and the first USA appearance of *The Beatles*; both shows put the viewer ratings for CBS sky high for years to come. Comparatively few people appeared *many* times, but if they did, they were the type of performer whose act evolved and changed. Comics, singers, ventriloquists and dancers made frequent appearances along with the 'hot' celebrities of the day, unless they did something to offend Sullivan, and then they were banned from ever appearing on the show again.

Behind the scenes, Ed Sullivan's personality was similar to the one he showed on the screen, that is to say, rather dry. He was a friendly character, but his deadpan expression and serious delivery of jokes, earned him the nickname, "Old Stone Face."

One evening on his show, after Augie and Margo had performed a particularly difficult routine, Sullivan, applauding them off the screen, turned an impassive face to the television audience and said, *"I used to do that dance, but I hurt my back."*

Along with his quick wit, he also had a reputation for holding a grudge. If, for example, a performer did something on Sullivan's show against his wishes, he would ban them from ever appearing again, no matter who they were. Jackie Mason, the comedian was one such performer. At the end of the time scheduled for Mason's act on the air, Ed Sullivan, off camera, made a winding motion with his hands toward Mason, which is the silent sign to 'wind up' the act. Mason was not ready to finish and he gave 'the finger' back to Sullivan as he continued his delivery. It was the last time Mason ever appeared on the *Ed Sullivan Show,* and it messed up his career for several years to come, as many other venues refused to book him.

When singers had a phrase or word in their songs which sounded a little *risqué,* Sullivan would ask them to change it for the sake of his audience, and if, during their performance, they stuck to the original words - sometimes it happened by accident - no amount of excuses or apologies would change his mind. They would never be allowed back, and he never forgot!

On the other hand though, his heart was big. He made stars out of many people who appeared on his show, and when dancer Bill "Bojangles" Robinson died penniless, Sullivan paid for his funeral. More interestingly, when the CBS 'higher-ups' tried to discourage him from inviting black performers, he refused to go along with them, and introduced many great acts to the general public in America, some for the first time; *The Temptations*, Aretha Franklin, *The Supremes* and Nat King Cole are just a few examples of talented people he greatly admired in the black community of entertainers, and whom he had on his show. Another 'first' was with foreign performers, who were exposed to the American public for the first time on the *Ed Sullivan Show.*

∽∽∽∽∽∽∽∽∽∽

It was an American performer, though, who Augie and Margo appeared with on one of his shows, and whom they particularly remember. It was said, in fact, that most people who met her never forgot her - and she made sure of that.

The scandalous Tallulah Bankhead's acting career had been quite successful over the previous fifteen years, in movies and on the stage in both London and New York, but her dedication to being outrageous at all times was beginning to take its toll by the time Augie and Margo met her.

She had spent years drinking gin and bourbon like they were water, and had long lost the notion of self control. During her entire life, since childhood, people expected her to be outrageous, and she always obliged.

Over her career, which began in the 1920's, she became a star of all the mediums, stage, screen, radio and television. In England, where she lived for eight years, acting in London's *West End*, she had an enormous cult following of young working-class women, who idolized the young, beautiful American woman who led a totally glamorous life, and was free to do or say anything she wanted.

Her female fans came in droves to see her perform on stage, sometimes standing in line for forty-eight hours until the box office opened. They came not especially to see the play she was in, but to study her mannerisms, clothing and hair styles, which they slavishly copied in their own world. The fact that her fans tried to emulate her never worried Tallulah. *"Nobody can be exactly like me."* She frequently immodestly proclaimed. *"Sometimes, even I have trouble doing it!"*

Bankhead adored the attention. Before and after a performance, or even during one, when she was applauded, she never failed to turn to her fans, blowing them kisses, and saying, *"Thank you, dahlings,"* in her affected English accent. Even the phrase itself was coined by her fans, and later by the country at large, when it became (and still is) quite common for British people to call even brief acquaintances darling.

People were mostly shocked by Tallulah's flagrant disregard for modesty. She was known to take off her clothes at the drop of a hat, and she slept with anyone who wanted to sleep with her, both males and females. A famous expression of hers was, *"The good girls keep diaries; bad girls never have the time!"* And bad she certainly was, indulging herself in everything that took her fancy, including drugs. When asked on one occasion if cocaine was addictive she laughingly replied, *"Of course not. I ought to know. I've been taking it for years."*

Her appearance on Ed Sullivan's show was in 1964, when she had clearly become a caricature of her former self. It was one thing to be a young, vital, beautiful woman, having one affair after another, using decidedly coarse language and acting in a vulgar way, but a sixty-two-year-old woman, who smoked over a hundred cigarettes and drank two bottles of *Old Grand Dad* bourbon daily, was quite another proposition.

Getting Ms. Bankhead to rehearse *and* remember proved to be quite difficult!

The day she was to appear, she arrived for the pre-show rehearsals with Augie, Margo and the rest of the guests. The director gave her instructions on which side she should enter the set and where she should stand, and all went well up until the final rehearsal, when she did everything wrong. When Ed Sullivan and the director politely corrected her, she blew her top and started raving at everyone, *"Do you realize to whom you are talking? I am Tallulah Bankhead - how dare you tell me what to do!"*

Sullivan kept his fingers crossed that she would remember her cues for the actual live show, but true to form, she was predictably unpredictable, and walked on the set behind the host, making him turn around to greet her, and generally kept everyone on pins and needles during her appearance, for fear of what she might do, or say, next.

Her wit, however, was still intact. When the baseball player Earl Wilson, famous for his own quotes, made a dig at her cigarette smoker's hoarse, raspy voice, he said to her, *"Are you ever mistaken for being a man on the telephone?"* She immediately replied, *"No, dahling, are you?*

The *Ed Sullivan Show* lasted longer than Tallulah. She died in New York, from double pneumonia, in 1968 at the age of sixty-six. The *Ed Sullivan Theater*, in New York City, from which his show was broadcast, is now the home of the *David Letterman Show*.

Augie and Margo were close friends with Ed and his wife Sylvia for years, and were sometimes greatly amused by his back-stage comments.

.... The Opening Act

When the comedians Allen and Rossi, who are reputed to have appeared on the show forty-four times, made a slightly obscene remark on one occasion, Sullivan paced up and down behind the scenes, with both hands holding his head. *"What's the matter with them?"* He was heard to say, *"Don't they know this is a fucking family show?"*

~~~~~~~~~~~

Another booking in Augie and Margo's first year as professionals was at the *Hotel Pierre* on Fifth Avenue in Manhattan, which is one of New York's original 1920's skyscraper hotels. They danced in the hotel's elegant *Cotillion Room*, famous in this decade for the filming of Al Pacino's *tango* scene in the movie *Scent of a Woman*.

The featured singer at the hotel was a blonde, stunningly beautiful German-born French chanteuse, named Lilo. At the time, she was also starring in the leading role of Cole Porter's musical, *Can-Can*, on Broadway. She was not, however, a very happy performer.

Out-of-town reviewers, prior to the Broadway debut of the show, hailed Gwen Verdon's performance, and said it out-shone the show's star, Lilo. Verdon, playing Claudine, was the second female lead, and when Lilo heard about it she demanded that Verdon's role be cut to only two featured dance numbers.

With her role slashed to barely more than a member of the chorus, Verdon threatened to walk out of *Can-Can* before the show premiered on Broadway, but she was there on opening night, and her *Garden of Eden* ballet number stopped the show. The applause was so thunderous that the surprised dancer ran from her dressing room and took a curtain call in her robe! For that performance she received a pay raise, and later, legitimately 'stealing' it from the Star of the show, her first Tony award!

After *Can Can,* Lilo performed in one more musical in America, but it failed soon after it opened, and Lilo returned to singing in nightclubs and cabaret shows around the country, her dream of being a big Broadway singing star, dashed. She eventually married a Count, but wanted more than anything to continue performing and singing on stage.

Sadly, some time later Augie and Margo saw her in Las Vegas, where she was still pushing herself as a big star, but to get noticed she seemed to think she should be naked. They saw her once, spraying perfume all over her naked body in the dressing rooms, presumably hoping to attract some producers!

Gwen Verdon became known as Broadway's best dancer, and in 1960 she married Bob Fosse, the famous choreographer.

~~~~~~~~~~

George Abbott went often to *Roseland* or *The Palladium* to see Augie and Margo perform. He was always ready to guide them, and became a wonderful mentor. He advised them to take a full-page advertisement out in *Variety*, listing their accomplishments. *"Everyone reads Variety,"* he said, *"and it will be worth every penny you spend, to let people know about you."* Abbott was right. Offers for work came pouring in, but Augie and Margo should not have worried, they never stopped working from the day they turned professional.

Another person who helped determine their career in those earlier years was a producer/talent scout for Steve Allen. The producer's name was Nick Vanoff, and after seeing Augie and Margo perform at the *Eden Roc*, in Miami, he asked Allen to come and see them. Allen was so impressed that he immediately offered them a spot on his show.

Steve Allen was the creator and original host of the *Tonight Show*, and was himself, an incredibly multi talented entertainer. His career spanned over fifty years, and at that time he had his own show, featuring variety acts. From being an actor, to a comedian, a jazz clarinetist, to poet, writer and lyricist - he is said to have written thousands of songs - Steve Allen knew and appreciated a talented person when he saw one, and in this case he saw two!

Augie and Margo were, naturally, thrilled to be invited on his show, but their anxiety level went way up when the ever creative Steve Allen told them what he required them to do. Since his show was being televised in Miami at the time, he wanted a tropical atmosphere, which included having Augie and Margo dance on the beach!

Allen could do almost anything, but it was clear he was not a dancer. He understood that performing twists, jumps and turns on the sand would lead to holes being drilled, so he provided them with a platform on which to dance; however, that was where his understanding ended. The platform was only five feet long and thirty-two inches wide, a size that would severely curtail the creative movements of most of Augie and Margo's routines.

Another interesting facet to consider was that Steve Allen wanted the platform to be placed only inches from the water's edge. Augie and Margo took it all in their stride. They worked up a dance routine to accommodate the limited space, but when the time came around for them to perform, an evening breeze sprang up.

The fact that it kept them cool as they danced, was a welcome asset, but blowing unexpected flurries of salty spray over them, and little drifts of sand onto the platform, made gritty scratching noises under their shoes and hampered traction.

Somehow, it all worked out. They created exactly the atmosphere Steve Allen was looking for. One would never know, from the video of the show, the difficult circumstances of the routine.

Amorous and exotic Latin music plays in the background, while two young lovers, with eyes for each other only, pitch and sway to the movement of palm trees on the beach, the waves clearly visible, lapping within inches of their feet.

Not one step was incorrect. And as the beat of the music defined their moves, dancing there under the stars on that warm Miami night, while they entertained millions of viewers on national television, it is quite possible that the song dancing in their minds was not Latin, but the most popular one that Steve Allen ever wrote - *This Could Be the Start of Something Big*.

~~~~~~~~~~

In 1958, Steve Allen, remembering the versatility of Augie and Margo, asked them to appear with him in Havana, Cuba. This time, however, he had something different in mind for them.

Tybee Afra, their friend from *The Palladium,* and singer Celia Cruz went with them, and they also took their son, Richard, and stayed at the beautiful *Hotel Habana Riviera,* from which Steve's show was being broadcast. The hotel, which was seventeen floors high with a pool and a large cabana on the roof, was reputedly built with mob money and was said to be half-owned by George Raft, the film actor.

At that time, Havana was largely run by the Mafia and huge money interests in the United States. It was a city of gambling, drugs and prostitution, frequented by the rich playboys of the world, including many corruptible politicians and people of power.

In order to keep the money flowing, and the influence pedaling alive and well, hotel owners made sure their guests were well entertained and happy, so they hired the best acts they could, and made Cuba a very desirable place for entertainers to be seen.

Augie and Margo had been in Cuba before, and they knew the drill. MCA had already sent them to perform at the huge and stunningly beautiful *Hotel Nationale* in Havana. Situated on a hill overlooking the ocean, the hotel was, and still is, famous for its outdoor entertainment events, and it was for one of these events that Augie and Margo had been booked.

The contract was for four weeks, for which they were being paid $1,200 a week, but they had been advised that it was quite possible the government in Cuba would try to take some of that money. The dictator Fulgencio Batista ruled the island with an iron fist, but since he received a large cut of the gambling profits he allowed casinos to operate in Havana. Similarly, if he could twist the arms of American tourists or performers visiting Cuba to give up some of their own well-earned dollars, it was all the same to him.

In order to make sure that entertainers on the island had fair pay, their USA contracts were written twice, and in the case of Augie and Margo, the amount of money they were to earn was split in half to $600 on each contract; but only one of those went with them to Cuba!

The hotel event, along with Augie and Margo, starred Ilona Massey, a singer/actress from Hungary who had her own television show at that time; and a group of acrobats named *The Charlavelles.*

Every day after their performance, an immaculately dressed man sought out Augie and Margo and told them they were wonderful and how much he had enjoyed their dancing. His Spanish was perfect, to the extent that they thought he was a Cuban, and clearly, from his businesslike demeanor, he appeared to be some kind of administrator at the hotel. They thought perhaps he had something to do with the hiring of the acts.

They became quite friendly with him over the month they were there, finding out that his name was Santos, and they made a habit of stopping to chat when they saw him at different locations around the hotel.

Everything went beautifully at the *Nationale* from the point of view of the show. The hotel staff was delighted with everyone's performance, but when it came to the time to leave and return to America, Augie and Margo were visited by a government official, who demanded $900 from each week of their $1,200 contract! They protested, and told him they only had a $600 contract, but he refused to believe them until they produced it, and then he insisted on them paying him $500 of every $600 they had earned!

They were devastated, but no amount of protestations warmed the heart of the bureaucrat from the government! Looking around in desperation for help, Augie saw Santos, their friend who had been so complimentary about his and Margo's dancing, so he ran over to him, told him about the situation and asked if he could help. *"Leave it to me."* Santos said, entering the room where Margo stood with the government man.

While Santos spoke quietly to him, Margo joined Augie to wait outside. They had no idea how the conversation went, but it was all over in a few minutes, and Augie and Margo were informed by Santos that everything had been straightened out, and that they would be keeping the entire $600 a week, as stated on their contract.

They were delighted, not to mention surprised and impressed, that Santos had so much influence with the Cuban government, but later they discovered just who their new friend was, and their surprise diminished a little. His full name was Santos Trafficante!

Christine Hamer-Hodges

∼∼∼∼∼∼∼∼∼∼

The important thing about Steve Allen's show, on the occasion that he invited Augie and Margo to appear on it, is that he was pioneering the first ever live broadcast from Cuba, and he wanted it to be a show to remember. With that in mind, he invited a number of well-known celebrities to be on the show with him, including the now veteran actor, Tom Poston, who appeared frequently with Allen; singer Steve Lawrence, who would begin performing with his wife of one year, Eydie Gorme, two years later in 1960; Lou Costello, the comedian, who had broken up with his partner Bud Abbott the previous year, due to huge problems with the Internal Revenue Service, forcing them both to sell their large homes and many possessions; and Augie and Margo, who were by now appearing all over, and definitely on the "up" ladder in the world of entertainment.

Tybee Afra, and Celia Cruz also appearing, were in the same position as Augie and Margo. Not yet famous but incredibly good and hugely appealing to the local Cuban population.

Steve's show was being broadcast in the hotel's nightclub and cabaret room, located on the top floor of the hotel, but Steve had an idea that he wanted Augie and Margo to perform their act on the roof! Not the roof of the hotel though, that would have been too easy; from the roof of the cabana, located on top of the hotel roof!

Having absolutely no nerve, especially Margo, when it came to dancing, they agreed to Steve's request, and went up to the roof of the cabana to inspect their new 'stage.' The hotel was only eight years old, but presumably no one had intended that any people, other than workmen and a few stray pilots, should see the sky-high vision of bitumen and tarpaulin which kept tropical rains from leaking through the cabana roof. To put it mildly, the roof needed a little TLC!

Steve asked the hotel management to tidy it up a little, and make it more presentable, so not only did the hotel staff oblige, but a couple of days before the show was due to air, they finished the job by painting the roof a delightful shade of bright blue!

The Opening Act

Everyone on Allen's staff was pleased that the hotel had co-operated so nicely. The show had been well advertised and would draw huge numbers of people, including many of the rich and famous, to see the historical event.

Steve Allen had written the musical arrangement for *Bell, Book and Candle* one of Augie and Margo's very special dance routines, and the day before the show they went up on the newly painted roof to rehearse their exact positioning. To their dismay, they found the tropical heat had not been helpful in drying the paint, for it was still sticky. There was only one solution: To remove the paint - pronto!

A team of workers got started immediately, and using a mixture of water and ammonia they mopped away at the painted roof until it was no longer a hazard - at least, as far as they were aware.

However, the timing of the whole procedure was getting a bit tight, to say the least, and Augie was becoming concerned as show-time drew nearer, and he had not been able to inspect the finished results. People were arriving in limousines to see the show before he got his chance. He and Margo had seen a flurry of activity when Mamie Van Doren, the blonde bombshell sex symbol of B rated movies, (her last one being *Born Reckless*) arrived, and he decided it was 'now or never.'

It was a bit of a sprint from the nightclub floor to the top of the cabana. First he had to run to the door leading out to the hotel roof, then along the length of the pool to the cabana, and then, having entered through the cabana door, he had to go up a spiral staircase to the roof. By the time he got half-way up the stairs, he was panting and had a dry throat, but fortunately, one of the workers had left a bottle of water on a step near the top of the stairs, so Augie thankfully reached for it and put it to his lips.

The large gulp he took was somehow halted when it reached the back of his throat - about the same time that he felt his mouth was on fire! He managed to spit out the liquid, which was certainly not water, but the flames in his mouth kept burning so much, he simply didn't know what to do.

Somehow, he got back down to Margo and told her she would have to perform alone, but even as he said it, he realized it would be an impossible thing for her to do. They were a couple. That was how they danced, had *always* danced, and there was no way he could expect her to step out on that roof and go it alone.

By this time, they both realized there had been clear ammonia in the bottle. The show had already begun, so Augie rinsed his mouth in real water this time, and he and Margo returned to the roof, to dance one of the most difficult performances of their career.

The view from that height was breathtaking, and looking at the video of their performance one would never know how much Augie was suffering, and how worried Margo was. They danced divinely, and the fact that another little matter was also going on to test their nerve at the same time, only served to show their true professionalism. It was the sound of rebel mortar fire, and guns, exploding on the outskirts of the city!

After the show, Augie went straight to the hospital! The doctors washed his mouth out with egg whites and made him hold his mouth open to let the air heal it. The experience was not pleasant, and for years afterwards Augie sniffed everything before he drank it!

Little did everyone know that within months, Fidel Castro, who was leading his revolution against Batista in the villages and countryside of Cuba, would overthrow the dictator. They had no idea that soon, all the American driven activities in Havana would come to a screeching halt, and that within three years, a huge anti-aircraft gun against American planes would be a permanent fixture just outside the entrance of the famous and elegant *Habana Riviera Hotel*.

CHAPTER SEVENTEEN

David Baumgarten very quickly began to appreciate the popularity and professionalism of Augie and Margo. He teamed them up with orchestra leader Xavier Cugat and his singer wife, Abbe Lane, and although the young dancers still felt naive and inexperienced, they were able to 'cut their teeth' with a band leader they grew to love very much, crossing the country many times to perform with him at different venues.

Cugat, like Augie's father, had been born in Spain. He was brought to Cuba by his family at the age of three, and as a child became a highly skilled violinist. When he moved to Los Angeles as a young man, he was employed as a cartoonist with the *LA Times* during the day, and in the evenings he kept busy playing music and setting up a band. As an artist, he was also extremely talented, and his work at the *Times* was eventually syndicated across the country, while his caricatures were shown in magazines and galleries, as well as newspapers.

Augie and Margo own an impressive painting by Cugat, and they also treasure two of his famous sketches of bull fights. One, he gave them, and the second, he made them buy! He was already getting quite collectible by then!

Cugat's music became popular countrywide in the early 1930's when he recorded the huge hit, *El Manicero - The Peanut Vendor*, which started the *Rhumba* craze that swept the country, earning Cugat the title, *King of Rhumba*. After that, came the Perez Prado song *Cherry Pink and Apple Blossom White*, which he also turned into a hit, giving his audiences the opportunity to dance to a song of love and romance. Once he was popular and in demand, Cugat spent his entire professional life 'on the move.' Augie said he was the only guy he knew, who could literally go to sleep while standing up! And he did it in very noisy places, like airports and train stations!

Cugat became resident band at the *Waldorf Astoria*, while having several commitments in Los Angeles, which included movies and a radio show. Augie and Margo became his official dance team and traveled with him for ten years, during which time they developed a great personal friendship with him.

Abbe Lane was his wife when they first knew him, though Cugat had already been married before. The conventional wisdom was that Abbe was his third wife, but in fact there had been three before her! His first and second wives, Rita Montaner and Carmen Castillo, were actresses, though Rita was also a very good pianist. Cugat's third wife was a model named Lorraine Allen. He was a notorious womanizer, especially liking young girls, but the gorgeous Abbe Lane had stopped him in his tracks.

He had heard her sing in a Broadway show when she was in her late teens, and afterwards he went backstage and asked her to come and audition for his band. Immediately, he signed her up to be the band's singer, and later, when she was twenty years old, he married her. She was a tall, stunningly beautiful redhead, with a sinuous body, and hips which she undulated as she sang. Through her twenties she developed a very sultry style, which added much to the band's popularity, and earned herself the title of "The Swingingest Sexpot in Show Business."

Despite the fact that she was married to Cugat, he was savvy enough to know that her sexy presence in his band was a huge advantage, so he was perfectly happy when his wife said things like: *"Jayne Mansfield may turn boys into men, but I take them from there."*

~~~~~~~~~~

Abbe was the real love of Cugat's life, and he bought her a 28 carat diamond ring to prove it, which was an amazing thing for him to do, since he also had the reputation of being an extremely shrewd businessman - to the point of being stingy!

Augie and Margo became great friends with both 'Cugie' and Abbe Lane, but after being married for fourteen years, Abbe fell in love with a Hollywood talent agent named Perry Leff, and divorced Xavier Cugat. She married Leff, and they had two sons, and though she later made a couple of very popular records, she basically chose family and marriage over career, and is happily married to Leff to this day.

Shortly after his divorce to Abbe Lane, Cugat met a young woman working in a bar in Los Angeles. She had come from Spain some years before, and her name was Charo. She was able to play the guitar, indeed she claimed to have studied under Andre Segovia and, falling for her rather voluptuous looks, Cougat took her under his wing and decided to coach her, understanding that his audiences still liked that sexy type of woman in a prominent place in his band while they were playing the popular 'hot' Latin music.

To begin with, Cugat put Charo on the stage, dancing a type of *salsa* to his music, which she could do well, then he decided to train her as a singer. Augie and Margo never said, but a very good friend of theirs who knew the group socially, confided, *"When Cugie first got Charo to sing, she sounded like an old crow."*

It wasn't easy to put a voice where none existed, but as she was able to play the guitar, her voice was coached to the point where Cugat was able to bill Charo as a "Folk Singer," and that is exactly what he did. He also encouraged her to project her sexy image; and although it did not come naturally to her, as it had with Abbe, when Charo shook her breasts and shoulders one night, and pouted her lips while saying *"Coochie, Coochie, Coo,"* she got such a big reaction from the men in the audience, that Cugat told her to develop that aspect of her performance, as he privately thought it made up for a huge lack of talent.

The same friend of Augie and Margo also said that despite her stage image, Charo was a very nice person behind the scenes, as Augie and Margo also maintain. *"When she took all that stuff off and behaved naturally, she was really very sweet."* The friend said. Then he added, *"But Abbe was the one he really loved. If she had as much as crooked her little finger in Cugie's direction, he would have dropped Charo like a hot potato!"*

Charo certainly tried very hard to please Cugat, and to get the image he wanted for the band. Piling her hair up on her head, in a tousled

Brigitte Bardot look, and wearing skin-tight gold lame pants and low cleavage tops, she even went to the extent of stuffing a wad of chewing gum under her top lip before going on stage, to give herself a "pouty" look.

Cugat always had his eye on the business side of the band, and his brother, who took care of their day to day management made sure they ran a very tight ship. Never a slave to tradition, Cugat preferred following music trends rather than remaining true to one form of Latin music, like the *rhumba*, which had first made him popular. In other words, he was willing to make artistic compromises, but they had to be good. He was a total perfectionist, and had a real sense of showmanship, making sure his band always looked immaculate and "showy," even down to the bright scarlet linings of their jackets, which became visible as they played.

Eventually, in 1966, Cugat and Charo were married. They held the wedding nuptials in Caesar's Palace, and were the first people ever to do so. Charo continued singing for the band, but in spite of the fact that Augie and Margo did not personally experience any difference in Cugat's popularity, the press releases of the next few years reflect the fact that critics felt that he made a huge mistake letting Charo front the band. By 1969 the comments had become quite harsh; in December of that year, Dino, a critic in *Variety Magazine* wrote of Charo that she was *"The last of the red-hot Kewpie dolls, with jungle cut blonde tresses and screamingly suggestive outfits covered with tassels."* It was almost as though Cugat wanted to turn her into a caricature.

Charo insisted that she was born in 1951, despite the fact that a certificate registering her birth was found in Spain, and recorded the fact that she was born in 1941. If her claim is true, she would have been fifteen at her wedding!

Both Augie and Margo and other sources who knew the couple are positive she was in her mid-twenties when she married Cugie. Perhaps they should have been consulted when Charo actually took the matter to Court in the United States and persuaded the Judge to officially record her birth as being in 1951!!

The Opening Act

The marriage lasted for twelve years and it was quite a volatile one. The couple never minded who heard them when they argued in public, and it put quite a few of their friends off spending time with them. No-one thought it was a love match.

Sometimes Charo would press the muscles on Augie's arm when they were off-stage and squeal her appreciation. Augie was not a tall man, but very strong. In response to this, Cugat would open his jacket and take a big roll of bills out of his inside pocket. *"Charo,"* he would say, holding up the roll in the air, *"what do you want? That - or this?"* Charo hesitated not one moment. *"I take the money!"* She always said.

~~~~~~~~~~~

A year after they appeared for MCA at the *Waldorf*, Baumgarten booked Augie and Margo to open in Las Vegas, for Gisele MacKenzie, a singer from Canada, who was a regular entertainer there. Her resonant, crystalline voice was impossible to mistake, and because of it, she acquired a reputation of being the greatest female vocalist of her generation.

Several years earlier, MacKenzie had been seen performing in Las Vegas at the *Flamingo* hotel, by Jack Benny, where he also saw and appreciated her other accomplishment - that of playing the violin. He was so impressed with her, that he invited her to tour with him for two years, and subsequently gave her a permanent spot on his *Jack Benny Show* where they played duets together, with Benny using her as a straight act opposite his own, hilariously inept, violin playing.

Benny became Gisele MacKenzie's mentor and he certainly brought her into the spotlight alongside himself, giving her wide recognition and endless opportunities, which resulted in her becoming one of early television's biggest stars.

~~~~~~~~~~~

The engagement Augie and Margo had been booked for at the *Waldorf Astoria*, set something of a precedent for them. As David Baumgarten had correctly said when he told them where they were performing, they were not starting out in some *"crummy joint."*

If the standard of a venue was high, it also meant high wages, so Augie and Margo were not only delighted to be getting work in places that most performers only dreamed of, they were suddenly earning real money. When they had danced in the Catskills they were paid $50.00 a night, but in New York's Waldorf Astoria it was $500.00, a fortune in comparison.

Like rare and desirable artwork whose value is determined by the highest bidder, once performers appear at the top places in the country, it follows they can command a certain level of pay; in other words, starting out at the top, also set a precedent for their salary.

Already, Augie and Margo had appeared on television shows and in some of the most elegant clubs and hotels nationally, so when they were booked to play the *Town and Country Club*, in Brooklyn, New York, they were still paid top dollar.

The *Town and Country* was not necessarily the most elegant nightclub in New York, but it was close, and it was certainly the biggest. In fact, it was the biggest night club in the country, seating over 3,000 people. On weekends its staff and kitchens were capable of hosting multiple weddings, sometimes up to twenty-seven a day!

The club's owner, Ben Maksik, made sure that he hired the very best performers he could. His audiences made great critics. It wasn't that they were hard to please, they just appreciated real talent, and even the professional entertainment critics knew that if somebody bombed at Maksik's *Town and Country*, they would probably thereafter go downhill fast!

People who frequented the club, however, were rarely disappointed with the entertainers. Stars like Tony Bennett, Judy Garland, Billie Holiday, Bobby Darin, and numerous others of a similar caliber had performed there, and were happy to do so. In 1957, the year that Augie and Margo were booked to play at the *Town and Country*, Jerry Lewis did his first solo live performance there. He had dissolved his partnership with Dean Martin the previous year, and had gone on to make two movies and a hit record, but performing his comedic act in front of a live audience was something he initially shied away from.

Scoring the record hit had been a big surprise. He had covered Al Jolson's *Rock a Bye, My Baby* on a Decca recording, and it ended up in the Top Forty. Lewis was, of course, well known as a spoof singer, imitating his ex-partner Dean Martin and others in his goofy, pseudo-juvenile comedy acts, but singing 'straight' songs was a new concept. The success of his hit, inspired him to add some songs into his new, one-man act, and the *Town and Country Club's* audience would be the first one to hear it.

Lewis was nervous about 'going it alone,' despite the fact that he had been immensely popular with Dean Martin as his partner, but intuition told him that playing to his somewhat vulnerable and exposed side could be highly successful.

He was right. He began his performance by singing *I'll Go My Way by Myself,* which brought cheers of genuine enthusiasm from the crowd, and resulted in his act having an appealing quality that a straight comedic role would not have given him.

It is a matter of record, that immediately after his break-up with Dean Martin, Jerry Lewis's career went from strength to strength, especially in the business of acting and making movies, but although he sang straight songs again, and his 1956 album, *Jerry Lewis Just Sings* was a best-seller in the record charts, his voice was not known to be good.

Biographer, Arthur Marx, rather unkindly likened his singing to *"The croaking of a parched parrot,"* which may well have been the case, but if Jerry didn't know *how* to sing, he certainly knew *when,* and the people who saw his one-man debut, at the *Town and Country Club,* in Brooklyn New York, wholeheartedly agreed!

~~~~~~~~~~

When Augie and Margo appeared at the *Town and Country*, another actor/ comedian was there, but this time he was in the audience, and it was his reaction to them that arguably set the pattern for the rest of their professional lives.

Danny Thomas, who later became a producer of many television shows, as well as a great philanthropist, was very impressed with Augie and Margo's dance routine. So much so, that after the show he went back-stage to compliment them.

He asked who their agent was, and explained that he would like them to open for him at the *Sands* hotel, in Las Vegas. At the end of their Brooklyn engagement, Augie called MCA to let David Baumgarten know about the conversation, and found that Danny Thomas had already called!

Naturally, Augie's impression was that Danny Thomas must have been keen to have them, so when it came time for the agents to negotiate the booking, Augie's impetuous bird personality flew into action! Crossing his fingers, and struggling to calm his breathing, Augie told MCA to inform Jack Entratter, the general manager and entertainment director at the *Sands*, that since Danny Thomas had actually asked for them, he and Margo wanted to be paid $1,500 a week!

To put his daring move in perspective, by the time Augie and Margo were invited to appear in Vegas, they were earning $1,000 a week, an incredible amount of money for two relatively new people in show business - especially dancers. It seemed to them that they were already on the crest of a wave, but in fact, they still had a long way to go and would soon be named the highest paid dancers in the country!

However, had Augie realized exactly who Jack Entratter was, he might have held back a little on his hardball request! Negotiating with *him* was almost the same as trying to reach an agreement with The Mob! Except that in this case, Augie hadn't even reached a point of negotiation - he just laid down an audacious demand.

Entratter was no fool when it came to business. In the early 1930's he had started out as a doorman/bouncer in New York's ritzy *Copacabana Club*, but within a very short time he was the general manager, with a slew of friends - influential movers and shakers on both sides of the law.

The Opening Act

Known as the quietly efficient manager, who was always to be seen out front at the *Copa*, as it was called, Entratter made it his business to schmooze with the top people who frequented the club. He went out of his way to ensure that his patrons and entertainers had everything they needed, and he soon rose to the point where he held a controlling interest in the *Copa*.

At thirty-eight years old, he cashed out his stock and took an opportunity to get involved in the brand-new *Sands Hotel* in Las Vegas, which opened its doors in December 1952 with Jack Entratter as the general manager and entertainment director.

It was rumored that Entratter owned a twelve percent interest in the *Sands,* but the truth was that he actually owned only two percent. The remaining ten were in his name only and actually belonged to two New York mobsters, Vincent Alo, who was known as "Jimmy Blue Eyes," and Doc Stacher.

Other mob members were also involved, but as people with criminal records, official ownership in the hotel would endanger the casino's gaming and liquor licenses. As a result, Entratter fronted the stock and the position of general manager for Stacher and Alo who were the real decision-makers; except for the entertainment aspect of the hotel, where Entratter had the last word.

Performers at the *Sands,* presented their acts in the *Copa Room,* so named after the New York club, and since Jack Entratter had been popular amongst the big name stars who entertained there, he relied on their loyalty to come and perform at his new venture in Las Vegas.

From the outset, he presented the biggest names in the entertainment business he could find, and when they arrived at the hotel, he treated them like royalty.

Amongst the New York crowd, show-biz elites like Danny Thomas and Lena Horne had been regular performers at the *Copacabana,* so on opening night in December 1952, in the new *Copa Room* at the *Sands,* Entratter asked Danny Thomas to top the Bill.

Appearing with Thomas were the *Copa Girls,* modestly billed as the "Most Beautiful Girls in the World," Jimmy McHugh, the prolific lyricist, Chuck Nelson, actor/comic and Judy Collins, who at that time was a classical pianist and only thirteen years old.

It was in the 1960's that Collins became interested in folk music and took up the guitar, but by all accounts she was a highly gifted pianist, whose public debut, when she played Mozart's *Concerto for Two Pianos,* had been that same year she played at the *Sands.*

~~~~~~~~~~

There is no doubt, the driving force behind the world-wide acclaim that the *Sands* hotel was the "in" place to be in Vegas, was down to Jack Entratter. In retrospect, many people even gave him the entire credit for putting Las Vegas 'on the map.' The following year, in October 1953, Frank Sinatra debuted at the *Sands,* and later became a regular fixture there, as well as a part-owner, though his share was highly complicated by its entanglement with mobsters - as was his life.

Entratter's extensive contacts with members of the national Press and celebrities alike, gave him enormous 'clout' which made most performers feel that, as long as they had appeared at the *Sands,* they had reached their zenith.

It was into this lion's den, then, that Augie Rodriguez stuck his head, as a relatively unknown, albeit fabulous young dancer, and demanded through his agent to be paid what amounted to a small fortune.

Entratter was astounded! Dancers never, *ever,* earned that kind of money. He told Danny Thomas that he wouldn't dream of paying that much for dancers, and asked Thomas to negotiate Augie's demands down.

It didn't work! When Thomas personally called Augie and asked him to compromise, offering $1,250, Augie turned him down flat, citing the fact that he and Margo had already been earning $1,000 at the *Flamingo,* and $250 more to play at the *Sands,* just wasn't good enough. Amazingly, Entratter backed down, and agreed to Augie's demands.

Afterwards, Augie and Margo could hardly believe their good fortune, but during the first weeks of their appearance with Danny Thomas, Entratter gave them a wide berth; actually, he completely ignored them!

'Where was he?' They fretted. 'This expansively genial man, who was already a legendary host to his entertainers; why did he not come to welcome them, settle them in, make them feel relaxed and comfortable, as he did with everyone else who performed in the *Copa Room*?'

Entratter was barely forty, but he was a big man with heavy, unsmiling features, and usually had a cigar gripped between his teeth, which gave him something of a tough-guy image.

Still young and relatively inexperienced, Augie and Margo were overwhelmingly concerned that Entratter was avoiding them because he didn't like their act. Here they were in this big, fancy hotel in Las Vegas, getting paid a small fortune, and the entertainment manager who booked them wouldn't even speak to them!

They agonized over their decision to have demanded such high pay; at least, Augie did, since he was the one that dug his heels in, and they began to think their time in Vegas might be sweet, but it would it be very short!

Then one day, two weeks after their first appearance, Jack Entratter came backstage. They felt better as soon as they saw him, but the feeling didn't last. Entratter barely spoke, past muttering acknowledgment of their presence.

Now they *knew* they were in trouble! Two more uncomfortable weeks went by, and then, one month to the day after their first performance, when they came off-stage he came to their dressing room.

They stood nervously, waiting for him to speak, not knowing *what* he was going to say. It seemed they waited for a long time, but as he stepped toward them with a twinkle in his eyes, smiles broke out on their faces. Entratter put a hand on each of their shoulders. "*You guys are wonderful,*" he said.

CHAPTER EIGHTEEN

The Rodriguez team had already developed their brilliant *mambo* dance into a routine which included the poise and strength of *ballet*, the ease of *jazz* dance, the dramatic moves of *modern* and the romantic, fiery styles of the *flamenco*.

Augie made it look easy when suddenly, in the middle of a routine, Margo ended up high in the air, balanced on his hand, and Margo made it look easy with her slow, controlled movements, snaking up and around Augie's shoulders and then sliding to the ground, or spinning like an ice-skater on her knee, while Augie touched just the tips of her fingers. The strength and muscle-control each of them possessed was amazing. They were, in a word, phenomenal!

By this time, they had clearly turned their act into very personalized routines, using their own music, which gave them a totally unique performance - one which the entertainment critics were beginning to notice and admire.

It would be wrong to give the impression there were no other dancers on the entertainment circuit at that time. Indeed, there were hundreds, all pursuing their own claim to fame. Many were extremely talented, but it can be argued that the majority of them danced their own style and remained within its boundaries; keeping it 'pure,' as it were. Theoretically, in the arena of dance, the rules were just waiting to be broken, and Augie and Margo were recognized by critics as being the pioneers.

~~~~~~~~~~

The early years of their career were spent on the road, touring at home and overseas, bringing baby Richard with them; living for weeks, sometimes months with top celebrities from around the world. They tell wonderful, surprising and humorous stories, but have never been unkind or judgmental about a single well known celebrity, and they got to know several very well indeed.

These artists truly understood Augie and Margo's significance as 'openers' for their highly publicized acts. First and foremost, they were sensational entertainers who could warm up an audience in an instant, but the important thing was that as completely unique performers, they didn't steal the spotlight. Their consummate talent, and genuine warmth, humor, and honesty, made them perfect traveling companions, and before long they were in great demand.

In 1957, Hal Prince, the well-known producer and director, asked them to be in a show he was co-producing with Robert E. Griffith, which would debut in the *Winter Garden Theater* on Broadway. He wanted Augie to play the part of Bernardo, a leader of a gang called the *Sharks*, and Margo was to be Anita, Bernardo's girl and best friend of a girl named Maria.

It was, of course, *West Side Story*. Augie and Margo were so busy with engagements and commitments that they had to decline the offer and the parts were later taken on by Chita Rivera and Ken Le Roy.

~~~~~~~~~~

In the same year that Augie and Margo appeared with Danny Thomas, Jerry Lewis had presented his solo performance at the *Town and Country* in New York, and Dean Martin was booked to appear at the *Flamingo* in Las Vegas, so it was only a matter of time before Augie and Margo would get to know both of these performers very well indeed.

Not only was Jack Entratter engaged in booking entertainers for the *Sands*. He also had a hand in providing big names for other Las Vegas hotels, so six months after their *Copa Room* debut, Entratter arranged for Augie and Margo to open for Dean Martin.

Because his name was well known, Dean Martin's agent put him back to working clubs in Vegas, but this would be his first performance, and Martin was still an unknown quantity when it came to performing alone.

All the arrangements were made, and then suddenly Entratter changed his mind. He decided that, as Dean Martin was appearing without Jerry Lewis, perhaps Augie and Margo would overwhelm or outshine him. Everyone knew Dean had a great voice, but for years he had been part of a double act; now, he may find his new format very difficult and be disadvantaged as a solo act.

As an alternative, Entratter chose that another well-known star, one who would be opening at the *Copa Room*, should have Augie and Margo open for him instead. This second star was also hampered with a recent and unwelcome problem, but since the age of three, when he debuted on stage, and at five years old was touring the country as a vaudeville entertainer with his father and uncle, he had been credited as being a performing phenomenon.

He was 'a natural.' For years, he had proven he could dance, sing and act, and no one could compete with him on any level. At least, that's what most of the world thought - but not him: never him.

Sammy Davis Jr. had recently recovered from a car accident, which broke several bones in his face and lost him the sight in his left eye. It was 1954, and he was on his way from Las Vegas to Los Angeles, to record the theme song for a Tony Curtis film, titled *Six Bridges to Cross*.

The result of the automobile accident was that Sammy's eye had to be surgically removed. He took to wearing an eye patch, but never liked the fact that it drew the kind of attention he despised. He wanted to be referred to as a great performer - not just remembered as *"The kid with the eye patch."*

Frank Sinatra insisted that Sammy recuperate at his home in Palm Springs. He had been Sammy's friend since 1941, when the two of them met in Detroit. Sammy was performing with his father, Sammy Davis Sr. and his uncle, Will Mastin, in their dance troupe, *Will Mastin's Gang*. They were opening for the immensely popular bandleader, Tommy Dorsey, in his show at the *Michigan Theater*, where Dorsey was showcasing Frank Sinatra as the band's vocalist.

Sinatra and Sammy became instant friends, and over the following years, when Frank Sinatra had opportunities to visit new venues, or to meet influential people in show-business, he offered Sammy the same chances he had. For example, in 1952, the newly-integrated *Copacabana* in New York billed Sammy as the first black American to perform there, which he was, and he performed together with Frank.

That is not to imply that Sammy Davis Jr. was not spectacularly popular in his own right. After recuperating from his accident at Frank Sinatra's home in Palm Springs, at Frank's insistence, by 1955 he was ready to return to the stage, where he sang a string of songs that became huge hits. *That Old Black Magic, Something's Gotta Give* and *Love Me or Leave Me* are still standard ballads to this day, and when Sammy made them hits it earned him an enormous following of fans on both sides of the racial divide.

The following year, in 1956, Sammy Davis Jr. made his Broadway debut in the musical, *Mr. Wonderful*. He starred in over 400 performances, and made a hit of a song from the show, *Too Close for Comfort*, another perennial favorite.

By 1958, when Augie and Margo had "cut their teeth" in Vegas, Sammy Davis had already returned to acting and films, and although he was always conscious of it, he learned to live with the fact that he only had one eye.

He told Humphrey Bogart one day about his fear of only being remembered for his eye patch, and Bogart convinced him to get a false eye and throw away the mask. For Sammy Davis it was a huge hurdle to jump. The man who had more talent in his little finger than most entertainers would ever have was an extremely insecure person inside.

~~~~~~~~~~~

Sammy's life had been a huge achievement of talent over circumstance. He was brought up first by his paternal grandmother, and from the age of three by his father and his uncle Will, after his dancer mother, Elvira, abandoned the family. Both his father and uncle were dancers, and his father didn't want to lose custody of him, so when the tiny boy was three, he took Sammy with him as they toured around the country performing vaudeville.

Almost immediately, Sammy Jr. began showing exceptional talent, in both singing and dancing. When he was seven years old, Bill "Bojangles" Robinson met the touring group, and was so impressed with Sammy that he gave him tap-dancing lessons.

Although he never went to school of any kind, Sammy learned a lot from his father and uncle but was largely self-taught. He never experienced prejudice until he joined the military at age 18, because his family shielded him from it; telling him such things as, when white people made offensive comments, that people were jealous of him because he was such a good performer.

When, at age 18, he entered the U.S. Army, and was confronted with racial blocks and remarks every time he turned around, Sammy was completely shocked. His family had protected him so much, that he really had no idea about the cruel and prejudicial segregation practices that existed all over the country.

After having his nose broken twice in the military in purely racial conflicts, Sammy's perception of the nature of the real world truly began to hit home. He gave back as good as he got, though; his frame was small, but all the years of dancing had made him strong and wiry, and he could bob and weave with the best of them. His nose might have been broken, but he wasn't always on the losing end. Talking to a friend about that phase of his life, he once said, to paraphrase, *"Since I didn't start the fights, I didn't fight back with no Marquis of Queensbury rules!"* However, the constant taunts didn't make his time in the military a happy one.

To help counteract the situation somewhat, he joined an Army entertainment unit, and suddenly he found that everyone was decent to him. As a performer and traditional song and dance man, who could also act and do amazing impersonations, he was more 'acceptable' under the spotlight; so from then on, Sammy decided it was better to use his talent as his weapon!

The emotional stress and hurt feelings, though, persisted, and became a sense of outrage that he drove inside; so in order to forget it was there, he turned to anything that could filter out the pain.

As a smoker from a very young age, he quickly became a chain-smoker, getting easily through four packs of cigarettes a day. He also turned to alcohol and drugs, and when they ceased to have the desired effect, there was always sex.

Despite his small stature and lack of striking good looks, Sammy Davis Jr. was never at a loss for women - and he went for the beauties! After working once with his father and uncle in Canada as a teenager, he had experienced an interracial attitude that was much more free and easy than in North America, and he had been very attracted to some blonde fair-skinned Canadian girls he met while touring around. From then on, blonde beauties always fascinated him.

It's hardly likely that everything which happened to him while on tour, affected his later experience with women negatively, but he was certainly encouraged to think that more than one woman in attendance was OK, from a very early age.

Many of the cities visited by *Will Mastin's Gang* when Sammy was young, had very strict child labor laws. To overcome this, the little boy was billed as, *"Silent Sammy, the Dancing Midget"* and his dad and uncle made sure after their shows, that he was seen parading around backstage with a rubber cigar between his teeth, and a woman on each arm! Just in case any inspectors were hanging around after the show to check on the performers.

The lack of a mother in his childhood, undoubtedly, also repressed part of Sammy's personality, and although too complex to explain away in a few sentences, it is almost certainly relevant to the fact that he could never have enough women in his life. The more blonde and

gorgeous they were, the happier he was. One could say they were drawn to him because of his talent and fame, indeed, some were, but many of them genuinely loved him.

It was a tragedy for Sammy that having one woman in his life was never enough, and it was terribly sad for the women who really cared. Part of the problem he faced was, understandably, from his own people. If he loved a white woman, he was considered to be betraying his own race, and they made sure to let him know how they felt about it.

He found himself, often, in impossible situations. Sammy had known many good white people, some of whom were his close friends, and he knew they bore no preconceived opinions of him as a human being, so instead of turning his discovery of prejudice into hatred of all white people; he sought a spiritual explanation instead.

When he was at a low point during his recuperation after the accident, he got to know a Rabbi, who visited him in the hospital. The Rabbi was so caring and interesting to talk to, that Sammy turned to the Jewish religion and found some answers to the many questions he had. When he left the hospital, he began to study Judaism, understanding that Jewish people had also experienced prejudice and sought to overcome it; so along with the practical help of some of his Jewish friends, including Milton Berle, he found many answers to his spiritual needs. The result was that in 1956, he decided to convert.

Sammy Davis was nothing, if not pragmatic. Converting to Judaism was not popular at all amongst his fellow African-Americans, but it made *him* feel better inside. Using his tremendous sense of humor, he became self-deprecating, referring to himself as a 'broken-nosed, one-eyed, black Jew,' which to a large extent quieted his critics; at least, it did for a while, until the following year, in 1957, when he started dating the actress Kim Novak.

It was at that point that he met, and became friends, with Augie and Margo.

~~~~~~~~~~

They had met briefly before, in the Catskills, where Sammy was performing and Augie and Margo were dancing. Chita Rivera, whom they knew well from the Katherine Dunham School, had introduced them. Sammy Davis Jr. was already a famous artist, and Augie and Margo were still pretty shy, truly wide-eyed kids, so although their conversation had been limited to *"Hello, nice to meet you."* They never forgot that brief encounter.

They assumed, on the other hand, that Sammy had forgotten, since he never mentioned the incident when he saw them again in Vegas. Augie and Margo decided, also, not to remind him of their meeting. He had met so many people in his tours around the country; so why on earth should they tell him, they thought, and perhaps make him feel bad?

Sammy was the kind of person who "took" to people, and he instantly took to Augie and Margo when they started working with him. The feeling was reciprocal. Once they knew each other, they immediately became fast friends and confidantes.

At that time, a loose alliance of Sinatra's associates, dubbed the *Rat Pack*, had begun performing regularly at the *Sands* in Las Vegas, though Sinatra had made his debut there in October, 1953, a year after the hotel had opened. There are varying stories as to how the name *Rat Pack* came about, but the most likely one, is that it came from another gathering of Hollywood elites, named by gossip columnists as the *Holmby Hills Rat Pack*. This was a group of drinking friends, including Frank Sinatra, who latched on to Humphrey Bogart and Lauren Bacall. When Bogart died, Sinatra continued the custom of the group, only this time he surrounded himself with his own friends and named them the *Clan*. The group consisted of Dean Martin, Joey Bishop the comedian, actor Peter Lawford, Sammy Davis Jr. and, in the early days, Shirley MacLaine.

The problem with the word *clan*, though, was that it had an undertone of racism, and Sammy was bothered by it so, as Frank agreed with him wholeheartedly, he changed the name to the *Rat Pack*. To use Sammy's exact words, *"I wanta go on record that I ain't belongin' to nothing that's called a clan!"*

The Sands hotel in the 1950's was the first to hire Frank Sinatra, and soon after, all his friends in the business followed. Sinatra, of course, had a personal interest in *The Sands*. It is said he owned a 9% interest in it, but it is less well known that 75% of that investment belonged to Chicago gangsters.

Frank's career had taken a big dive during his first marriage, when he was considered all but a has-been, both as a singer and an actor, but after he married Ava Gardener, she begged Harry Cohn to give Frank a role in *From Here to Eternity*, which earned him an Academy Award for Supporting Actor. Receiving the award brought him back on top, but forever after he was indebted to the mob.

It is true that other performers, people like Tony Bennett and Al Martino, also had their venues and bookings manipulated by mobsters, whose hands were in almost every aspect of Las Vegas, but at the end of the day, their connection and lack of independence did not run as deeply as Frank's did.

Primarily, of course, the city of Las Vegas and its hotels were developed for gambling, but it soon became obvious to the hotel owners that helping their patrons to relax and enjoy good food and fabulous entertainment, was conducive to encouraging a sense of well-being and, therefore, a feeling that they would return to the tables and win!

In light of this revelation, other hotels began to hire big-name entertainers also, and over the years it could be argued that Las Vegas hotels have overtaken all the rest in the world. By providing the absolute ultimate in entertainment for their guests, it has reached a point, now, that visitors to the city go to be entertained almost as much, if not more, than they are there to gamble.

Augie and Margo Rodriguez, the young adagio dancers, would have most likely been stunned with disbelief, that forty seven years after dancing in Las Vegas at the newly constructed *Sands* with the *Rat Pack*, they would be back again. Dancing, amazingly twice a night, with the world-famous *Cirque du Soleil* in one of the hottest shows in Vegas!

CHAPTER NINETEEN

From an early age, both Augie and Margo were exposed on the street to varying amounts of one stimulant or another. It would be easy to say, *"By some miracle they were sober,"* but a comment like that would completely demean their decision making. They *chose* to be sober.

They had family members, friends and fellow performers who were drawn to the habit, some with disastrous consequences, and so at a young age they made a conscious decision that they preferred to avoid and refuse all but the occasional glass of beer or wine.

While socializing and enjoying the company of many people whose habits either frequently incapacitated or totally annihilated them, they knew where their own line was drawn in the sand, and it paid off for them big time! How many people of their generation can clearly remember what *really* happened fifty years ago, and be fit enough to still be performing two shows a night?

Drinking in general amongst performers, both top-name and not so well known, was par for the course in the world of entertainment, but it seemed to Augie and Margo that in some cases, the bigger the stars became the more they seemed to drink.

Since their first encounters with Frank Sinatra, Sammy Davis Jr., Dean Martin and Liberace, who all had a pretty high tolerance for alcohol, they also knew stars like Peter O'Toole, Tallulah Bankhead, Peter Lawford, and Judy Garland, who drank the booze like mineral water and still, somehow, managed to perform on stage.

Judy Garland in particular was able to carry out near miracles, turning in powerhouse performances which resulted mostly in near-hysterically worshipping audiences. However, on one occasion in 1968, Augie and Margo were performing with Dean Martin, Frank Sinatra, Mickey Rooney and Judy Garland in the TV Show *"Dick Clarke's World of Talent,"* and they were able to see at first-hand just how close to the edge Judy really was.

At that stage of her life she was already rebellious and difficult, a trait directly attributable to her drug and drinking habit, but she was also by then a very nervy and restless person with a career that fluctuated like the Stock Market. Sometimes she was capable of delivering a completely magnificent performance, but at other times she could be astonishingly mediocre. The incredibly phenomenal entertainer that she had been to her audiences practically all her life had recently been the recipient of cat-calls.

Cracks had begun to appear when she appeared on stage in Europe, when she had either been too ill or bombed out to perform. Although most of the time she was able to pull the cat out of the bag for her audience, actually sitting on the stage sometimes, and gaining the love and sympathy of her fans that way, she became consistently late or sick as her diminishing health failed her.

Garland had been a child star at the same time Mickey Rooney was, and they were teamed together as youngsters in many musicals and films, but having her old friend with her on Dick Clarke's show, did nothing to help her insecurity and her heightened highly-charged emotional condition.

The preparations prior to the show were almost like a party, with Frank and Dean drinking plenty and fooling around when Augie and Margo rehearsed. While the director was asking for *"Lights, Margo, music,"* in that sequence, Sinatra and Martin would call out a changed order when Margo attempted to go on stage. They both enjoyed teasing the Rodriguez dance team as much as they bantered with Sammy Davis Jr. and ended up calling them Sacco and Vanzetti, after the two notorious Italians from Massachusetts who were accused of killing two armed guards in a payroll robbery.

The poor director had a hard enough job handling the *Rat Pack* crowd, but perhaps seeing everyone else 'having drinks and fun,' made Judy more than happy to go with the flow.

As she rehearsed, she persistently stepped off the stage to drink, against all admonitions from the Director, so by the time she was scheduled to go on and perform she was totally bombed. Augie and Margo, along with everyone else, were astounded at her condition. No-one could imagine that she could pull out of her completely inebriated state and carry on. It would take a miracle.

Up until it was her turn, the show went without a hitch; but she was the star and the last one to come on stage. It would be fair to say that everyone held their breath!

Two stage hands went to her dressing room, and taking hold of an arm each, they carried her slumped body to the wings, holding her upright until the introductory music struck up, at which time they literally shoved her forward to the front of the stage. The miracle happened. Judy staggered a little, blinked at the spotlights and sub-consciously flipped the 'magic' switch. The legend lived to perform another day!

Sadly, only a year later, Judy Garland died. She had married her fifth husband, Mickey Deans, a London nightclub manager in March of 1969, and three months later he discovered her in their apartment, dead, of an overdose of barbiturates.

Judy's life is well documented, and the tragedy of her dependence on drugs, could be traced all the way back to her childhood when the powerful movie studio bosses were perfectly happy exploiting and feeding their child prodigies with stimulants to keep them acting at all hours, and then sleeping pills to make them rest. Her life and, sadly, her death, became a disgraceful testament to the controlling ways and lack of decency demonstrated by many movie moguls.

~~~~~~~~~~

When Augie and Margo first met Dean Martin, it's worth repeating that they were relatively new on the scene. Dean Martin, as it happened, had actually done very well alone. Starting to perform solo in Vegas in

1957, the year Augie and Margo were paired by Jack Entratter with Sammy Davis instead of him, Dean Martin surprised Entratter and several other skeptics, when he showed them he could stand very nicely on his own two feet.

On his first night at the *Sands,* crowds of people came to see if Martin would sink, and by the end of his show there was no doubt in anyone's mind that not only could he could float and swim, but do a very acceptable rendition of the butterfly, the crawl and the back-stroke as well! Everyone loved him, and he went on to be one of the most popular acts in Vegas for the next three decades!

Experienced enough in the art of charming and delighting an audience from his days with Jerry Lewis, to the extent that they had become the most financially successful comedy duo in history, Martin knew intuitively before his first solo appearance that he had to develop a character which set him apart from other singers and entertainers in the industry.

Enough publicity had been given to the break-up of his partnership with Lewis to warrant some careful consideration on Martin's part, and he eventually came up with a brilliant concept which would also serve to alleviate any opening night jitters.

He decided to perfect the laid back facade of a lovable drunk, which worked perfectly for his nightclub act, where he came across as amicably inebriated and a charming womanizer. This gave the men in his audience a "buddy" with whom to relate, and the women, an astoundingly handsome man who sang romantic songs of love to them alone.

Just performing as a nightclub singer though, was not enough for Dean Martin. As the perceived weakest link in his ex-partnership, he was determined to regain the status he truly believed he had owned and deserved even before teaming up with Lewis, and to do that he needed to get back into motion pictures.

A part in the movie *The Young Lions,* made in 1958, was exactly what he wanted, and after successfully persuading his agent at MCA to engineer a role for him, his co-stars, Montgomery Clift and Marlon Brando, became invaluable, albeit unknowing, instructors for him in their craft. The movie turned out to be a huge success, and Martin, having been given one of the coveted dramatic roles of the decade, proved himself to be a fine actor; more than holding his own opposite his counterparts.

Very much a part of the *Rat Pack*, although he was a friend of Sinatra, Dean Martin did not like to be thought of as a dependent member of the group. He was no sycophant, and let it be known he was only in the *Pack* because *he* chose to be!

He soon became known as "The Eternal Essence of Cool," and people started calling him the Chief Deputy, to Frank's, Chairman of the Board. The success of his performance in *Young Lions* proved to be the foundation of Dean Martin's comeback, which turned out to be nothing less than spectacular, and, surprisingly, only one person had been able to predict it.

Jackie Gleason, the comedian and actor, dubbed "The Great One," who immortalized the role of Ralph Kramden in the television series *The Honeymooners,* was convinced that Martin would eventually surpass Lewis in popularity. His reasoning was smart but required very little analyzing. Dean Martin was handsome, he could sing, he moved well and he had perfect comic timing!

Gleason was absolutely correct! By the mid-1960's, Dean Martin was enjoying the fruits of a titanic career. Not only was he a top movie actor – he actually starred in 36 motion pictures – a recording star and nightclub attraction, he also had a weekly television show on NBC and owned a chain of Italian restaurants called *Dino's*. All this, as Jerry Lewis's star was beginning to fade.

~~~~~~~~~~~

Martin himself was quite critical of his baritone voice. He made no secret of the fact that he had modeled his singing style on Perry Como and Bing Crosby, and despite the fact that he couldn't read a word of music, during his career he recorded 600 songs and more than 100 albums, including many major hits.

His believable portrayals of heavy drinkers in the late 1950's movies, *Some Came Running* and *Rio Bravo*, gave many people the impression that Dean Martin was an alcoholic, which led to widespread rumors that were never fully borne out. Certainly, his exploitation of being a half-soused crooner didn't help to alleviate the gossip, and the reputation remained with him until the day he died.

Augie and Margo were very soon paired with Dean Martin as his opening act, and were also included with him and the *Rat Pack* at major venues across the country, so they got to know him as well as everyone else in the group. When they first met him, they found a very friendly and pleasant person who never let his popularity elevate his ego. He was as charming to his fellow-performers as he was to his fans. Over the years, as they grew to know him better, they understood him as a complex person, somewhat reserved and private off-stage, but never one to be pretentious or putting on airs.

Even though Sinatra was considered to be his best friend, unless they were performing together, Martin only saw him a couple of times a year, preferring to be at home with his family, watching television, playing golf or dining out. Though he cultivated the womanizer image in his act, he was not essentially that kind of guy.

Married three times, his first marriage in 1941 to Betty McDonald, with whom he had four children, a boy, Stephen Craig, and three girls, Claudia, Barbara Gail and Deana (Dina), lasted nine years. In 1949, he married Jeanne Biegger, a former Orange Bowl Queen, and fathered three more children. This time two boys, Dino Paul and Ricci James, and a girl, Gina Caroline, who married Carl Wilson from the singing group *The Beach Boys*.

His final marriage, almost twenty five years later, to Catherine Mae Hawn, a beauty salon receptionist, lasted only three years, during which time they adopted a daughter, Sasha. The marriage was dissolved in 1976 when Martin realized that Catherine was only interested in his money and celebrity.

~~~~~~~~~~

Most, if not all, of the biographies and editorials written about Dean Martin state that his legendary drinking habits were a ruse; that the glass of "Scotch" placed on the piano during his nightclub act every evening was nothing more than fruit juice. *"It's no secret,"* it says in several editorials about Dean, *"that Martin was sipping apple juice not booze most of the time on stage."* It has also been stated by a family member, that had he actually drunk that much alcohol every night he would have been unable to perform.

Logically, that makes sense; but Augie and Margo tell another side to the story, which certainly gives one pause for thought. In the case of Dean Martin, like his fellow performers in the *Rat Pack,* booze was an integral part of their routine. Dean may not have been strictly an alcoholic, but the story that he only had juice in his shot glass when he performed his act was not quite accurate.

At the start of their career, the pair of young dancers, Augie and Margo Rodriguez, were in awe of the titans of entertainment for whom they performed as an opening act and then socialized with after the show. Augie is the first one to say they were still pretty naïve; so when he and Margo either opened for Dean Martin, or were on the same bill he was on in a variety show, they accepted him for who he was and assumed his half-soused crooner image was just an act.

Dean was always very friendly toward them. He even showered attention on their little Chihuahua, Jackie, who traveled with them. Every time Dean saw Jackie in the corridor outside the dressing rooms, he always stopped, bent down and barked at him, until Jackie was so thoroughly excited he started hysterically barking back; at which time Dean would yell, *"Kill, Jackie, kill!"* Bringing everyone running to see what all the fuss was about. Dean was a fun guy, a nice guy and Augie and Margo liked him a lot.

After completing their first act, Augie was always pleasantly surprised on returning to the dressing room, to find a bottle or two of apple juice waiting for Margo and him. It became a matter of habit; when it started Augie put it down to the back-stage staff, but then at different venues the apple juice continued to appear.

Augie hung around the room one day to find out whom he should thank. Their refreshment-giver turned out to be Dean Martin, who went back-stage before his second act to do a switch! He gave Augie a big wink, and said nothing; which is exactly what he knew *they* would do!

~~~~~~~~~~

For Sammy Davis and other black performers, in Las Vegas in the early days, along with the rest of America, he was met with racism at every turn. It even went to the point that initially he was not allowed to stay at the *Sands*, where he was performing.

With Sinatra, Dean Martin and the rest of the group, he was bringing huge revenues into the hotel, so after a while, Sinatra put his foot down and insisted to Jack Entratter that Sammy be allowed to have a room there along with everyone else. Entratter obliged and slowly, very slowly, after that things began to improve for the black entertainers and visitors who entered the small desert town in the middle of nowhere.

At the time Augie and Margo started opening for him, Sammy was heavily involved with the actress Kim Novak, but their relationship was coming to an end, and Sammy was genuinely distraught. He told Augie and Margo that he really loved her, and she him, but there were cruel twists of fate driving them apart. Despite the fact that they were both famous people, their careers were threatened to the point of annihilation, and it was mainly because people behind the scenes were anticipating that their own revenues from the couple would be wiped out if it became generally known they were together.

Although racial issues were undoubtedly at the heart of the problem, both stars were eventually compromised to the point that they had no choice but to do as they were told, especially since their lives and futures were settled behind the scenes, by the Mafia.

The story was simple. Kim Novak had been selected to be the next big star for *Columbia* pictures, by no less a person than Harry Cohn, one of *Columbia's* founders. Rita Hayworth was *Columbia's* glamorous blonde star at that time, incidentally, discovered by Xavier Cugat, but

Cohn was getting tired of the rebellious behavior and histrionics she displayed. He decided instead, to groom Kim Novak as the next "Blonde Bombshell", putting Columbia in competition with *20th Century Fox*, who had Marilyn Monroe, under contract.

When it came to running his company, Cohn was notoriously demanding and rigid. People said he ran his studio like a private police state, and he was often referred to as "King Cohn" for that reason. When he found out that his new protégé was running around with Sammy Davis Jr. he attempted to nip it in the bud immediately.

Segregation, being alive and well at that time, meant that a large majority of the American public would have been horrified to know the truth about the dating habits of the gorgeous and glamorous Miss Novak, and probably shun *Columbia* pictures for decades.

Cohn was in no way prepared to let that happen, Kim Novak was hot property. The problem was, that he was counting on the affair to be like most of the others in Hollywood, shallow and transitory, but Sammy and Kim were actually involved in something much deeper and were more than reluctant to let anyone, even Cohn, dictate to them.

For a while, Sammy continued seeing her any way he could. They had a direct telephone line to each other, so at least they could talk, and they sneaked around, trying to avoid being seen, but it was very difficult, actually, impossible. They were two of the highest profile celebrities in the country, not to mention the fact that they were visible breakers of the racial barrier on top of everything else.

One night, Sammy dressed up as the boyfriend of Kim's black maid, so he could get into her apartment, and everyone in his crowd hooted with laughter when they saw him, realizing the lengths to which he was willing to go, but it became impossible in the end. Sammy really had no choice in the matter. His very life was dependent on being a performer, he knew nothing else, and by then the rumors had started everywhere.

There was no doubt his black brothers and sisters were furious that one of their first fellow African-American brothers to become ultra-popular, on both sides of the racial divide, had chosen to walk around town with a gorgeous, white, film star on his arm.

The comments from his fellow blacks hurt him a lot, but at the same time, Sammy was performing in what was then, virtually a white mans world, and the "top men" who called all the shots on the entertainment circuit around Vegas, also did not like to see him getting too comfortable with the likes of Kim Novak. He was told in no uncertain terms by the mob elites that he had better not be seen romantically involved with a white woman, or his gigs would come to a screeching halt.

Sammy Davis, despite his undisputed talent, was in a hell of a position. Unlike Dean Martin who was able to call his own shots, Sammy was constantly and unwillingly put in the position of being a sycophant to Frank Sinatra; a reputation which persists to this day, as portrayed in the latest *Rat Pack* movie. And sadly for Sammy, it all boiled down to racial intolerance.

In the end it was easy. Harry Cohn's first attempt to break up the couple had failed, but Cohn had long been known to have ties with the Mafia, especially John Roselli, who had a multitude of connections in Hollywood and even helped Cohn finance his partnership in *Columbia* some years earlier. A word in the right ear in Vegas had soon started things moving.

Very soon a young black dancer named, ironically, Loray White appeared (rather, was pushed) on the scene, and rumor has it that she was paid $25,000 to play along. Sammy did what was expected of him; kicking and screaming all the way, he married her!

There is no doubt that the mob forced him into the marriage with White, and several people in different biographies and editorials about Sammy have made various statements about the type of threats he received if he chose to disobey them. That, 'his other eye would be poked out' or that 'he would be killed and buried in the desert,' but the truth is that it only took a 'gentle' word in his ear.

He didn't need to be told: with all the bad publicity, and his lifestyle even reaching the ears of people in high political places, he knew his relationship with Kim Novak was doomed.

His marriage to Loray White was in 1958, the year that he starred in the movie *Anna Lucasta* with Eartha Kitt and James Edwards, a talented and dignified actor who lead the way for black male actors in breaking stereotypical roles, being portrayed as subservient, indolent or illiterate.

Along with Sammy himself, his co-stars were all struggling to break new ground in their endeavor for racial equality, but in spite of the fact that they were talented and sought-after in the entertainment industry, they all knew where the line was drawn in the sand. It was going to take a lot more effort and understanding by all fair-minded citizens, before true success could be theirs and the line was obliterated for ever.

The day of Sammy's marriage to Loray White was a disaster from the word 'go.' Harry Belafonte was Best Man, and he had quite a job trying to keep Sammy off the bottle!

He was not very successful: Sammy was walking around wailing, *"Why can't I marry the woman I love?"* And everyone within earshot did their best to prevent his bride from hearing him. According to Sammy's former personal assistant, Arthur Silber, on the night of the wedding Sammy put a gun to his head and threatened to kill himself, until Silber overpowered him and knocked the gun out of his hand. That information, however, is not substantiated, and others believe that even if he did that, Sammy was just plain drunk and acting out.

The child Loray White was rumored to be carrying was never born, and Sammy Davis turned to his career, becoming heavily involved in the making of the movie *Porgy and Bess*, which was directed by Otto Preminger and starred Sidney Poitier as Porgy and Dorothy Dandridge as Bess.

The movie was a huge success which, perhaps, helped to give Sammy Davis the courage to escape his failure of a marriage. Less than a year after the wedding he filed for divorce; which cut him free from a woman he didn't love, but led him on the road to a permanently confused love life, and mistaken notions that sex alone would be the answer to all his emotional problems.

CHAPTER TWENTY

In 1960, The *Rat Pack*, were making the movie *Oceans Eleven*, on location in Las Vegas. It was a real bonus for the *Sands* owners, because during the day the group shot their movie, and in the evenings they performed at the hotel. A routine sprang up between them, where Frank would be performing his act and then suddenly Dean Martin would enter the nightclub and yell at him to stop, that he had been 'on' too long! It was a real shock for the audience.

Initially, it had been an impulse on Dean Martin's part, and Frank, for a moment or two, was completely frozen on stage. Frank was not a spontaneous person but, of course, Dean had spent years sparring on stage with his ex-partner Jerry Lewis, and he was brilliant at throwing verbal curve-balls. The first time it happened, the audience was as stunned as Frank, to see such audacious behavior directed at their idol, Frank, the undisputed King of Sing. Horrified, they waited with bated breath to see what Frank would do.

Fortunately, Frank quickly realized what his buddy was doing and, naturally, it became a perfectly orchestrated part of the act, with the nightly audience being treated to a wonderful jibing back and forth between the two singers. Each night was different, a little unpredictable, with Sammy sometimes joining the others and creating uproar in the crowd with his imitations of Frank. Though it was said, that although Sammy could 'get' the voice perfectly, he was never quite able to achieve the languid 'distance, yet presence,' that Frank alone had on stage.

~~~~~~~~~~

Meanwhile, after making *Anna Lucasta*, Sammy went on to make *Porgy and Bess,* with Sidney Poitier, and it was a huge hit. Both movies served to establish Davis even more as a Star, and by the time *Oceans Eleven* was being discussed and cast, he was well accepted and totally recognized as a legitimate member of Sinatra's *Pack*.

Perhaps it was that fact which gave him the courage to ignore the opinions of his black fans, and dive, once again, into an association with a blonde, white woman.

May (pronounced My) Britt was a twenty-three year-old actress when Sammy Davis first saw her, in 1959, at the *20th Century Fox* Commissary. She had been discovered working as a photographer's assistant, seven years earlier in Sweden, where she was born, by Carlo Ponti, who later discovered and married Sophia Loren. Ponti took her to Italy where she made a few minor films before moving to America, where she was given a role in the movie, *Murder Inc.*

May Britt's impact on the Hollywood acting scene was minor, to say the least, but she was a beautiful young woman whose looks completely swept away Sammy Davis Jr. when he first set his eyes on her. He often spoke about it, saying her delicate freckled skin, pale blonde hair and stunning figure made her the most beautiful woman he had ever seen, and that he could spend an entire day just looking at her; watching her walk around.

In 1960, on May's 24th birthday, Sammy bought her a beautiful diamond cocktail ring, and several weeks later they announced their engagement. It was a complicated time in America's history to do such a thing, in more ways than one!

First, because at that time thirty-one States in the country had laws preventing interracial marriage, and second, because for the past two years the entire *Rat Pack* had been deeply involved in promoting the then Senator, John Kennedy, who was running for President.

It is no secret now, that the Senator's father, Joe Kennedy, who had several connections of dubious origin across the country, sought the help of Mafia kingpin, Sam Giancana to secure the union vote for his son in the Chicago area.

Frank Sinatra, being a 'friend' of Giancana, was also drawn into this arrangement, and became involved in supporting and publicizing the Senator in Las Vegas, where he regularly came to schmooze with the big shot vote catchers, when they were in town.

The *Rat Pack* all did their best to make the Senator comfortable when he visited the *Sands,* but Frank went out of his way to keep Kennedy happy! One day, Augie and Margo were sitting in Frank's suite with a small group of friends when the telephone rang. Someone picked up the receiver, and after listening for a while, he said, with a puzzled expression on his face, "Who's 'number two? This guy says he's 'number one' and he wants to talk to 'number two'."

With that, Frank jumped out of his seat and ran to the phone. This happened on several occasions, and the gang soon found out that 'number one' was Kennedy. Sinatra, 'number two', had promised to send call-girls to his suite, before he came down to socialize with everyone, and if the girls didn't arrive promptly, Kennedy got very impatient and called Frank, telling him to find out why they were late, and to hurry them up. Kennedy was obsessed with sex, to the point that he wasn't willing to go to work on promoting himself until he had been 'serviced', and Sinatra was well aware of that fact.

As a presidential candidate, in 1960, when Kennedy was visiting Palm Springs where Sinatra's estate was located, Frank introduced him to his own mistress, Judith Campbell. Campbell, born Judith Inmoor, had been married to the actor William Campbell, until she met Frank in 1958, when she divorced her husband and began a relationship with Sinatra.

Upon meeting Kennedy, Judith Campbell promptly became one of his mistresses, and continued to be one throughout his presidency, which was bad enough; except that where deception is involved, ugly things can happen. After Kennedy became entangled with Campbell, Giancana got wind of it. He asked Sinatra to introduce Judith Campbell to him as well, and another affair began. As easily as that, the man who would be President had laid himself wide open for everything from blackmail to murder.

~~~~~~~~~~~~

The reason Sammy's engagement to May Britt was so controversial, was not just the racial implications it posed, but that it had now become a political hot potato for Senator Kennedy.

Sammy and May wanted to marry in early November, with Sinatra as the Best Man, but the Presidential Election was also in November, and as Sinatra was a known friend of Jack Kennedy, his father, Joe, was adamant that Sammy's wedding be held after the election. Joe was convinced that if Frank was seen in all the national papers as Best Man at Sammy's wedding, his son would lose huge numbers of the white vote, and therefore, the election itself.

Sammy had no choice but to agree, and finally he and May Britt married on November 13th. 1960. At the time, May was twenty-four years old and Sammy Davis was thirty-four. Sinatra was Best Man, and along with a group of good friends, including Shirley McLain, Augie and Margo attended the wedding.

Joe Kennedy was probably right about the white back-lash. The vitriolic outrage across the country, following the wedding, including death threats, forced the newly-wed couple to hire bodyguards, but their bravery in going through with the event deserves mention.

They were actually very happily married. May Britt gave up her career to have a child, a daughter named Tracey, whom Sammy adored. When Augie and Margo went to see May and the new baby in the hospital he was ecstatic: *"Look how beautiful she is,"* he said to them *"her hair isn't nappy!"*

Over the next three years she and Sammy adopted two African-American boys, Mark and Jeff. Unfortunately, with the schedule that Sammy had, the couple rarely had time together, and traipsing three children across the country in order to be together was not easy.

May also disliked the way the *Rat Pack* poked fun at him on stage. It was supposed to be Frank's way of making prejudiced members in their audience see how narrow-minded they were; but sometimes the jabs got very close to the bone. Sammy always told May not to be sensitive, that Frank and the rest of the crowd loved him and they were only joking; but underneath his bravado she wondered how her brilliant husband must *really* feel, and she continued to hate it.

Inevitably, May ended up taking care of the children, and Sammy, 'on the road' was unable to rein in his roving eye. Sometimes, even when May was on location with him, Sammy would have a couple of girls in tow, concealed within his entourage.

Six years after the wedding, Sammy and May Britt separated, and two years later, in 1968, they were divorced. It was ironic that a year before their divorce, in 1967, the Supreme Court abolished the law banning interracial marriage.

~~~~~~~~~~~

Augie and Margo worked and traveled together with Sammy, or Sam, as they called him, for many years, and became the ones he turned to when his innumerable relationships exploded. It got to the point that he would not do a show unless they agreed to open for him, and they did so for almost twelve years, traveling with him all over the world. Sammy never failed to let them know how much he loved them, and how fortunate he felt to know people he trusted.

They became more than friends - they were like family. Augie often says that the two men he has loved most in his life were his father and Sammy, and it is clearly so. The tears in Augie's eyes when he talks about either man speak more truth than a thousand words. Without doubt, those were the men who loved Augie unconditionally, and his sensitive nature understood that, every time he looked into their eyes.

Many conversations Augie and Margo had together with Sammy will go to their graves, but the bottom line is that Sammy Davis, for all his undeniable talent, was a man who always felt enormously inadequate.

If one asks either Margo or Augie to compare Frank Sinatra and Sammy Davis Jr. Which one had the pure personality? Who had the most talent? Their answer is immediate and absolute. Sam.

"Frank," they say, "was wonderful. His voice was great, like velvet, and he held an audience in the palm of his hand, but he was aloof and lacking personality off-stage. Sam, on the other hand, had it all. He could sing; he could dance; he could do impressions that brought the house down and he could act. He was brilliant: Bringing audiences to tears - sometimes of laughter, sometimes of sadness.

His personality bubbled over the stage and into the crowd; he loved them and they loved him. And after the show, he was just the same with everyone he knew. Larger than life, that was Sam."

He was also extremely generous, to the point of lacking common sense; spending money like water, always picking up the tab, no matter how many people were in the group, no matter how much food and drink had been consumed. Augie often used to tell him that he was too generous; that sometimes he should let Augie, or others who offered, pay the bill, but Sammy would never hear of it. For him it was a point of honor.

All through the 1960's Sammy's career went from strength to strength. In 1962, he made the movie *Sergeants 3* with the rest of the *Rat Pack*, including Joey Bishop and Peter Lawford. He also scored a major hit with a song from the Broadway musical *Stop the World I Want to Get Off.* Written by Anthony Newly, *What Kind of Fool am I?* Was a song that Sammy loved, and it became a perennial favorite with his audiences who always requested that he sang it.

In 1969, he gave one of his most memorable screen performances in the musical *Sweet Charity,* which was directed by Bob Fosse, and starred Sammy as Big Daddy Brubeck, Shirley MacLaine as Charity and Chita Rivera as Nickie.

Many books and articles have been written about him. Some are greatly exaggerated. Several people have claimed to know everything about Sammy - from cradle to grave - and because he was such a frank and communicative character, they really thought they did.

The truth is though, that although he talked openly to people whom he met in the course of his life, he kept his deepest insecurities well hidden, and only brought them out when the people he trusted most were around him. Often, in the middle of the night!

When Augie and Margo were on tour with Sammy, on many a night after the show; after the 'after-show' party, they would have arrived back to their hotel room around 2 or 3:00 A.M. and be sound asleep in bed, when the phone would ring. Sammy.

The conversations would go something like, *"What are you doing, Augie?" "We're sleeping." "You're lucky, I can't sleep." "Well, try to Sam, we were up all night, we're tired. Good night, Sam." "It's no good, I have tried. Come on, Augie, wake up Margo and let's go out."*

Inevitably, after a little more back and forth, Margo was shaken awake and out they would go. Depending on which city they were in, and how late it was, they either went to the hotel's half-empty night club, or stayed in Sammy's suite if the place was dead! Wherever they ended up, Sammy would want to talk.

It didn't matter how much praise he may have received for his performance the night before, or who had been to see him back-stage and fawn over him; and everyone from Za Za Gabor to Richard Burton did that. It was for his feelings of inadequacy which came in the middle of the night - the demons in his head that needed to be silenced - that he needed Augie and Margo.

Sitting around a table, drinking coffee, or something a lot stronger, and smoking one cigarette after another, Sammy would begin to talk about his fears and his feelings. He talked about the women he either had, or wanted, in his life, and he talked often about his insecurities, of which there were many. His looks; his ability to act; his color; his size; his lack of education; whether people really liked him. The list went on, Sammy talked and sometimes he cried like a baby. And all the while Augie and Margo listened. Sammy compared himself constantly to Sidney Poitier, who was a good friend of them all. He was envious of Sidney's good looks and incredible acting ability, and thought himself inept in comparison.

They would tell him, truthfully and assertively, that he was wonderful. That he had no need to be so down on himself, that his fans adored him;

but Sammy was impossible to convince. Eventually, getting nowhere on that tack, Augie would remind him of some funny incident, or some crazy circumstance they had found themselves in during their travels, and in a while Sammy would be all smiles again. Before long they were all roaring with laughter, recalling, for example, the time they were in England.

~~~~~~~~~~

Augie and Margo were dancing at *The Savoy Hotel* in London, and Sammy was working in the West End. *The Savoy* was, and still is, one of London's grandest hotels. From the moment it opened in 1889, its guest list was akin to reading *Who's Who*. With stunning views over the River Thames, the artist Monet, a frequent guest, is said to have painted over 70 canvases on his visits there.

Everyone who entered the doors of *The Savoy* was treated like Royalty, who themselves were frequent guests over the years, especially on the eve of the Coronation, when Elizabeth ll was crowned Queen. The grandest Ball of the Century, it was said, was held at *The Savoy*, hosting Kings, Queens, Princes and Princesses and Royal personages from all over the world.

When he was in London, Winston Churchill visited *The Savoy* every week, and Augie and Margo knew that was true, because when they were performing there, they met him in the elevator! Just nodding at them in acknowledgment, he stood silently, chewing away on the end of his cigar. Late at night after the show, they met with Sammy and whoever had been to see him backstage.

There were always people to meet in London; some of them were hangers-on, some were old friends who happened to be working there and others were well-known people in their own right who just wanted to be seen around Sammy. He was not called "Mr. Entertainment" for nothing. Just having their names linked together with his in the social columns of the London papers was enough to keep some of the old theater hacks happy.

Sammy was quite the opposite. Although he liked the people who came to see him, it didn't matter how famous they were, or were not. He treated everyone in the same friendly way. Airs and graces did not impress him; in fact, they made him feel downright uncomfortable.

Augie and Margo asked him several times to come and see them at the *Savoy*, and Sammy, several times, said no. *"The staff there wears white gloves, and walks around on tippy-toes."* He said, and Augie and Margo laughed, and then compounded the problem. *"Even the audience wear gloves,"* they added, *"and they eat tiny little cucumber sandwiches with no crusts on the bread. They all say 'mamba' instead of mambo, they won't allow you to wear shoes with black rubber soles, and they don't allow loud music."*

Sammy was astonished, still fixated on the first thing they mentioned. *"I don't believe you. Who wants to be applauded,"* he giggled, *"by an audience wearing <u>gloves</u>?"* It was a friendly banter between them. They knew that Sammy would come in the end, if only to prove Augie wrong, besides, the famous *Bluebell Girls* were opening the show, and they knew Sammy wouldn't be able to resist coming to see them!

One afternoon while they were dancing for the 'Tea Crowd,' Augie and Margo saw Sammy hiding behind a pillar, trying not to be seen. It was too much for them to pretend they hadn't seen him, so they managed to dance past the pillar slowly enough for Augie to say, as he nodded towards the audience seated around tables, drinking tea, *"What did I tell you? <u>Gloves</u>!"*

Sammy roared with laughter! He was invited several times to perform at *The Savoy* over the years, but he always turned the opportunity down. He just couldn't get over those gloves.

Despite its 'toffee-nosed' reputation, *The Savoy* had a few events under its belt which Augie, Margo and Sammy could certainly relate to. In 1925, George Gershwin had been there, giving London its very first performance of *Rhapsody in Blue* in the hotel's Grand Ballroom, and even before that, in 1923, *The Savoy Orpheans Band* and *The Savoy Havana Band*, became the first to broadcast regularly from a hotel.

As far as the people who stayed there were concerned, Augie didn't feel that he had too much in common with them, but he *did* have the same name as the very first chef in the hotel, at least, the first name - it was Auguste Escoffier!

~~~~~~~~~~

Another story they enjoyed having a laugh about, was when they were all in Miami. Augie and Margo were performing at the *Eden Roc* with Harry Belafonte, and Sammy was finishing up a booking at the *Fountain Bleu,* which Frank Sinatra was going to continue with. On Sammy's last night, during the closing show, Frank was going to take over on stage from him. It was set to be a fabulous show, normally only seen in Vegas, with the two great titans of entertainment on the same stage; and Augie and Margo planned to run next door to the *Fountain Bleu* after their performance to see the event for themselves.

As always, their own last show ended late, so by the time they arrived next door, the hotel nightclub was packed with people and Augie and Margo had standing room only. They managed to catch the last of Frank's show, but afterwards it was so mobbed with hangers-on, that they went back to their hotel. When Sinatra arrived anywhere, as Margo says, *"It was like God was in town."* So making contact with Sam or Frank that evening was impossible.

Next day, they received a message that Frank was giving a big party at a Miami Steakhouse, before his official opening show, and they were invited. A driver was sent to collect them. Augie wordlessly described the driver by pushing his nose to one side with his left hand and bending his right ear forward with his right hand; it is how he usually describes members of the Mafia. Sitting next to the driver was his blonde girlfriend, probably a show girl.

When Augie and Margo entered the car, both the driver and his girl got excited when they recognized who they were. *"You guys are great,"* they said, and enthused about their act all the way to the restaurant, which was pretty much taken over by the entire Sinatra entourage.

Frank's table had about fifteen people sitting around it, and Augie and Margo sat there with Sam and his then wife, May Britt. The minute they arrived, they saw that Sammy was not very comfortable; not everyone knew, but when Sammy was on edge he would cover his good eye with his hand, so that he could pretend he wasn't in a particular situation.

Augie and Margo called him "The Old Seeing Eye," because in spite of his lack of vision at times like that he could still hear everything! They wondered what, or who, was bothering Sammy at the party, so glanced around to see if they knew anyone there. Suddenly, a tall immaculately dressed man across the room caught Margo's attention. Their eyes locked, and recognition dawned.

Santos Trafficante strode across the restaurant to Frank's table, walked straight up to Margo and Augie and warmly welcomed them. Frank's eyes opened wide in amazement.

Bear in mind that at that time Augie and Margo were still young and relatively new in the business. When Trafficante had returned to his table, Frank said in utter surprise, *"You know him?" "Sure,"* said Augie casually. *"He helped us out with a little problem we had one time, in Havana!"*

~~~~~~~~~~

After the party in the restaurant, Frank went back to the *Fountain Bleu* to do his show, and a small group of friends, with Sammy, May, Augie and Margo, went up to his suite to wait for him. It was the first opportunity since the previous night that Sammy had gotten to talk to Augie and Margo without Frank being around.

Sammy had clearly been bottling up something he wanted to tell them. He'd had a gleam in his eye and a cheeky grin all evening, and after a couple of drinks he began to talk. *"Guys,"* he started, *"you know I love Frank. He's my idol. But I gotta tell you - last night, I had a standing 'O' and he bombed!"* And with that, he leaped up on Frank's bed and began jumping up and down, yelling *"He bombed! He bombed!"*

No one could help being pleased for him, and they let him know it. Cheering and laughing, everyone was in high spirits, Sammy jumping away like a kid in a school dorm, and hoots of laughter coming from the surrounding group - at least they did, until they suddenly realized that Frank had entered the room!

The silence was deafening! Margo felt faint, and Frank, frowning, looked like thunder, but Sammy didn't miss a beat. Before Frank had finished saying, *"What the hell's so funny?"* Sammy had leapt off the bed and was grabbing Frank around the waist, laughing insanely, as though he couldn't wait to share his joke with him.

Margo *still* felt faint, but Sammy started to tell a story about a fat guy in the audience the night before, and everyone took his cue and started laughing again, more in relief than anything else.

Frank's fairly humorless temperament didn't really respond, but Sammy's quick wit had saved the day, and he tucked the memory of his triumph over Frank into the back of his mind.

Unless, of course, he was in one of his very low moments, and then he switched to instant recall and mulled it over. Laughing and chuckling about it at some unearthly hour of the morning, while he smoked cigarettes and drank coffee with his friends - Augie and Margo.

CHAPTER TWENTY ONE

One night at the *Sands*, Liberace came to see Augie and Margo dance. He was performing at *The Riviera*, and had heard about the young couple who were opening for Sammy Davis Jr.

After the show he went backstage to tell them how fabulous he thought they were, and he asked who their Agent was. Next day, he called MCA and arranged for Augie and Margo to open for him during a long up-coming engagement he had, starting in Kansas City, at the second largest theater in the country, the *Starlight Theater*, and then moving to New Orleans.

MCA booked Augie and Margo to alternate their show for Liberace, with another one for Jerry Lewis, who was appearing in Washington D.C. at the *Carter Barron Amphitheater*, a 3,750 seat theater gifted to Washington fifty years ago by the Federal Government, so for several weeks, they traveled back and forth, opening for both performers on different dates.

Liberace's opening night was one to remember for Augie and Margo. First, they were struck by what a gentleman he was, and how much he did to accommodate his audience and fellow performers, despite the fact that he was the star of the show. He was incredibly popular with the ladies, and never refused to sign an autograph, sometimes sitting for hours, writing kind personal messages for his patient fans, who gathered in droves wherever he was performing.

The Opening Act

The lead singer for Liberace's show probably remembered well her opening night in Kansas for years to come. During her performance, in mid-"*Aaaaaaahhhhh,*" when her mouth was open at its widest, an insect flew in and landed in the back of her throat! She was hysterical after the show, but Liberace could not have been kinder or more understanding.

During the engagement in Kansas, Liberace decided to introduce an International flair to his show, and Augie and Margo were perfect people to help him. On opening night, his fan club was in attendance, and Liberace pulled out all the stops for them. He had Margo wear a spectacular white gown, which she still remembers well, and he introduced them as South American dancers and asked Augie to speak only in Spanish to the audience.

He also wanted to present a *Polka;* not exactly their style of dance, but they were willing to work up a routine. One of Liberace's greatest hits was the *Beer Barrel Polka,* and his fans always expected it to be part of his program.

Ray Arnett, Liberace's Stage Director, choreographed a dance for Augie and Margo, but the only problem was that they needed the entire stage on which to perform. Liberace's gorgeous Lucite piano was in center stage, as always, but for the polka routine he instructed the Stage Manager to move it right off to the side, giving Augie and Margo the entire stage. It may not seem such a big deal to a layman, but for a major star to give his young, relatively unknown guests the spotlight was quite unusual, and a typical gesture of just how generous a soul Liberace was.

Over the years, Augie and Margo became great friends with Lee, as they called him, and Ray Arnett, his loyal Stage Director. They visited him at his home in Los Angeles, where he had a pool shaped like a grand piano, and in Las Vegas, where they got to know his many friends, and one of his young lovers, who not only packed all Liberace's costumes for him, but also made sure there were bottles of liquor tucked in alongside the carefully tissue-wrapped satins, furs and rhinestone extravaganzas!

∼∼∼∼∼∼∼∼∼∼

In March 1959, Toni Arden, a singing star whose recording of the song *Padre* had just sold one million copies, was booked to play the luxurious *Café Cristal* in the one-year-old *Diplomat Hotel* in Miami, and Augie and Margo opened for her.

Arden was considered to be a highly talented singer - very well known for the variety of moods she brought to her songs, but on opening night in the *Café Cristal*, just her rendering of that hit song alone brought such enthusiastic applause from the audience, that it seemed they might be satisfied hearing her sing only that.

George Bourke, entertainment editor for *The Miami Herald* gave a glowing review for Toni Arden, and of Augie and Margo he said, *"We've used this line before but it is still applicable - every time we see them they seem twice as good as the time before in their execution of exciting modernistic dance that defies description. Here, too, is an example of artists who don't merely dance - they entertain."*

It was certainly true that they just kept getting better and were in great demand. That same year, Augie and Margo went to London to perform with Sammy Davis Jr. in a Royal Command Performance at the *London Palladium*; Latin music and dancing had a huge following in the UK by then, and they were received with great enthusiasm.

Everyone in England knows that royal personages are always present at a Command performance, but it was not common knowledge on that particular occasion that Queen Elizabeth and Prince Phillip would be in attendance on the *Palladium's* opening night to proclaim the start of the season.

The Queen was pregnant with Prince Andrew at the time, and she was reluctant to let the general public see her in that condition! Opening night was always glamorous and extremely well publicized, so she and Prince Phillip must have slipped into the theater unheralded, to avoid the inevitable clamor and candid shots of the Press.

However, the performing artists were informed of the Queen's presence, so at the end of the show when they came out for their curtain calls, after bowing to the house, they then turned and bowed toward the Royal Box, which caused quite a joyous stir and commotion amongst the audience when they realized who was there. During the 1950's, Latin dancing was highly popularized in Britain by Princess Margaret, who had friends and distant family members living in Barbados and throughout the Caribbean. She frequently vacationed there, some said in order to 'let her hair down,' and it was in those islands that she learned the *Samba*. The Princess brought her love of the dance back home, and continued to give flamboyant demonstrations of it at social events, soon making it the 'in' dance to know amongst the British social elite.

~~~~~~~~~~~

The *London Palladium* shows were always a lot of fun for Augie and Margo. They did several over the next decades, mostly with Sammy, and sometimes with other members of the *Rat Pack* and of course British artists.

Des O'Connor was one performer they came to know well. Formerly a Red Coat at a British 'Holiday Camp,' O'Connor was the kind of entertainer who had a good-natured temperament, even when master-comedians Morecombe and Wise made him and his singing voice the butt of their jokes – which they did often!

The *London Palladium* variety shows were the first television performances O'Connor made. He started out as a crooner, and was very popular with the ladies, but his talents leaned more towards light comedy and hosting shows and it is possible that a certain lack of confidence in his own ability made him a lot more nervous than he appeared. A singer with a relaxed laid-back style, his fans may have been surprised to know that he never went on stage without being violently sick beforehand!

Also performing in the show with Des O'Connor was Henny Youngman, the fast-talking British comedian of the famous one-liners, like: *"I told the Doctor I broke my leg in two places and he told me not to go to those places!"* and *"I was so ugly when I was born the Doctor slapped my mother!"*

Augie asked Youngman one day why he spoke so fast in the first show of the evening, and Youngman, who had an answer for everything, explained that during the early performance which began at 6:00 P.M. the audience was hungry and bad-tempered. *"Why make them suffer?"* He said to Augie, *"It's much better that I talk fast and get the act over with quickly, so they can go and get their dinner!"*

After the shows, several well-known people came back-stage to 'meet and greet' everyone, and Augie and Margo really learned then how much Brits liked to party! Peter O'Toole, the actor of Irish/Scottish descent, who by his own admission was born in Leeds, England, and not Connemara which is widely believed to be his birthplace, came every night to hang out with Sammy Davis and the rest of the *Palladium* crowd after performing in *"Hamlet"* with Richard Burton.

Sometimes Burton came too, but after a few hours of drinking and partying he went home. Not so Peter O'Toole. From what Augie and Margo could see he never ate and he never went home to sleep! He would consume huge amounts of alcohol and then make a real nuisance of himself by not leaving. Worse still, he started to fawn over Sammy Davis, kissing and slobbering over him, much to Sammy's revulsion!

They were performing in London for a month, and night after night he attempted his pathetic seduction, until Sammy could stand it no longer and told everyone, *"Keep that bastard away from me!"*

On another occasion when Augie and Margo were in London, Sydney Poitier contacted them when he came into town. He needed some good quality shoes, so Sammy told him about his favorite store in Mayfair.

Sammy was a very snappy dresser; he liked the best clothing and footwear and was willing to pay for it. Ordering three or four custom made tailored suits at a time when he went to Hong Kong, shirts and ties by the dozen whilst in Italy and hand-made leather shoes when he was in London.

Poitier was just stopping over on his way back to New York, therefore time was short and Sammy was unable to go shopping with him, so he asked Augie to take Sydney instead.

The shoe store was on Bond Street, home to the most expensive and elegant shops and boutiques in London, with more Royal Warrant holders (suppliers to the Royal Family) than anywhere else in the city.

Inside the store, the surroundings were plush and the service impeccable. The sales assistants, all dressed in immaculate suits, were courteous and deferential to their customers; they were there only to please and to be of service. Sidney Poitier, describing the shoes he was looking for was, of course, afforded the same respect, until the assistant serving him asked, *"Would Sir like to see the shoes in Black or Nigger Brown?"*

For a moment the silence was palpable; but Sidney Poitier, true gentleman that he is, said nothing, putting the comment down to pure misguided ignorance, which it probably was, since the assistant continued his polite conversation, completely oblivious of the offensive remark he had made!

Poitier was a very different person from Harry Belafonte who took every opportunity he could to criticize America and white people. Everyone in their wide group of friends and fellow performers liked him, but many felt that he spent far too much time grandstanding. It often seemed he couldn't go though a day without spewing out his resentment of one thing or another.

Certainly he had experienced the harsh side of life growing up, partially, in Harlem; his father Harold Belafonte was a seaman, married to a Jamaican domestic worker, Melvine. They had two sons, and were so poor that they sent the boys back to Jamaica to live with relatives for five years, which might have made Harry feel disenfranchised and unwanted; perhaps to the point of blaming the country in which he was born.

In any event, the civil rights that most fair-minded people advocated for American blacks did not go far enough for Harry Belafonte. He quickly developed a strong political sense of activism which seemed to affect everything he said or did.

In the early part of his career, the singer and actor Paul Robeson had a huge influence on Belafonte's life. Himself a civil rights activist, he taught Belafonte that turning one's art into a 'history lesson' would make people listen and take notice, so Belafonte shifted his desire to act to the singing of folk songs like *Matilda* and *Banana Boat Song*, which told stories of the people in the Islands, and proved to be a highly successful medium for him, earning him the name "The Velvet Singer of *'Islands in the Sun.'*"

It is well known that over the decades of his career Harry Belafonte enjoyed enormous recognition and success. With his second wife, Julie, who was a student at the *Katherine Dunham School*, and with whom he has two children, he has also worked tirelessly for human rights around the world, and in recognition of that, Belafonte was named a goodwill ambassador for UNICEF, but from his very early years as an entertainer, he injected political statements into his career.

Belafonte was dismayed when, in 1959, Poitier accepted the role of Porgy in the movie *Porgy and Bess*. He is reported to have considered the part demeaning to blacks, and although he supported Poitier he let him know, in no uncertain terms, that he would never have accepted such a role.

To some in the group it was nothing less than pure hypocrisy. His first wife, Marguerite, with whom he had two children was black, but having a white father and a white second wife, his criticism of white people and the country of his birth, sometimes became too much.

One day when they were all together, Sidney Poitier, whose home actually is Cat Island in the Bahamas, got fed up with Belafonte's ranting and, to paraphrase, he told him to *"Shut the fuck up! This country has been very good to you. You have made a very good life for yourself, thanks to white people."* Poitier said, *"If you don't like it for God's sake go back to the Islands and climb trees!"*

It was quite a shock for Augie and Margo to hear Sidney Poitier speak so bluntly. He was always tactful and a gentleman, the height of refinement, but everyone in the group thought that Belafonte had it coming, and they were secretly pleased that it was so succinctly stated.

~~~~~~~~~~

Five years after their professional career began, on February 18, 1960, Augie and Margo were honored with an award.

The American Guild of Variety Artists and the *Diners Club* held their first annual awards dinner in the grand ballroom of the *Hotel Astor*. The occasion was named the *AGVA 'Joey' Awards*, in honor of Joey Adams, president of the AGVA, and the occasion was held in order to award the greatest night club performers of the year. The top performers nominated in each category won a golden statuette, called Joey.

The AGVA, for which Joey Adams was the president, is a Union for people in Show Business. Adams was the originator of "Joey's Law", which prohibits AGVA members from entertaining in nightclubs that are not integrated. He was a 'larger than life' character with tremendous charisma and incredibly popular as a comedy star, but he became extremely controversial. He was a Jew; married to Cindy Adams the gossip columnist, and he spent many years, broadcasting on his own radio show on a Jewish network, singing Yiddish songs and writing for Jewish magazines, as well as raising a lot of money for Jewish causes. Indeed, he was *so* popular, that President John Kennedy appointed him the nation's goodwill ambassador for life.

The controversy arose when a few people in the media discovered that for many years, he and his wife Cindy had adopted Christian Science as their religion, and when they were confronted with the question as to whether or not it was true, they spent many more years trying to deny the fact. Joey Adams had, over his long career in show business, become something of a Jewish icon, and his fans were horrified that he had, in their minds, turned against them. Of course, he had not, but he and Cindy preferred to embrace Christianity as their faith, and they thought that telling people about their religion was a private affair.

Joey did a huge amount to further the cause of equality for African Americans in the country. He was a great friend of Martin Luther King Jr., and on one occasion he joined him on a civil rights march in Birmingham, Alabama. During the march, he, King and all the rest of the participants were pelted with eggs, tomatoes and defamatory remarks; later that day, when Adams and King were sitting together at dinner, Adams asked King how he handled his enemies. King replied, *"There's only one way. Love the hell out of them!"*

~~~~~~~~~~~

The grand ballroom of the *Astor* was packed with people, including Mayor Wagner of New York and hundreds of famous and important people from all over the country. Gene Knight, the Entertainment Editor of the *New York Journal-American*, said it was one of the greatest dinners he had ever attended.

Fifteen categories received awards, with Augie and Margo winning *Greatest Dance Team* of the year. It isn't necessary to mention every winner, but to name a few, gives an idea about the caliber of people with whom they were included.

Male singer: Frank Sinatra. Female singer: Ella Fitzgerald. Male comic: Jimmy Durante. Female comic: Carol Burnett. International award: Maurice Chevalier.

It was an amazing tribute, for a young pair of relative newcomers to be honored in this way, and it caused quite a stir - with everyone who had not heard of Augie and Margo, suddenly wanting to know who they were.

In the New York Post next day, an article appeared, headlined: "*Roseland Director Is Star-Maker*." Louis Brecker took the credit for having discovered them at his ballroom, and said he had insisted they perform for talent agencies, which is a slight exaggeration, but Augie and Margo were happy to let it be. After all, he *had* arranged for them to dance at *The Harvest Moon Ball*, which definitely created a huge opportunity for them; though David Baumgarten of MCA might just have disagreed!

∾∾∾∾∾∾∾∾∾∾

Shortly after the Joey Awards ceremony, the *Persian Room* of *New York's Plaza Hotel* had a Spanish Fiesta revue, lasting several weeks, for which Augie and Margo were booked. The Broadway critic, Danton Walker, described the show as being *"More packed with talent than many of the shows with bigger names,"* and referred to Augie and Margo as *"Whirlwind Dancers."*

Gene Knight, in his review in the *New York Journal-American*, went much further in his praise, saying, *"Augie and Margo shivered on in a number called 'Jubilation.' They followed with 'After Supper.' He in tight black trousers, she in clinging gold pants. Don't ask me what they danced after that but it certainly was sexy and much too short. They started slowly, but the tempo mounted. Margo is a slinking, sliding, coiling, embracing dancer. Augie is a panting partner. They are, indeed, dramatic dancers. And together they are poetry in motion."*

CHAPTER TWENTY TWO

In October 1960, one month before President John F. Kennedy was voted into office, Augie and Margo went to Detroit to perform at the Shubert Theater, opening for Marlene Dietrich.

The Shubert, originally the *Orpheum Theatre,* was an old-time variety theatre. Built in 1911, it was an elaborate building with an interior complete with balconies, boxes and ornate gilded plasterwork; but as burlesque and vaudeville went out of style, the name of the theatre changed several times, and by the mid-1950's live theater and concert performances were produced there.

Dietrich at that time was developing her singing career, rather than acting in films, which she had done since the age of nineteen; because in 1930, after appearing and singing as the heroine in the movie *The Blue Angel*, which was a great hit, her movie career began to slow down.

A fierce anti-Nazi, she became an American citizen in the mid-1930's and began to concentrate on her career as a singer, carefully crafting and maintaining her image as a sultry, heavy-lidded sex goddess, which she displayed in good taste and with a wry sense of humor. It was reported that she was 'AC/DC,' as Margot put it, and several females including Tallulah Bankhead were said to have been in relationships with her.

After entertaining the troops on the Front Lines very successfully as a singer during the Second World War, she turned her talents to the cabaret and theater circuit, and continued to develop her *femme fatale* image, by wearing clinging sequin-studded satin gowns and swan's-breast cloaks.

Burt Bacharach was the musical director who helped her direct her earthy, contralto voice to its maximum dramatic effect, since although she knew how to project herself on stage, her voice range was actually very limited. Bacharach, who was highly disciplined and a stickler for absolute voice perfection, was also Dietrich's pianist and bandleader, and he toured with her throughout the 1950's and first half of the 1960's.

The Marlene Dietrich show at the *Shubert Theatre* was a great hit. Critics raved about it, saying that the old theater had been brought to life. Marlene held the audience in the palm of her hand from the start, singing songs of sentiment and romance, including *Marie, Lili Marlene* and the raucous *Boys in the Back Room*.

Of Augie and Margo, Dorsey Callaghan, Dramatic Critic of the "Detroit Free Press," wrote: *"The spectacularly controlled dancing of Augie and Margo and their dancers was an exhibition of muscular grace beyond anything seen here in many years."*

~~~~~~~~~~

At the end of 1960, a series of events happened which had great impact, and resulted in historical changes in the United States, and in the world.

In November of that year, President Kennedy was elected into office, and one of the first things he did was to create and sign into law the Peace Corps. The world was relatively peaceful at that time, but it was a period of deep Cold War fears with the Soviet Union.

Kennedy was certainly a man with great ambition, and the following May he proved it by announcing a goal; to land a man on the moon and return him to earth by the end of that decade. In the same month, Kennedy met with the President of USSR, Nikita Khrushchev, but unfortunately the meeting ended badly. Three months later, in August, the Soviets built the infamous *Berlin Wall*, which divided the city of Berlin until its destruction in 1989.

Exactly one year later, in May 1962, Augie and Margo went to Washington, to perform a special show at the White House with Xavier Cugat, the Academy Award winning actress Shelley Winters, and Chet Atkins, for the President on his birthday.

Atkins was a highly accomplished singer and guitarist, who helped create the smooth country music style known as the *'Nashville Sound,'* and both he and Winters were hugely popular stars at that time. After the performance, President Kennedy came backstage to shake everyone by the hand.

Augie and Margo remember the evening well, for it was a great highlight in their career. He was very friendly and complimentary to them. When he reached Augie in the line-up, the President threw his arm around Augie's shoulders, saying, *"Man, what an act you've got!"* He told them he thought they were wonderful and that he had seen them perform several times on television.

Everyone observed that Kennedy was fascinated by a woman standing next to Augie and Margo in the line-up. It was Abbey Lane, who had been singing in Xavier Cugat's band that evening. All the way along the line, his roving eye kept alighting on her, and his expression made it very clear what his intentions were.

When it came to her turn for the President's hand shake, no one was surprised to hear Kennedy ask her who she had come with that evening: When she replied, *"My husband, Mr. President,"* he did not disguise his disappointment, clearly not knowing she was Cugat's wife; and it cast a somewhat tawdry veil over what should have been a sparkling moment.

The following year, in 1962, Kennedy's Birthday Party recorded a moment which will probably always be remembered in history. It was the party when Marilyn Munroe breathlessly sang to him *Happy Birthday Mr. President*, and all but confirmed her intimate involvement with him. By that year, the President's popularity was already beginning to wane. In the New York Times, no less, a piece by Walter Winchell said, *"The trouble with the Kennedys is that they are running the country like it was theirs instead of ours."*

Augie and Margo visited the White House again, in 1972 to dance for President Richard Nixon. This time it was quite different. The occasion was a Press cocktail party honoring a great friend of Nixon's, Dwight Eisenhower, for whom Nixon had served as Vice President during the two terms of Eisenhower's Presidency.

The connection between the two men became re-enforced in 1968, when Nixon's daughter Julie married the Eisenhower's son, David, after whom *Camp David*, the Presidential retreat was named. Although Nixon was polite and complimentary to everyone performing at the White House, he was also rather cool and distant; a person of a very different ilk was now presiding over the United States of America!

~~~~~~~~~~

By 1962, Augie and Margo Rodriguez were recognized as being the two highest-paid dancers in the country. The New York Mirror writer, John McBride, wrote in September 1962: *"Dance team of Augie and Margo's back after a hit stint at Puerto Rico's El San Juan. The couple started at New York's Palladium for peanuts. Now (after Ed Sullivan, films, Coconut Grove etc.,) they are the highest paid dance team in show business. . ."*

However, not only had the critics recognized Augie and Margo's talent. In October 1962, they received a compliment from Gene Kelly who, many people consider, was the dance icon of the 20th Century. If dancing for President Kennedy was a highlight of their career, this, surely, had to have been a close tie for second place.

Kelly, an actor and dancer, who taught Frank Sinatra to dance, was famous for his inventive choreography and the fact that he influenced the development of movie musicals, many of which he starred in. He had already at that time become a household name, from his highly successful starring role in *An American in Paris* and later for his puddle-splashing dance in *Singin' in the Rain* - one of Hollywood's most venerated moments.

In the 1960's he was beginning to direct shows, like *Hello Dolly*, and appearing on television in his show, *Going my Way*, and whilst in LA he quite fortuitously met Augie and Margo.

With many other Hollywood stars, Kelly was attending a benefit for WAIF, a charity and adoption agency founded by the actress Jane Russell. It was held at the famous *Hotel Ambassador* in Cocoanut Grove, Los Angeles, and Augie and Margo were there, dancing with Xavier Cugat's band.

After the show, Kelly came backstage to congratulate Augie and Margo, telling them they were the best dancers he had ever seen. It was a stunning moment, but what he said to them didn't really sink in until they actually saw it in print a few days later in *Variety Magazine!*

Also dancing in the city at that time, at the *Greek Theater*, was the world renowned *Bolshoi Ballet* who were on tour around the country. After their performance, the ballet company came to the *Ambassador* to watch the late-night show.

Sitting in the front row of the theatre along with the rest of the group, was their spectacular principal dancer, Maya Plisetskaya, who was married to the brilliant young composer Rodion Shchedrin. In 1958 she had been honored with the title of the *People's Artist of the USSR,* and was no doubt a great 'trophy' performer for 'The People' to put on display in the United States.

As she and Augie danced, Margo noticed out of the corner of her eye that the Prima Ballerina was watching the floor as she danced back and forth across the stage. Plisetskaya's eyes never wavered. They were fixated, rather like watching a ball in a tennis match, on Margo's feet.

After the show the Bolshoi Company came backstage, where they met Augie and Margo and showered compliments on them. Margo wanted to ask Plisetskaya why she had been so fascinated with the stage floor and her feet while watching their performance, but the ballerina volunteered an explanation before she had a chance to ask.

Taking Margo to one side, in a very strong Russian accent she said, "*I cannot <u>believe</u> what you do! You run, you turn, you jump, and you do every-think that I do: But you! You do it all in three inch high heels!*"

Walter Winchell, of *Variety Magazine*, was quick to agree. In his "Chatter" column he said, *"Augie and Margo's pashy 'man-and-woman' stuff more exciting than the entire Bolshoi troupe to this spectator."*

The Opening Act

∼∼∼∼∼∼∼∼∼∼∼

Several performances in the early sixties had Augie and Margo not only paired with members of the *Rat Pack*, but also with Harry Belafonte. Since their first opening together at *The Waldorf*, they had enjoyed a good working relationship together and made a highly successful team which, again, did not go un-noticed by the critics. Paul M. Bruun, of the *Miami Beach Sun*, gave them a glowing review which sums up so many in Augie and Margo's vast collection.

After being highly complimentary about Belafonte in a February, 1961 performance at the *Eden Roc* in Miami, he turns his accolades to the dancers who opened for him. *"Augie and Margo open the show. Now everybody who patronizes the Café Pompeii knows these audiences aren't the world's most courteous, nor are they quiet, except when the star is on stage. They seem to have much more important things to say to each other than to listen to entertainers, or to watch dancers. From the moment Augie and Margo came on stage, everybody paid close attention to them, and with excellent reason, they are nothing short of sensational. They dance three numbers. She makes one costume change, and the audience becomes slaves. She is a cross between a clinging cat, a snake, and a solo dancer, and he executes with precision, routines that are their own. Words fail to create pictures of their routines, they have to be seen to be appreciated and enjoyed.*

Harry Belafonte and Augie and Margo will be at the 'Eden Roc Hotel' for two weeks. If there is a vacant seat during these 28 performances, then lovers of great entertainment have either lost their appreciation of artists or have gone broke."

∼∼∼∼∼∼∼∼∼∼∼

Harry Belafonte, who was always interested and active in political issues, was a great friend and supporter of Martin Luther King, so when King was struggling to gain equal rights for African-Americans Belafonte became very involved with him in helping to raise money for the cause.

A *Benefit* for King was planned at *Carnegie Hall* in New York, called *Night of a Hundred Stars*, so Belafonte obtained an invitation for Augie and Margo to appear, and it was quite an honor for them.

The show was exceptional in that it was a very long one, lasting three hours, and they were positioned to close the end of the first half. It was a highly coveted position on the program, since although most people's attention span does not last very long, they generally remember the beginnings and ends of show segments.

The crème de la crème of the entertainment business were slated to perform at the *Benefit,* and not only were Augie and Margo unique in that they were relatively unknown performers; Harry Belafonte sent them a telegram, *"How does it feel to be the only dance team in the show?"*

Augie and Margo met Martin Luther King after the *Benefit* and they recall him as being 'Very nice, warm and friendly to everyone and really grateful for what they had done for his cause.' The only thing that really surprised them about this giant of a man was his stature; he was only about five foot two or three inches tall!

He wrote a 'Thank You' letter afterwards, to Augie and Margo, which they treasured and gave to a family member for safe keeping. Unfortunately, it went missing and is one of the few pieces of memorabilia from all their years in show business that they no longer have.

∼∼∼∼∼∼∼∼∼∼

In November 1963, when he had barely served more than one thousand days in office, President Kennedy was assassinated. Santos Traficante, the Mafia chieftain, who had been recruited with Sam Giancana by the CIA in 1960 to assassinate Fidel Castro, had prophesied that President Kennedy was *"Going to be hit;"* though it's a matter of pure speculation as to how he knew.

Augie and Margo were in Las Vegas at the time, opening for Sammy, and they remember how the entire city, not to mention the country and the world, was devastated at the news of the President's murder.

The *Sands* Managers, along with all the other hotel owners, had a discussion which resulted in the lights being lowered on *The Strip* and many hotels closing down for the day. For the next few days the hotels operated in a very discreet style; Augie and Margo did not dance, but Sammy went on to perform a much more low-key act than was normal for him.

With no jokes or dances, Sammy apologized to the audience that the full show was not being performed, and then he went on to sing some of his most moving songs, clearly paying a tribute to the slain President.

For Augie and Margo the first night Sammy came on was a night to remember. Because they had the evening off, they were able to go and watch him perform; it was the first time they had ever seen him on stage from the perspective of the audience, and he was phenomenal. At the end of his act, with not a dry eye in the house, Sammy received a standing ovation that didn't want to end!

The *Sands* was becoming a legendary place to see Frank and the *Rat Pack*, although all the hotels in town fought to get the big names. After the second show of the evening, the chorus girls were expected to mix with the stars; it was part of their contract that they had to be seen around the performing celebrities until at least 2:30 AM, and if Frank was at the *Sands* all the showgirls from the entire city congregated there to see him. Joey Bishop, Dean Martin or Sammy Davis were considered to be a huge coup, but when Frank was in town the draw was incredible – everyone who was anyone came to Vegas; it was as though Royalty had arrived.

Augie and Margo remember one occasion when Jack Benny and Edward G. Robinson, the actor who brilliantly portrayed gangsters, came to town. In fact, Augie has a hard time recounting the story to this day; it makes him laugh so much! He and Margo were opening for Sammy at night, but during the day and after the shows everyone got together.

One day the men spent the morning in the sauna; Frank, Sammy, Dean, Augie, Edward G. and Jack Benny. They all sat there on pine benches in the steam, with a towel around their waists; swinging their legs and looking at each other.

Everyone started telling jokes and poking fun at each other's less desirable features on display, which made Augie roar with laughter. As the youngest and fittest one in the group he could afford to laugh, and he was tickled pink that this group of acting and comedic icons was ad-libbing in such an impromptu way. The jokes were coming thick and fast, everyone was laughing and then, suddenly, it went quiet.

Jack Benny was looking at Augie – looking him up and down. Just that alone was enough to set Augie off laughing again. The sight of Benny watching him, jutting out his chin with his legendary sideways expression, a meager towel around his waist and swinging his very thin legs was more than enough to do it; until, with his flawless comic timing, Benny started to talk.

He began to make admiring and envious remarks about Augie's body, saying how firm and muscular he was and that he would give up everything for a body like Augie's. He remarked that he couldn't understand how dancing alone could have created such a Greek God-like figure, but since Augie *was* a dancer it must be the case; so Jack Benny decided to get to work right away.

Clambering down from the bench, he tucked an end in his brief little towel around his waist, to secure it as best he could, raised his arms above his head, put his skinny legs together and began to do knee-bends, twirls and plies.

Augie, in paroxysms of laughter was by now rolling around on the floor. After everyone had been poked fun at, Jack Benny, consummate comedian that he was, was not going to let the kid in the group get away with a free pass; but he was perceptive enough to make himself look like a clown while he did it!

~~~~~~~~~~~

The idyllic days of the *Rat Pack* at the *Sands* could have continued for a long time, but as often happens when people become too comfortable with the status quo, events can change and turn life as they know it upside down.

The Opening Act

In the summer of 1967, aviation pioneer and millionaire Howard Hughes bought the *Sands*. His accountants and lawyers handled all the transactions behind the scenes, as it were, and on the given day, as soon as the money was handed over to the *Sands* owners, the Hughes team moved in at midnight and immediately took over.

At that point, the staff of the hotel and casino stayed put, but never having been in the casino business before, and imagining they were only dealing with gangsters and gamblers, the Hughes people froze all casino transactions the moment they took over at midnight, and did an accounting of everything in the *Sands* that was not moving!

By the time dawn arose, a new and long list of rules had been handed in to the casino, and the emphasis was mostly on casino credit. No longer could the croupiers take it in or give it out!

A few weeks after the casino takeover, Frank Sinatra was scheduled to play two shows a night and, as always, during the day before the 8:00PM show he went in to the casino and asked a croupier he knew to give him some chips on credit, as he had done many times before. When he was refused, he was not only surprised but annoyed, so he went to another table and tried again. Once again he was turned down, and this time he became angry.

Making an effort to get in touch with Jack Entratter to straighten things out and get the service he was used to getting, Frank became more and more frustrated and angry, as each time he called Entratter's office the boss was evidently 'unavailable.'

Augie and Margo often mentioned that Frank had a short temper, and also that he drank a lot, so by the time it came around to do the 8:00PM show, Frank was living up to his reputation; mad at everyone and refusing to go on stage.

At that time, Frank, Augie and Margo and several others in the show were sitting in the *Garden Room*, one of the hotel restaurants. Frank was still trying to reach Jack Entratter, but Cohen must have got word that Frank was refusing to perform, so he came into the *Garden Room* to find out what was going on.

Frank immediately confronted him, getting tough and yelling with rage, he picked up a chair and slammed it down. Cohen was not about to have a scene in his restaurant. People would soon be getting interested to see what all the fuss was about and casino staff and patrons would be intensely curious to see Frank in the middle of a brawl; so to stop the problem short in its tracks, Cohen drew his fist back and punched Frank right in the mouth, knocking him down to the floor.

Everyone froze in their seats; no one dared help Frank as he lay there. After a while he struggled to his feet and wiped a great deal of blood off his mouth; he also played the 8:00PM show!

One week later, after some hasty negotiations, Frank Sinatra left the *Sands* hotel forever and went to *Caesars Palace*. His parting message was that the *Sands* would 'go under.' He was right. It took a while, 29 years to be exact, but it did go under eventually. Sheldon Adelson, a wealthy property developer and the owner at that time, decided the competition in the city was becoming too hot to maintain the old style and ambience of the *Sands*, so he decided to demolish the old hotel in June, 1996, and build a new mega-resort.

Standing on the site of the *Sands* now is a $1.5 billion, *Venetian Resort-Hotel-Casino*. Mr. Adelson has brought the famous Italian city of water to the *Sands* site, in the desert of Nevada.

CHAPTER TWENTY THREE

PALLADIUM CLOSES

Between engagements, whenever they were in New York, Augie and Margo visited *The Palladium*. As far as they were concerned it was like returning home; their best friends were still regulars, and the fans they had accumulated, long before becoming famous, were always there to see them and marvel again at their dancing.

Their hard work and dedication had resulted in a performance which had a distinctive flavor that no one else could match, and when they were in town people just couldn't get enough; lining up outside *The Palladium* for hours in order to get in to watch their brilliant, ground-breaking choreography.

Dance Champion, Billy Fajardo, is one such person who credits Augie and Margo with his own passion for dancing, saying he was a disciple of Augie's since being a very young man.

Augie and Margo may never have discovered their own capability of performing dance if it hadn't been for Maxwell Hyman and the three fabulous bands he hired each week, who belted out the brassy, hot, swinging *mambo* music, which had turned out to be the foundation stone of their lives.

Even though they had a soft spot for *Roseland*, it was *The Palladium* and all the people there who had helped to shape their lives, given them confidence and fortified their dream; they were family.

~~~~~~~~~~

Coincidentally, another man named Rodriguez, who came to America from Cuba during the early 1950's, is credited as being the first person ever to develop *son montuno*, or Cuban music. His full name was Arsenio Rodriguez, and his grasp of music and rhythm was said to be remarkable; perhaps because as a child he was blinded by a horse kicking him in the face, which may have led to him having a heightened sense of hearing.

In any event, Rodriguez became a musician and band leader, and earned himself the name "The Blind Marvel." He composed almost two hundred songs, and

reinventing the *son*, he added instrumental solos to extend it, and increased the importance of new instruments like trumpets, congas and piano, which gave birth to detailed and rhythmic dance music.

At about the same time, a musician and singer from Cuba, named Benny More, picked up the ball thrown by Rodriguez and further developed the genre by adding *bolero*, *guaracha* and *mambo* influences. More was known as "The Fantastic Man of Rhythm," and a festival that bears his name is held every year in Cienfuegos, Cuba, to honor him.

A lot more could be said about both men and their incredible contribution to the development of *son montuno*, but perhaps the greatest tribute paid to them is the fact that their involvement lives on in the music itself.

The great bands that came to *The Palladium* became legends; and amongst the thousands of dancers, half-crazed by the mysterious music, their feet moving to the syncopated complex sounds, were many who laid down the blue prints of Latin dance for decades to come.

~~~~~~~~~~

One year, Augie and Margo came back to see everyone, and were told that one of the bouncers, Yumpy, was dead. Of the three brothers, Yumpy was the gentle giant; the big softie. He was the brother who always told Augie and Margo when he had seen them on television - he followed their career like a close relative.

At *The Palladium* he had always been their biggest fan, the one who truly understood the importance of their desire to dance at the *Harvest Moon Ball*. They were very upset. A bastion of their youth was gone, and would forever after only be a fond memory.

Yumpy died from a knife wound, but his gentle character shone through his tough-guy image to the very end. The stabbing attack that killed him was delivered by his jealous girlfriend, who had caught him fooling with another girl.

It seems it was an innocent flirtation on his part, he still loved his girlfriend; but when the cops came, and bent over a dying Yumpy as he lay on the floor, he made sure to let them know with his last breath that his girl was not to blame, it was an accident. He haltingly told them that he and his girl were playing around with the knife and that during their horseplay the knife had slipped.

~~~~~~~~~~

By 1962, the place where it all started for Augie and Margo had become the Mecca of New York's most progressive dancers. The thousands of devotees who went every week, which included people of diverse ethnic backgrounds, servicemen from every branch of the military, literary figures and artists, actors, musicians and Hollywood stars, had all inspired a Latin music revolution that impacted people around the world.

Tito Puente was especially conscious of the importance of dance, which he felt was a critical component in keeping the music alive. His premise was always the same; *'Teaching dancing is giving life to music.'* The *bossa nova* was a classic example of music dying, because no dance was developed for it, and he never wanted that to happen to the *mambo*! While playing his intricate, spontaneous 6/8 rhythms, pulsating and beating on well-tuned skins, the choreography of the dance was always in his mind.

Dance Studios sent their students to *The Palladium*, where they could learn by watching the great dancers. The mix was captivating: Ballet dancers, Broadway stars, Latin dance teachers; all together, and all were there to watch the mamboists 'do it right.' *The Palladium* had reached its Zenith and was staying there; those were truly the Glory Days!

Palladium music went global, and the Latin bands became household names in Britain, France, Germany, South Africa and even as far away as Hong Kong and Japan. The competition between them at home in America, though, was still rife. To keep up the pace against each other and satisfy their adoring fans, Machito and the two Titos would warm up before coming on stage at *The Palladium* across the road at the *Ed Sullivan Theater*, so by the time they were ready to take over from the previous band they were so hot they smoked!

The best dancers, who always stood around in an area near the band, were ready to dance up a storm as soon as the band struck up. All they wanted was to see which band would bring out the best in them, and the band leaders knew it. The fans, who couldn't get enough of the excitement, sat around on the floor to watch and cheer on their adored favorites, and everyone else packed around the sitting group, yelling and stomping their approval.

The high-strung music was the "height of hit." For a long time it seemed that almost everyone listened or danced to it, and the real enthusiasts became known as *mambo nicks* - the Italian version of beatnik.

The ballroom was always packed with people. It was chic to be seen there, whether you danced or not. Stars, artists and celebrities were as much a part of the scene as everyone else. Ava Gardner, an enthusiastic dancer, was often there, as was Sammy Davis or Marlon Brando, who often sat in on bongos with the *Machito* orchestra; or "Mongo" Santamaria, the famous drummer and composer of *Afro Blue,* who frequently sat in with Tito Puente. On any given night, it was not unusual to see Duke Ellington, Kim Novak, Jackson Pollock or the entire cast of a Broadway Show, who would go there to relax after their own show had ended for the night.

~~~~~~~~~~~

New York's extraordinary dance club, known as *The Palladium,* could have flourished for years, but one day, quite unexpectedly, the dream that had once been Maxwell Hyman's own, and which he ultimately shared gladly with hundreds of thousands of people, came crashing down around him.

Just as a random un-stubbed cigarette, carelessly tossed into a waste basket, can destroy an entire building, something that was equally careless and random brought down the most remarkable multi-cultural phenomenon in American history.

It was an impetuous comment, made by the secretary of a powerful city lawyer, who remarked to her boss that on a previous evening at *The Palladium* she had been offered drugs. That was it!

The next night, in the middle of an exciting dance program, being viewed by a full house, two busloads of police parked around the corner outside Dizzy Gillespie's *Birdland,* and they all swooped together into *The Palladium* in a surprise raid.

Crashing through the doors simultaneously and yelling, *"Police! Raid! Don't anybody leave, just get against the walls and stand still!"* It would have been a miracle if everything had remained calm; bedlam broke loose as anyone with marijuana tossed it under tables or stuffed it in back of sofas. Some people flung themselves behind the stage or tried to bolt for the exits, where they hoped to get rid of illegal weapons or dope, and many were genuinely hysterical with fright.

The police started hauling some of the spectators away, while others were being harshly interrogated right there on the dance floor, and for the first time ever, the band stopped playing. This time, they knew it was different; they knew that the dance was over.

To the extent that the police knew drugs had been present there on many other occasions, it was an unjustified raid, but this time, unlike in the past, there was no warning they were coming.

Perhaps the lawyer had friends in high places in City Hall who had something against Maxwell Hyman. Certainly, there were dance club owners who had friends in City Hall, and whose own clubs were, perhaps, not doing as well as *The Palladium*, but whatever the reason was, no-one ever found out, and Hyman was never able to open his club again. Time and again, the City refused to allow him to renew his liquor license.

Ironically, he had just spent $25,000 on a new dance floor. The nightly routine of hundreds of dancers jumping up and down to the music had severely punished the old structure, causing Hyman to replace it with a new, reinforced one.

It seems almost too coincidental that a brand-new lease of life for *The Palladium* would be welcome knowledge for its competitors. The wheels of power were certainly set in motion, and a perfectly legitimate reason was used to hammer nails into the coffin, when Maxwell Hyman was repeatedly refused permission to re-open the home of the greatest music in the country.

Suddenly it was over. The closure of *The Palladium* brought about the official end of the *mambo* era, and all because the music revolution begun by Mario Bauza and Machito, and ignited by Tito Puente and Tito Rodriguez, had lost the most famous venue in the world to play. The leading exponents of Latin music and their insatiable dance audiences no longer had a home.

∼∼∼∼∼∼∼∼∼∼

Of course, the music continued to be wildly popular in America and around the world, and the bands continued to flourish. *Libre* was their founding principle; free music, based on Afro-Cuban roots that allowed a more relaxed, jazzier more urban sound. *Mambo* music evolved, and a younger crowd of Latinos gradually became interested in a similar version called *salsa*, which has since in its own right become a worldwide phenomenon, though the traditionalists, especially dance purists are very specific in their preference for *mambo*. "Mambo," they say, *"had variations – slow, medium and fast – so dancers had an opportunity to express many different facets of the dance. Salsa, on the other hand, is all fast and has no creative possibilities."*

Tito Puente was quite distressed when *salsa* started becoming popular, and he continued to maintain that people don't dance to lyrics, they dance to a beat. The complex rhythms of *son montuno* were deeply ingrained in his creative soul, and the simplicity of *salsa* threatened his mantra that *"If there is no dance, there is no music."* He loathed the name salsa. At any opportunity, he told people that *salsa* was something he put on his food - *mambo* was his music.

~~~~~~~~~~

Augie and Margo were away when Maxwell Hyman finally closed the doors of *The Palladium* for the last time. Just like a flop show, the final curtain had fallen and only memories remained. They heard from all their friends that many tears were shed, and they themselves felt quite devastated.

Mr. Hyman, as they always called him, had been a real father figure to everyone including them. In spite of the one miscommunication they had with him, they knew he did whatever he could to keep his dancers happy. He embraced their culture as though it was his own; they had really loved him and they knew he loved them.

They thought of all the people who had met there, courted each other and fallen in love there. Even after they were married those couples had made the pilgrimage back every week, to dance and thrill the younger people who loved to watch them move expertly on the floor.

Augie and Margo wondered where all these people would go, and they thought about their many friends who, when they came back to Manhattan, would no longer be able to meet them on the left side of the dance floor: Little Georgie, the Bloomingdales stock clerk; the tall handsome Puerto Rican boxer and ex *Golden Glove* winner, Joe Vega, so fast on his feet; Tybee Afra, who loved dancing so much she had gone on, like them, to ballet school; Fat Harry Bruce, the three hundred pound light-footed dancer who never missed a Wednesday night dance contest, and always brought four or five shirts to change into as he perspired so much; Marilyn Watson, who they all called "Olive Oyl" because she looked like Popeye's girlfriend, and her dance partner, Ernie Thuma, who was very tall and thin, just like her, except that he was black and she was white. Watching them both dance was like watching a Fellini movie!

Then there was Cuban Pete, the man with the fast feet and arm movements, who had inspired Margo, Larry Selden, the meticulous ex marine and the *Mambo Aces*; all of them great friends, and part of the fabric of Augie and Margo's lives. Some of them would continue to dance and carve out a career for themselves; others would get involved in the drug scene and bring their hopes and talent to a screeching halt, or worse, like Joe in the *Mambo Aces,* die of a heroin overdose.

And Harry Fine, the wonderful photographer who owned a camera store in mid-Manhattan, who had spent every spare second at *The Palladium* with his wife, Rose. He and Rose were both tremendous dancers and loved the *mambo*. Sometimes, even if he was about to take a photograph, when Harry heard a terrific beat, he would drop his camera, grab Rose and get on the dance floor! He was a wild one, dancing just like the pro's, turning and jumping on the beat.

He had given them stacks of wonderful photographs of themselves dancing at *The Palladium* and *Roseland* from the very early days on. Augie and Margo owed Harry a lot; every one of those photos was worth a heap of wonderful reminiscences.

Some of the most promising dancers from *The Palladium* allowed drugs to dominate their lives, turning themselves into shells which only held their talent, and allowed them simply to look backward at what they had done. Not able, at all, to see what could have been. Augie and Margo Rodriguez were so thankful that they had a great career and their whole lives to look forward to.

On the site where *The Palladium* stood there now exists an office building, forty floors high, but Augie and Margo only care to remember how it was. In the days when thousands of dancers were driven to jump up and down in sheer exhilaration, until they nearly brought the floor down into the drug store below! Their memories are still very strong. They remember everyone; they will never forget.

CHAPTER TWENTY FOUR

The next years were a kaleidoscope of events and experiences. New countries were visited, new foods were sampled and people Augie and Margo had only known as names, as famous entertainers, became entwined in their lives and hearts - especially Sammy Davis and Xavier Cugat, each of whom they traveled with and grew to love over periods of more than a decade.

Richard, their son, traveled with them until he started school, at six years old; at which time he boarded at *Rumsey Hall*, a boarding and day school in Washington Connecticut, which took children from kindergarten through age fifteen.

Located in a beautiful part of New England with 147 acres alongside the Bantam River, Richard enjoyed school and the routine it offered; the hardest thing about being away was just before leaving, after a weekend with his grandmother in New York or a trip with his parents. He hated the "goodbye" part, but as soon as he was on the train and heading back to school he was fine again; being athletic like his parents he fit in with sports and activities so kept busy and occupied. There were always vacation times to look forward to, when he went back on the road with mum and dad.

Of course, with all the world travel at a young age, Richard was sometimes exposed to some unusual lessons in life. One year when he was about seven he went to Denmark with his parents while they were performing in Copenhagen with Sammy Davis. They took him to the famous *Tivoli Gardens*, an enormous amusement park which was opened in 1843.

The founder of the park, Georg Carstensen, said that *"When the people are amusing themselves they do not think about politics,"* and he made sure that 'the people' certainly could be amused. The park is filled with story book features: exotic oriental-style buildings including a theater, a large lake, entertainment areas, flower gardens, an antique scenic railway, merry-go-rounds, band stands and cafes.

The park attracts thousands of visitors every week, including some unusual ones, and while Richard was in the open air theater with his parents, a very exotically made-up female impersonator came on stage and began to bend his body into amazing shapes. When Richard asked his mum what sort of person that was, Margo explained to him it was a contortionist. For many years, every time Richard saw gay people or anyone who acted or looked a little 'different,' and he saw plenty in the world of entertainment, he would ask his mother if he or she was a contortionist!

Richard's childhood memories are happy ones, and some of his favorite remembered moments are the times when his parents received standing ovations. He was a very proud son. As a little boy, he grew to care for Xavier Cugat and Sammy Davis in the same way his parents did when they were all on the road together; it was just like being in part of an extended family, all of whom gave him affection and attention.

He speaks fondly of Sammy playing with him when they toured, and best of all after the shows how Sammy would take everyone out to dinner and then bring them back to his suite in which he had set up a mini-theater, where everyone would watch movies.

It is fascinating to hear the events that stand out in Richard's mind, during his childhood, considering all the remarkable experiences he must have had. Like all show business children, it is their world, the only one they know, so as long as they feel loved and secure they accept life as it is; but an intriguing lesson in hypocrisy stuck in his mind after touring Italy with his parents and Xavier Cugat.

He was five or six years old, and he remembers the tour being a long series of one-nighters. One night in Sicily, after the show, a long line of young men were standing outside the theater waiting for the performers to leave. As soon as Cugat's wife, Abbey Lane, and his mother started walking past the guys, they began cat-calling and jostling to pinch their behinds. It was quite a shock for everyone, and though it might be considered acceptable behavior in Italy, it was completely out of order for American women to have to put up with it.

Richard proudly watched him mum stop dead in her tracks and let them have it! Language barrier or not, she told them loudly enough and in no uncertain terms that they'd better stop, or else!

Later, in another Italian town, the show was going to be televised. His mother needed to wear for some routines, a leotard, because it was easier to perform her acrobatic maneuvers. The costume she had was blush colored, and it caused a great deal of trouble for the producers of the show when they saw it. They told Margo after much discussion that she couldn't possibly wear it on Italian television because people would think she was naked.

In the end, Margo had to wear a leotard with sequins, while her little boy wondered, completely logically, why it was that in Italy complete strangers, men, could actually think it was OK to pinch his mother's behind, but at the same time she couldn't wear on television a perfectly respectable costume in pink that covered her, quite literally, from head to toe!

From twelve to fifteen years old, Richard came back to New York and attended the *New York Military Academy*. His athleticism extended to being very light on his feet, like his parents, and he excelled at cross-country running and wrestling, but although in his early twenties he took a little ballet training, it was purely to get fit and strong after some inactive years of studying in College. He never had a desire to follow in his parents' footsteps.

They were a wonderfully happy family. Movies of them all together, with grandparents, aunts, uncles and cousins, showing them at the beach, in parks, family homes and around hotel pools where Augie and Margo were performing; everyone with smiling faces and loving arms.

.... The Opening Act

At home, boxes and boxes of photographs and movies, showing him with his mum and dad, splashing in the water or practicing their routines on the beach; Augie standing at the ocean's edge and holding Margo aloft on one hand; his fearless mother with arms and legs spread wide in the air, while he stood in the sand to watch them, his hand shading his eyes from the bright sun as he watched his mother, looking like a star against the sky.

He adored his grandfather, Augustin, and treasures the memory of staying with him in Spain for several months after Augustin had retired there. His gentle influence over Richard was so memorable that Richard freely admits he still thinks fondly of his grandfather several times a week, just as his father, Augie, does.

After Military School, Richard spent a couple of years in High School and then went to the *Bronx Community College* to study Medical Laboratory Technology, where he earned an associate degree. He then went on to *Pace University* to get a degree in Biology.

After graduating and sending out endless resumes, no appealing jobs were forthcoming, so his cousin got him interested in computers and he decided to get certified in computer technology. After qualifying, he was hired by ADP (Automatic Data Processing Inc.) and he has been contentedly employed there for twenty six years.

Richard's temperament is calm and steady, and although nothing from his eventful somewhat turbulent childhood made him unhappy, he chose to live a tranquil life in familiar surroundings.

In August 1990, Richard married his wife, Maria, who he met at his company, ADP. They are the proud parents of Jennifer, aged fifteen and Justin, aged 13, who, his grandparents think, is quite a keen acrobat............

~~~~~~~~~~

In 1968, Sammy Davis and May Britt divorced. Davis admitted to his wife that he had been having an affair with a dancer and actress named Lola Falana, who he had 'discovered' in a nightclub. Davis gave Lola a featured role in his Broadway musical *Golden Boy* and later brought her to Las Vegas where she remained as a dancer for many years.

In reality, Sammy was unfaithful to May long before Lola came along, sometimes bringing one or two girls along on trips right under his wife's nose; so it was purely a matter of convenience to use Lola's name.

Almost as soon as the divorce was over, Sammy began another relationship with a young woman who was dancing in the chorus-line of *Golden Boy*. Her name was Altovise Gore. When Sammy told Augie and Margo about her, they were amazed. They had known Altovise at the *Katherine Dunham Dance School* where she was a student, and at the time they knew her she was seven years old!

It was a huge age difference between Altovise and Sammy, twenty years in fact, but she was beautiful and smart and she loved him. Sammy loved her too, but even more importantly he wanted a black wife to please his fans, so in 1970 they married, with Rev. Jesse Jackson officiating at the ceremony.

The year before, in 1969, Augie and Margo decided to give their act a new dimension. They teamed up with another couple of experienced dancers, Hal and Barbara Loman, whom they had met years before in dance class.

It was an exciting time for the Lomans, because shortly after their union with Augie and Margo they were booked to tour Europe with Sammy Davis and his entire entourage. A very beautiful singer named Fran Jeffries also showed up on the bill.

Jeffries was a talented actress and singer who, up until 1961, had been one half of a double act with her husband, band singer Dick Haymes. That year they parted company both as a singing act and husband and wife, and Fran was gifted enough in her solo capacity to bring her act to some of the most prestigious clubs and hotels around America; the same places that, amongst many others, Augie and Margo, Sammy Davis, Frank Sinatra and Dean Martin were booked to perform in.

She was smart enough to develop a singing technique that was classic, stylish and romantic; an approach to music that fit in perfectly with the famous *Rat Pack,* who were an easy-going but mature contrast to the popular and rebellious rock and rollers of that time.

The first album she released on going solo was called *Fran Can Hang You Up the Most* which was soon followed by two more albums, and when a *Playboy* review raved about the last one named *This Is Fran Jeffries* it set the seal on her lush, sexy, romantic voice, and considerably advanced her career.

Her divorce to Haymes, who was twenty three years older than she, was finalized in 1965. By then she was hot property! In the previous year, she had appeared and sung in the Peter Sellers movie *The Pink Panther,* and her song from the movie *It had Better be Tonight* was included on the soundtrack album released by Henry Mancini.

The following year she appeared in the movie *Harum Scarum* with Elvis Presley and Mary Ann Mobley; a production that only won two and half stars and was described by critics as being cheesy. However, despite the bad reviews and the brainless lines she was required to deliver in her small role, Fran was portrayed as being "Red Hot Sexy" a description that kept her image very well preserved.

~~~~~~~~~~~

When Sammy and his co-performers took off in a private jet for the 1970 European tour, quite a large support group accompanied them, including Sammy's pianist Lloyd Mayers and Fran Jeffries's hairstylist, a charming gay man named Bruce.

They flew first to Sweden, and before they touched down on Swedish soil, Fran Jeffries and Lloyd Mayers were making eyes at each other. Lloyd was quite a guy; known as *The Silver Fox*, he played piano for Sammy Davis for eleven years and was also a pianist for Duke Ellington's band. Quite possibly he had met Fran before, but that would be speculation; whether he had or not, by the time they began the tour there was a tacit agreement between them that they would be getting together.

Perhaps Fran was unaware of Sammy Davis's compelling urge to seduce practically every woman he laid his eyes on, but her sexy demeanor and beautiful appearance put her directly in his category of women to hit on.

True to form, within a short space of time Sammy was also getting laid by the gorgeous Fran. The only problem was that, especially in confined surroundings, two might be company but three is definitely a crowd!

Fran was fairly adept at playing the field; ironically, Romi Schneider's lover Alain Delon had fallen under her spell along with many others; but with everyone in such close proximity to each other on tour, the odds of carrying on two associations at once were rather risky to say the least.

One day the inevitable happened. It was afternoon nap time before the first show, and everyone was resting; everyone, that is, except for Fran Jeffries who was enjoying a tryst in her room with Lloyd Mayers. Everything was fine until out of the blue there was a knock on the door and a soft voice, Sammy's, asking to be let in.

The lovers kept quiet, hoping Sammy would think Fran was asleep and that he wouldn't disturb her, but they were disappointed. Sammy knew Fran was in her room and nothing was going to deter him from joining her. He banged and yelled louder, and Fran realized she had been caught.

She could stay quiet and hope he gave up, but by then she knew him well enough to know that at any second he could get the hotel staff to open her door; then suddenly she had a brainwave. She realized that Bruce was asleep in the adjoining room which had a connecting door to her own!

She must have said a little prayer that it was unlocked, because all at the same time she called out to Sammy that she was coming, opened the door to Bruce's room and shoved Lloyd and his bundle of clothes through it! When Sammy entered her suite, the expression on his face told her he smelled a rat, but she said she had been feeling unwell and that it had taken her a while to wake up and realize he was there.

The explanation might have satisfied him, but his suspicious look remained as he heard a male voice, no doubt Bruce's, articulating his amazement at the sight of a naked man suddenly appearing in his bedroom! Fran was quick to answer when Sammy asked, *"Who the hell is that?" "It's just Bruce with a trick."* She replied.

Fran Jeffries was very fortunate, she was never found out; but both Lloyd Mayers and Sammy Davis Jr. would have done themselves a favor and not looked like a pair of idiots if they had heeded the title of her first album, *Fran Can Hang You Up the Most!*

The combination of Hal and Barbara Loman with Augie and Margo worked really well. Hal and Barbara were great dancers and they even added a little singing into the mix, but the partnership didn't last long. Hal and Barbara had three children and the constant traveling was too hard on their family life, so about a year after joining up with Augie and Margo they had an amicable separation.

CHAPTER TWENTY FIVE

Traveling was more common than being at home for Augie and Margo from the mid 1960's to the late 1970's, and sometimes their journeys turned into real adventures. Once, when they had finished a show in Spain, instead of flying, they decided to rent an old RV and drive it to Munich where they had an engagement to appear on television with Petula Clark.

With a few days to spare before the show began, the opportunity to see all the spectacular scenery in that part of Europe was too good to miss; so estimating they should arrive in Germany comfortably, by the day before the show aired, they set off in high spirits.

It was a beautiful drive and the first couple of days went very well, but when they reached the mountainous region they discovered that the old RV was not too fond of steep mountain passes. Their speed slowed down considerably, and they found themselves constantly pushing for time which became more and more urgent as they approached the mountains into Germany.

Reaching each summit at a snail's pace, a stage of alarm had set in that they might not actually make it on time; so a need for increasing speed on each downhill run became paramount.

Suddenly, when they were going much too fast for safety on a very narrow incline, both doors of the RV flew open and the vehicle skidded and tipped sideways! It was fortunate that the doors *had* opened, because they prevented the RV from rolling down the mountainside!

After recovering from the shock, Augie and Margo gingerly continued their journey. The now dented RV did so well that by the time they reached the no speed limit Autobahn, they felt confident in again pushing the pedal to the metal, and were bowling along nicely when out of blue a loud clattering noise came from the engine. Augie steered across to the hard shoulder and the RV abruptly stopped.

Unlike many places, the German people are extremely helpful when they see a person in distress on the side of the road, so it wasn't very long before a kind man stopped to ask if they needed help.

Augie and Margo were more than relieved! In spite of the fact that the man's English was rather limited, they hung on to the hope that he understood the mechanics of cars better than they did, because they were now desperately short on time! Their hopes, however, were soon dashed as the man, peering into the engine, said one word that they understood, *"Kaput!"*

Thoroughly distressed, Augie struggled with his sign-language to ask if the vehicle could be fixed; and the man haltingly replied, *"No. No, you not understand. It is really kaput!"*

The look of dismay on their faces was enough for the man to become their rescuer. He gave them a ride to Munich, and they arrived just two hours before they were due on stage!

~~~~~~~~~~

In 1973, Augie and Margo traveled to South Africa, to open for Cilla Black, who was performing in a variety show at the *Colosseum* in Johannesburg and the *City Hall* in Durban. The bill consisted of a group of high standard acts, including the marvelous musical trio *Alberto de Luque Los Amigos de Paraguay*; an outstanding father and son wire-act, *The Thuranos*, who had come straight from the *Lido* in Paris; and two brothers, *The Pattons*, who were a breakneck speed comedic tap-dancing team, with wisecracking skills that were almost as fast as their feet.

"But the dance duo to really set the stage alight," says Peter Feldman, writing about the show in the Johannesburg Press, *"was Augie and Margo. They were vigorous exponents of a style that appeared to embrace ballet and modern jazz. Their teamwork was magnificent and their performance was imbued with fire and passion."*

Interestingly, several different reviews of the show spoke very highly of everyone except Cilla, the star. To be sure she was not panned, but although all the critics liked her quote, *'clear and agreeable'* singing voice and bubbly personality, referring to it as *'wholesome,'* they felt she spent far too much time chatting up the audience and trying to get them to participate in her performance, by joining in with her songs and clapping their hands.

The reviews made it clear that the audience loved her *"as if she were the family pet doing her piece at a birthday party,"* as one critic put it, but although they all observed a rather sparse collection of some of her best known numbers, they also agreed that a bit more singing and a lot less chat to the audience would have been greatly appreciated and made for a much better performance.

Talking to Augie and Margo about Cilla Black brought some unexpected but interesting remarks, including the fact that they found her, quote, *'a cold fish,'* which is rather surprising since she went to such great lengths to be friendly when she was on stage.

Basically, she kept to herself behind the scenes, and just said *"Hello"* when she came into contact with any members in the show, who were all extremely sociable and easygoing with each other. It seemed surprising that such a warm friendly person on stage should seem so cool and reserved towards the people with whom she was performing, but perhaps Cilla was feeling particularly insecure at that time as her singing career was actually in serious decline.

Since 1963, when John Lennon had introduced her to Brian Epstein, the manager of *The Beatles,* Cilla had experienced ten incredibly good years as a singer in the UK, and to a lesser degree around the world, but at the time she was in South Africa, she had not had a hit song for two years, and it was not clear where her career was going.

The lass from Liverpool had been so nervous at her first audition with Epstein in early 1963 that she failed it, partly because *The Beatles*, who backed her, did not play the songs in her vocal key; playing instead in their own. Shortly after though, Epstein heard her in a Liverpool club and signed her up immediately, making her his only female client.

The second song she recorded, in 1964, *Anyone Who Had a Heart*, was a huge hit, and became the biggest selling single record by a female singer, in Britain's history of popular music. It was followed by *You're my World*, another mammoth hit, which gave Cilla worldwide chart success, and is possibly one of the most remembered songs of her career.

Over the next few years, Cilla went on to make twenty consecutive Top Forty hits on the British charts until, sadly, four years after signing up with Epstein he died of a drug overdose. Robert Stigwood became Cilla's agent as a consequence of Epstein's death, but unfortunately, a part in a film which was a huge flop, *Work is a Four Letter Word*, put Cilla's career in decline.

Her singing popularity dwindled through the late sixties, but her good friend Paul McCartney wrote several songs for her, which did quite well and helped to keep her career buoyant, until *Something Tells Me*, recorded in 1971, became her last hit in the Top Ten.

Quite possibly, Cilla's reserve in South Africa was due to the fact that she was no longer topping the charts and, therefore, felt insecure; but whatever her reasons were she need not have worried. She went on to host a long-running variety show on television and built a career in that medium, eventually becoming the highest paid television presenter in the United Kingdom.

Her affable behavior toward the audiences in South Africa, which had truly responded to her affection and familiarity, confirmed the fact that she was capable of entertaining and pleasing people without even having to sing, and to this day she regularly warms the hearts of millions on British television.

~~~~~~~~~~~

Augie and Margo were so well received on the 1972 visit to Johannesburg that by popular demand the following year, they and *The Thuranos* were invited back by South Africa's biggest booking agency, named Quibell Brothers, to do a tour of the country.

The Thuranos were, and still are, a truly extraordinary family from Düsseldorf, Germany. Their family name is Thur, and the father, Konrad, and his son, John, present a kind of crazy wire act, a tightrope comedy, together. Other family members also perform on the wire, but the spectacular father and son act were the stars of the show.

Augie and Margo enjoyed very much being with them as they toured the country, and they became good friends, which made the entire trip a very pleasant experience. The tour was extremely successful. This time they mostly performed cabaret acts, which brought them into closer contact with the audience; and they also danced for the State President of South Africa, Jacobus Johannes Fouche, known as Jim Fouche, who was highly complimentary to them.

Press releases from the tour gave Augie and Margo rave reviews. Perhaps some of the enthusiasm was because visiting acts from the United States and Europe were a special treat; but many of the critics were just really pleased to welcome them back.

Of their performance at *Annabel's*, in Johannesburg's five star *Landdrost Hotel*, Michael Venables wrote *"We have seen them before on a large theatre stage in the supporting bill of the Cilla Black Show, but cabaret is, I would say, obviously their real métier and the act they are now presenting involves far more versatility than they were able to show then."*

Amongst other flattering comments, he also added something which really sums up Augie and Margo's expertise very well: *"Perhaps the greatest delight of their act is the way they manage to re-create the original excitement of two dance forms which have been the subjects of parody for so long that one had almost forgotten that they were ever taken seriously – the traditional Apache duet, which glowering Augie and smoldering Margo make as grippingly dramatic as it can ever have been, and the much-derided tango, which does, admittedly need great skill, personality and commanding stage presence if one is to be unaware of how closely it verges at times on the ridiculous.*

As these two strut, lunge and posture in the familiar steps they restore the dignity, passion and drama of the tango in a way that puts any thought of laughter out of one's mind."

During the tour Augie and Margo learned a lot about the country of South Africa. The experience was quite an eye-opener for them, if not for the entire cast of the show. In each town they visited, one day a week Mr. Quibell took everyone to a different part of the town to perform in theaters reserved for the black people only. Margo found the audience comparisons amazing.

Part of their act was to play musical instruments, to set the scene for the atmosphere of the dance. Augie was a formidable player on the bongo drums, keeping up a rhythm that would give most people a coronary, and Margo, whose early piano training had come in useful after all, played a terrific keyboard.

The enthusiasm of the black audiences was even more fervent than when Augie and Margo came on stage in the all-white theaters. As soon as the *mambo* music struck up the crowd went wild, and they continued to stomp and cheer all the way through their act. Augie and Margo loved and appreciated their passionate reactions, and in return they always pulled out the stops and gave their all.

The Thur and Rodriguez families had not only their friendship in common. Some very special attitudes also bonded them together, in the form of body fitness, determination, perseverance and perhaps most importantly of all the sheer joy of performing.

While Augie and Margo never gave up dancing, even during their 'retirement' period, the same can also be said of the Thurs. In 2004, the entire Thur family was still living and traveling together and, at the age of 94 Konrad was still performing, making him the world's oldest working artiste!

CHAPTER TWENTY SIX

Sammy Davis Jr. once said, *"I've done some things I wish I could erase. I invented mistakes."* And it's true that he certainly made a lot in his life. Augie and Margo spent many hours with him traveling on tour and after shows, talking and listening; advising him to lay off all the stimulants he thought he needed to get through his days – including sex. They knew how much first May, and later Altovise loved him, and how hurt they were by his sometimes quite unashamed behavior.

As the years went by, he began to show a predilection for bizarre sexual practices and pornography, but during the 1960's and 1970's, his blatant desire and partiality was to have affairs with almost any female he came into contact with. It was his favorite pursuit, and it was quite astonishing.

One woman with whom he had worked and had a brief fling was Eartha Kitt. He told Augie and Margo that he was engaged to Eartha, but if that was indeed the case it was very short lived. Eartha Kitt is a very independent woman, and playing second fiddle to Sammy Davis was probably decidedly *not* on her agenda.

Margo found Eartha Kitt quite a difficult person to work with, seeming to be very moody and unpredictable. Considering the fact that she had attended the *John Gregory School* at the same time they were there, and had also been on the same bill with them when they danced at the *Harvest Moon Ball*, the least they expected from her was a friendly greeting when they met and performed with her later in their career.

Surprisingly, though, it didn't happen. When they first met backstage and Margo said *"Hello,"* Eartha Kitt completely ignored her, so Margo assumed she didn't want to be bothered with being sociable, and avoided her when she could.

The next time their paths crossed, Margo walked on and said nothing, only to hear Eartha's voice calling behind her, *"Hey, stuck up, what's wrong? Can't you say hello?"*

~~~~~~~~~~~~

It seemed that wherever he was performing, Sammy watched out for the women who flocked to see him after the show, and it was almost like a challenge for him to set his sights on the least attainable one.

When the lady he desired almost inevitably let him know she was interested, he acted like a little kid with a box of chocolates, saying to Augie things like, *"She likes me Augie, Oh my God; I think she really likes me!"* Clearly, it was a huge self-esteem issue for him.

His marriage to Altovise had lasted, and they were both very contented, enjoying a happy family life when they were together. Sammy liked to cook for Altovise and he loved to have his friends to their home and entertain them. Later in their marriage Altovise knew that he had some bizarre sexual practices and fantasies, but she chose to 'let it be.' Sometimes when guests came over he showed them pornographic movies, and when that happened Altovise would just leave the room. She knew how Sammy was, but that kind of entertainment was not for her.

One of Sammy's well-known expressions is, *"Being a star has made it possible for me to get insulted in places where the average Negro could never hope to get insulted."* So his desire to get laid no matter what, was possibly the only antidote he could find to alleviate the pain of being snubbed by others.

Just getting to that stage of the game was one thing, but Sammy took it all the way, regardless of the consequences. On one occasion in Paris, in 1968, when Augie and Margo were performing with him at the *Olympia*, he met the actress Odile Rodin a young and beautiful actress who also made it clear that she wanted an affair with Sammy Davis.

The problem was that Odile was married to a very powerful man by the name of Porfirio Rubirosa. To be sure, Rubirosa was a notorious playboy whose reputation for seducing women was legendary, whether or not he was married at the time, but he was a man with many high-ranking contacts and an influence to be reckoned with.

Odile was his fourth wife, and he married her at the age of forty seven when she was nineteen years old; but his first wife was the one who afforded him the life he went on to enjoy. She was Flor de Oro Trujillo, the daughter of Dominican dictator Rafael Trujillo, and since he liked his son-in-law very much, Trujillo appointed him as a diplomat to France.

Rubirosa's marriage to Flor de Oro (Golden Flower) Trujillo did not last long, but his position as diplomat remained. Ramfis, the son of Trujillo was something of a playboy himself, and he and Rubirosa were great friends, so his influence also helped to keep his ex brother-in-law in the cushy position he found himself in.

Once in Paris, the suave and handsome Rubirosa soon earned himself a reputation as being an international playboy. He played polo with high society, drove racing cars and was a skillful pilot.

He soon married the French actress Danielle Darrieux, and she was followed by tobacco heiress, Doris Duke and Woolworth heiress, Barbara Hutton, two extraordinarily wealthy American women, whose divorce settlements entitled him to a small fortune.

Many things have been written about Rubirosa, including the possibility that he was involved in the assassination of exiled Dominican, Sergio Bencosme, in 1935, although his cousin Luis de la Fuente Rubirosa was actually accused of the killing. Four years later, in the streets of Paris, a mysterious shooting injured Rubirosa, but no-one was accused.

In 1956, a Professor from Columbia University, Vasco Jesus de Galindez, inexplicably vanished, and again Rubirosa was suspected of being involved in his disappearance, a supposition that Rubirosa vehemently denied.

It was true, however, that Rubirosa always remained fiercely loyal to Trujillo, the man who kept him wealthy and famous; so much so that when Trujillo's regime was sanctioned by the Organization of the

American States, Rubirosa tried to effect a meeting in neutral territory on a ship out at sea, between Joe Kennedy, father of the President, and Trujillo. The meeting failed when the United States Congress got wind of the plan and protested strongly against it.

There was no doubt that, had Rubirosa found out about his young wife's liaison with Sammy Davis Jr. he could have brought all kinds of unpleasant acts to bear on the entertainer. Augie and Margo knew this very well, because they knew from family members what Trujillo and his cronies were capable of; so they warned Sammy in no uncertain terms that he would be getting into very deep water indeed, if he messed with Odile.

Fortunately, scheduling of tours and other commitments dampened the lovers' ardor and they both went on to live another day. In 1965, Rubirosa was driving his *Ferrari* along the Avenue de la Reine, in Paris, when he lost control of the vehicle and crashed into a tree, killing himself at the age of fifty six. At the time, he was still married to Odile. Ironically, his ex brother–in–law Ramfis Trujillo killed himself in exactly the same way, four years later, in Spain.

~~~~~~~~~~~~

Life is full of coincidences, some of them very unpleasant, and Sammy Davis had more than his fair share. Two of the women he met in Paris and had affairs with were highly successful and extremely glamorous; but at the same time they suffered from severe depression and died tragic deaths at an early age. Romi Schneider was the first one.

Sammy was working with Augie and Margo at the *Olympia,* in Paris, where they met Regine Zylderberg, who was the creator of the first ever discotheque.

After her first successful disco in Paris, Regine went on to own luxury nightclubs all over the world, including a flagship American club in New York, where the likes of Jackie Onassis, Andy Warhol and Mick Jagger hung out together.

As much as she was an entrepreneur, Regine's other specialty was being a socialite who loved bringing famous people together, which earned her the title "Queen of the Night" in the American press; so when she met Sammy, Augie and Margo, she invited them to the Rothschild Mansion to schmooze with some celebrities and members of Paris high society.

It was a very memorable evening for Augie and Margo, for one of their idols, Josephine Baker, was at the event. Sammy knew her and introduced her to them; they were surprised to hear she knew who they were, and said she was honored to meet them - a feeling they completely reciprocated.

The international film actress Romi Schneider and her husband Harry Meyen were also present, and Regine introduced them to Augie, Margo and Sammy. Both Schneider and her husband were German born actors, but Schneider had created quite a national scandal in 1959 when she had fallen in love with French actor Alain Delon, and had left Germany to go and live with him in Paris.

Four years later, Delon dumped Schneider, dealing her a devastating blow which was hard for her to get over, as she continued to perform with him in films; but three years later she met Meyen and married him. Clearly she was still smarting from her relationship with Delon, for as soon as she and Sammy Davis met they had eyes only for each other.

Sammy could hardly believe his luck, and couldn't wait to tell Augie that he thought she wanted him. It is not well-known or even mentioned in accounts of her life, but Romi Schneider and Sammy Davis had quite a torrid affair, putting into jeopardy her marriage to Meyen with whom she had a son, David Christopher.

At the time, Sammy was in the final years of his marriage to May Britt, and although he fell really hard for Romi, the demands of both their careers kept them apart.

Romi Schneider's life continued to be turbulent. She remained married for nine years, until in 1975 she divorced Harry Meyen and married her private secretary, Daniel Biasini, with whom she had a daughter Sarah Magdalena, who looks startlingly like her beautiful mother and is herself now an actress.

Three years after that marriage the couple separated, and shortly after, in 1981, Romi Schneider received the hardest blow of her life when her son attempted to climb a fence at the home of his step-grandparents, and became impaled at the top which resulted in his death.

Romi was never the same again; she sunk into a deep depression and made statements like; *"I am nothing in life but everything on the screen."* Already a serious smoker, she took heavily to drinking, and the year after David died she was found dead in her Paris apartment. No post-mortem examination was carried out, but the rumor that she committed suicide by taking a lethal dose of pills and alcohol was the widely believed reason for her death. She was only forty-three years old.

~~~~~~~~~~~

The second glamorous star Sammy started a relationship with was Jean Seburg. He had just divorced May Britt, and Seberg had been making films and living in Paris since the late 1950's. By 1978, ten years after their affair, she was dead. Greatly appreciated by French audiences, who thought they were paying her the highest of compliments by letting her know that she didn't act like an American actress at all, she was first married to Frenchman, Francois Moreuil, then four years later she wed writer/director Romain Gary, who was born in Lithuania but moved to France with his mother when he was fourteen.

Seberg made it abundantly clear that she did not like the attitude of Frenchmen towards American women, explaining that they treated American women, 'As if they were breaking in horses, believing that they had to be combed, trained, run and beaten!'

Another very troubled person, Jean Seberg was a dedicated political activist in left-wing political groups including the Black Panthers. She traveled back and forth to America often, and was extremely popular in the United Kingdom. Her political influence in Europe was so strong that the FBI started hounding her, considering her a liability, and the result was that the stress she underwent during a pregnancy with Gary's child caused it to be born prematurely, and was stillborn.

After the death of her baby Seberg became extremely depressed and was hospitalized several times, trying on every subsequent anniversary of the child's death to commit suicide; once, in 1978, even unsuccessfully throwing herself under a train on the Paris Metro.

She recovered from the stress and melodrama of that event, and appeared to have become calmer, even planning at the persistence of her fans to return to filmmaking; but the following year she went missing for two weeks and her decomposing body was eventually found in the back seat of her car in a Paris suburb. The autopsy said that she died of a massive dose of barbiturates. She was forty one years old.

~~~~~~~~~~

Sammy was reckless in some ways, but it didn't alter the fact that he was immensely kind to everyone and very popular backstage wherever he went. In Las Vegas on one occasion, Donald Rumsfeld, who was then Secretary of Defense in the Cabinet of President Ford came backstage to congratulate him and mentioned he would also have liked to see Elvis Presley during his visit to the city.

It happened that Sammy was one of Elvis's few celebrity friends. They really enjoyed each other's company, and especially loved to do imitations of each other when they were together.

Presley was performing in another part of town, but Sammy immediately called for his driver and took Rumsfeld across Vegas to where he was performing, and introduced them to each other.

In London, when Sammy was at the *Palladium* with Augie and Margo, Richard Burton and Liz Taylor came backstage to see him. Burton did all the talking, Margo recalls; Elizabeth was not at all chatty or friendly, but maybe that was because Richard Burton referred to her as "fatty," an item that did not go un-noticed by the American Press!

The next time Sammy was in London playing *The Talk of the Town*, he and Augie took show tickets for Richard and Liz around to the *Dorchester Hotel*, where they were staying, to save them the exposure. It was a typical kind act of Sammy's; he bent over backwards to please everyone.

On another occasion in the early 1960's *The Beatles* came to see the show, and Sammy invited them to dinner that night after they visited him backstage.

They went to one of Sammy's favorite places in London, the *White Elephant Club,* where, as happened most nights, he booked a table for up to twenty people, most of them stage or screen celebrities and artists from the *Palladium* show.

That evening, only Paul McCartney and Ringo Starr had been able to go to dinner, and Augie and Margo remember how shy they seemed. Clearly, they idolized Sammy Davis, so were for the most part quiet and in awe of him and the rest of the company around them. Additionally, they were still young and relatively new on the popularity front, and that night they discovered that Terence Stamp's brother, Chris, was about to launch another group of musicians on to the music scene; a group called *The Who*.

Another group of people sitting around the table that night were already extremely used to being popular. *The Dallas Boys,* five young men who had all been friends at school in Leicester, England, had hit the pop charts singing live music in four-part harmony during the early fifties. Arguably, they were Britain's first 'boy band' and a pop phenomenon during the fifties and early sixties.

Immensely popular with the opposite sex, they were indeed an original, cute, clean-cut, cheeky pop group, and the ladies loved them – all the ladies – the young ones *and* their mothers.

Some of their hysterical fans might have changed their minds about them, if they had seen what Augie and Margo saw behind the stage at the *Palladium* where the boys were performing with them. Some of the details defy discussion, but one word can sum it all up. Orgies!

Seeing a few bawdy romps in the hay behind the scenes was nothing new for Augie and Margo, but the popular *Dallas Boys,* apparently, ran away with the first prize for crude and lewd. It could, though, have been the last time that the five squeaky-clean boys got so much back-stage attention, for standing in the wings were four mop-topped young scousers who were about to redefine the popular music scene forever. Their new definition of guitar playing and singing had just been launched, and almost overnight the harmonizing style of songs delivered by *The Dallas Boys* would begin to sound old-fashioned.

That evening, however, it was all quite overwhelming for those two rather awkward young men, Paul and Ringo, who were almost certainly completely unaware of the fact that it would not be long before they would themselves become the world-wide idols of millions!

∼∼∼∼∼∼∼∼∼∼

Sitting at the table next to Augie and Margo that night were Peter O'Toole and Terence Stamp, a young actor who had also recently become enormously popular and successful. He had made his debut in Peter Ustinov's movie adaptation of Herman Melville's *Billy Budd*, which had earned him rave reviews and a nomination for an Academy Award.

Suddenly, everyone wanted to know who this good-looking young man with icy-blue eyes was. Top producers and directors were clamoring to give him roles and his love life was all over the Press, airing details of his affairs with glamorous women like Brigitte Bardot, Julie Christie and supermodel Jean Shrimpton.

As was his habit on that type of occasion, Sammy inevitably picked up the tab at the end of the evening, but he knew how Augie felt about it. Augie's position was that night after night, no matter how rich and famous Sammy's guests were, no matter how much they ate or, more pointedly, drank, they were always happy to do it on Sammy's dime and never offered to take care of the check themselves. It bothered Augie a lot and on that night, as in the past, from his position at the far end of the table he signed to Sammy that he would pay the check.

Sammy, as always, firmly shook his head; but on that occasion he let Augie know that he appreciated and understood the offer. With a knowing wink he tossed his comment across the table *"Don't worry Augie."* he called, *"Everyone gets another freebie!"*

Once again, Sammy footed the bill, and added another several hundred to the huge five million dollar pile of debt that he would accumulate before he died.

One evening at a party at John Mills, the actor's house, Maurice Chevalier took Sammy aside and told him he was concerned. Warning him that he was endangering his health, Chevalier told Sammy he should stop burning the candle at both ends; but his warning fell on deaf ears, Sammy was hardly likely to change at that stage of his life.

CHAPTER TWENTY SEVEN

In 1978, when Augie turned fifty, he remembers the day and the moment he actually decided he was getting older. He and Margo were performing in Montreal and one evening, during their amazing routine where Margo ends up high above Augie's head, held aloft on his right hand, he suddenly became conscious of the fact that he would not be able to do it for very much longer. It was a stunning realization, but he knew he had to discuss the situation with Margo and that between them they would find the right path to follow.

The transition they made was not sudden, they just eased up a bit on their rigorously demanding routines until, in 1983, Augie and Margo retired from professional dancing and formed their own Production Company, *Augmar Productions*.

There was no real sense of sadness about leaving the professional stage because they had no *intention* of leaving it, their role would just be in a new and different capacity. It was time to move on; but they would remain in the only world they had known since their late teens and they were excited and pumped up about their future.

As time went on, *Augmar Productions* became more and more successful. The demand for their productions went from Canada to Atlantic City, to Puerto Rico and several cruise lines. Their heavy schedule meant they saw much less of Sammy Davis Jr. though they kept in touch with Altovise on a regular basis. Their schedule was demanding but they were living the life they wanted, and they loved it.

Only a few regrets surfaced after they had thought for some time about it, and none of those were significant, just a little disappointing. From a sentimental point of view, perhaps the biggest regret was that Augie didn't buy Sammy's Rolls Royce! Sammy had offered it to Augie several times for a very good price, but at the time, even though it was a great deal, it was still a lot of money from Augie's point of view and he felt it was a luxury he could not afford.

Another regret was connected to the *Tonight Show* with Johnny Carson, which was another highlight in Augie and Margo's career. They had a wonderful time during rehearsals, when Johnny became fascinated by one of their routines named *The Snake Dance*.

He decided that he wanted to try it live on television and dance with Margo, but as often happened on his show, the dance turned into one of Johnny's hilarious moments. Several years later, Woody Allen wanted to see the only tape Augie and Margo had of the event, and he never returned it.

The final regret was the loss of Martin Luther King's letter to them, and they still hope that one day it may turn up in the home of a family member.

~~~~~~~~~~~

So much had changed over the thirty years since *Augie and Margo*, the phenomenal dance act, had begun their career on the stage of the great New York *Palladium*.

Some of their old friends had already passed away, and others had left the business through ill health or simply because their once shining stars were beginning to tarnish in the face of fresh competition. Unless performers were willing and able to go with the flow, the chances were they would find themselves washed up somewhere; whether it would be in a rehab clinic in New York, a beach house in California or a mansion in Beverley Hills, it was all the same, life moved on.

In 1982, at the age of fifty-three, Tybee Afra, the girl who gave up everything for her love of dance, died. She had run away from home as a young woman because more than anything else she wanted to learn dancing, the pursuit of which her family completely disapproved.

Drawing the line from entirely alienating her family for a second time, she did not marry her other love, Joe Vega, at her parents' request since he was not Jewish, but she went on to learn ballet and to turn her talent into a successful career, which eventually made her family extremely proud of her.

She moved to Hollywood, and in 1957, she played the role of Fifi, in the movie, *Silk Stockings,* which starred Fred Astaire and Cyd Charisse. It was her only movie, but she stayed in California and became something of an icon in South America, as her Latin dance style was always admired. She had her picture on matchboxes in Cuba; and in Brazil, they named a flower after her.

Sadly, she contracted breast cancer, and it was confided to Augie and Margo that she died alone while listening to her beloved Latin music.

Liberace: their dear Lee, whom they had visited at his insistence, whenever they played the town he happened to be in at the time; his home in the Hollywood hills, which housed a magnificent crystal table made by Baccarat, and was filled with so many ornate treasures it was like a smaller version of the Palace in Versailles; his winter estate in Palm Springs, "The Cloisters" or the home in Las Vegas with his spectacular collection of vintage cars.

In 1984, whilst in New York, Augie and Margo went to see *Cats* on Broadway, and after the show they saw Liberace and his good friend Ray Arnett amongst the throng of people leaving the theater. Liberace was delighted to see them and very friendly, but Augie and Margo were shocked to see how gaunt he was beginning to look.

Two years later, in November, 1986, a good friend of theirs, adagio dancer Francois Szony, called them to say he had seen Liberace performing at *Radio City Music Hall,* and that after the show when he went backstage to visit, Liberace had asked after them. Shortly after that conversation, Ray Arnett telephoned Augie and Margo to let them know that Liberace was about to do his last performance, and that it would be at *Radio City.*

The audience was packed with many significant people in the entertainment business, including staff from William Morris and other big New York Agencies. Liberace had endeared himself to so many people during his career, and they all knew that this was probably the last time they would see him. It was a touching and poignant performance, which remained in the memories of everyone who attended.

Four months after the event, Liberace returned to "The Cloisters" in Palm Springs. He died there, peacefully, of complications from AIDS, in February, 1987, at the age of sixty seven.

Liberace was interred at Forest Lawn in the Hollywood hills, but a museum dedicated to his memory was later constructed in Las Vegas, where many artifacts from his lavish homes are now housed.

Flamboyant he certainly was, but his heart was bigger and glitzier than anything he ever owned, and Augie and Margo had loved him very much. They often talk about that last performance in New York, and remember when he played his favorite song from *Man of La Mancha*, '*The Impossible Dream,*' which always resulted in leaving not a dry eye in the house. It was the last time they saw him, and had to say goodbye publicly with hundreds of other people; but as they left the theater and thought of all the personal moments they had shared with him, they knew he had been aware of their presence.

Walking into the New York night air, they felt a sense of gratitude that they had been lucky enough to know him well; it was sad to say goodbye, but they found comfort in the fact that running through their minds and still ringing in their ears was his unforgettable closing theme song, *I'll be Seeing You.*

~~~~~~~~~~

The same year that Liberace died, Dean Martin's son, Dean Paul Martin, 'Deano,' died in a plane crash. After Deano's death, the man who preferred his private life anyhow, became a magnificent recluse. His health was already failing, and he no longer had the heart to perform.

Dean Martin died on Christmas Day in December 1995, and on his tombstone is the title of his single that knocked *The Beatles* out of the top spot on the charts, *Everybody Loves Somebody Sometime.*

Three years after Liberace's death, in May, 1990, Augie and Margo's beloved Sammy died. They had not seen much of him over the past several years, since their business had taken off like a rocket and they were as busy as they had ever been; while Sammy, on the other hand, was experiencing a career in decline. Having had successful roles in movies, topping the charts and also appearing in his own syndicated variety show in the 1970's, *Sammy and Company,* by the mid 1980's he was for the most part restricted to the casino circuit.

A comeback tour that was put together with Frank Sinatra and Dean Martin in 1988 was not successful, primarily because Dean was still grieving over the loss of his son, and was himself in ill health.

On one occasion Augie and Margo saw Sammy in New York, when they met coming out of a show at *Radio City.* He took one look at them and said, *"I thought you were dead!"* It was great to see him and catch up with all their news, just like old times, but they were shocked to see how ill he looked.

They vowed to keep in touch, and whenever they could, even if Sammy wasn't available, they called his mother, Elvira Sanchez, who lived in Atlantic City. She had re-entered Sammy's life by then and was an important support for him during his illness.

In 1989, Sammy played a highly acclaimed film performance in the Gregory Hines movie, *Tap,* which was a tribute to the legends of tap dancing, but it was to be his last role in a movie. It was a bittersweet year altogether; after 19 years of marriage, he and Altovise adopted a son, Manny, and later that same year Sammy was diagnosed with throat cancer. His final singing performance was shortly after the diagnosis, at *Harrah's* in Lake Tahoe, the day before he started radiation therapy.

He responded well to his treatment initially, the cancer appeared to be under control, but it flared up again several weeks later, and this time the doctors found a tumor in Sammy's mouth. It was a critical time and everyone knew it. A television special was planned to honor him, and twenty six entertainers paid tribute to him for two and a half hours. Augie and Margo were devastated that they couldn't attend. They had contracts to fulfill across the country, but were able to watch the live televised show.

Sammy and Altovise attended the event, and at the end of it Sammy got to his feet to acknowledge a standing ovation from the crowd. It was abundantly clear from the cheering and applause that they wanted to see him up on stage, so looking at Altovise he made a move towards it. *"Honey,"* she said, *"are you sure you can do it?"* He nodded to her, saying, *"My feet work. It's my voice that can't."*

He went up and joined all the entertainers on stage who were applauding him along with the crowd in the theater, showing him once and for all how much he was adored. Sammy said nothing, but did a little soft-shoe, and then he turned to the performers behind him and tossed an imaginary ball to Gregory Hines.

From then on his health deteriorated rapidly. He re-entered *Cedars Sinai Hospital* and was released after a month to go back to his home in Beverly Hills. There was nothing more the doctors could do for him.

Towards the end, Augie and Margo put on a production in Atlantic City and spent some time with 'Baby' Sanchez, as his mother was named. She was desperately upset at Sammy's condition, and told them he was a shadow of his former self, but very swollen from edema. She told them it was just a matter of time.

~~~~~~~~~~

Sammy didn't get philosophical at the end and try to analyze his amazing life, but a comment he made just before he died indicated he had enjoyed all the ups and downs he had experienced; *"I'm sixty four years old,"* he said, *"but I feel I've lived the life of a person at one hundred and sixty four."*

He died in his home on May 16th 1990, and before his body had been removed, hundreds of people were lining the streets outside. That night the lights on *The Strip* in Las Vegas were dimmed for ten minutes. The only other people to have been honored at their demise in that way were President Kennedy and Dr. Martin Luther King Jr.

The man who became known as *"The World's Greatest Living Entertainer"* was no more.

CHAPTER TWENTY EIGHT

The exterior and interior of the *Hotel and Casino New York New York*, as depicted by architects and designers, is a miniature representation of the city of *Manhattan*, with avenues of shops and restaurants and all the typical sight-seeing "musts" the real city boasts.

Opening its doors in 1997, the hotel and casino is the tallest one on *The Strip*, with a façade boasting a skyline that could only belong to *New York City*. The *Statue of Liberty* reigns supreme, while in front of her a permanent memorial to the victims of September the Eleventh reminds passers-by of that tragic day in our history.

The *Empire State Building* and a bevy of twelve interconnected skyscrapers housing rooms for 2,024 guests, lend real authenticity to the scene; along with a replica of the *Soldiers and Sailors Monument,* a 300 ft. long, 50 ft. wide *Brooklyn Bridge* arching majestically over a *New York Harbor*, complete with a tug-boat, and a *Coney Island* rollercoaster that guarantees to scare the dickens out of even the toughest of daredevils. If those certain risk takers *really* want to prove themselves, they can purchase for $25.00 an all-day Scream Pass!

The rollercoaster, which is situated in a *Coney Island* style amusement center, with arcade and carnival games and bumper cars, reaches speeds of 67 mph, and is the only one in the world with a "heartline twist and dive feature," which rolls 180 degrees hanging 86 feet in the air, and then dives back under itself, giving its riders the thrill of a lifetime to the force of negative g's; as proven by the audible squeals of fear and delight which can be heard from the street below.

Inside the hotel, the casino vicinity which houses all the usual gambling tables and over 2,400 slot machines, is based on a design of *Central Park,* with trees and streams surrounding its 84,000 square foot area. There is also an Irish/American pub with the appropriate food and entertainment, a *Park Avenue* section offering a delightful shopping experience for those who can afford the ritzy prices, a *Times Square* area, complete with an overkill of neon and flashing lights and a sing-a-long bar featuring dueling pianos, which is always packed to the hilt with tourists.

Close to the *Times Square* section, a series of typical miniaturized *New York* streets featuring *Greenwich Village* style delis, pizzerias and cafes attract the hungry visitors who long for a good pastrami sandwich or a real bagel. The eateries are also a magnet for the theater crowds, who can grab a bite to eat while they wait in line or after they have seen the show, for the *Zumanity Theater* is located alongside that area and the smaller *Cabaret Theater* is only a short distance away.

The *Zumanity Theater* in which *Cirque du Soleil* performs two shows every evening was custom built for the specific needs of the production, and is big enough to accommodate a large lobby based on the design of a classic opera house, a magnificent stage and an auditorium capable of seating an audience of 1,259 people.

Behind the scenes, probably the same amount of space again houses all the offices, dressing rooms and wardrobe facilities for the 90 minute production's very creative costumes; and of course the Green Room, where Augie and Margo Rodriguez waited with the rest of the *Cirque* cast on the evening of March 28th 2005, to make their stage debut after an almost thirty year hiatus.

People attending the two shows daily are advised to arrive half an hour before the official start, in order to enjoy the pre-show frolics; but they begin to line up in front of the theater long before that and, exactly like the crowds of enthusiastic people who used to line up outside the original New York *Palladium,* there is always a sense of anticipation and excitement in the air.

Alongside the box office which is adjacent to the theater entrance, a boutique selling *Cirque* memorabilia keeps some of the waiting theater-goers interested and amused. Articles of sexy clothing, suggestive accessories, chocolates for lovers, suspender belts, feathered confections, tee shirts and the like, pique the interest of the browsers as they try to imagine just what is in store for them at the show!

~~~~~~~~~~~

When the doors finally open, they enter a world of plush red carpet covering floors and walls, and exotic-looking people. Young hostesses with black angular haircuts, long black lashes and bright red Cupid's bow lips hand out souvenir programs and show everyone to their seats.

Dressed in black tee shirts which reach thigh-top and fishnet stockings held up with suspenders, the most surprising thing about their attire is that a nude figure is painted over the black shirts making the girls, at first glance, appear naked.

On the gently sloping lobby approach to the theater, high up in the wall, a large glass-fronted opening allows an intimate glimpse of a room, while a sexily-dressed 'Madame', seated on a chair behind the glass, heckles and jibes at male passers-by.

Occasionally, she picks on one man and using a few choice comments and innuendos, nails him to the spot and gets a dialogue started, which causes much hilarity amongst the gathering folks who stop to watch the fun.

Once inside the theater, which is designed to create a salon-like atmosphere, the audience begins to get a real sense of the show they are about to see. Surrounding the gilded circular stage, and positioned around the theater, plush red-upholstered love-seats, or 'duo-sofas,' some with candelabras, lend an intimate and sumptuous air to the scene.

Passionate red is the color of choice, everywhere: even in the carpeting which is patterned with Botticelli style cherubs; and under the curved bridge where the musicians are situated, festoons of silky scarlet draperies add a lush opulence to the heavily sensual atmosphere.

Having established the romantic aspect of the show, the next impression *Zumanity* producers achieve is one of bawdy comedy. Before the ninety minute production actually begins, human caricatures of some of the most extreme members in society frolic and gambol about the theater to warm up the audience as they are seated; and they begin interacting with the folks as soon as they are relaxed and comfortable.

The two large sisters from Brazil, Licemar and Luciene Medeiros, known as *The Botero Sisters*, dressed as French maids, totter uninhibitedly between the rows of seats offering in penetrating voices fresh strawberries, which they carry on trays. Skimpy black dresses and white frilly aprons barely cover their bosoms and bellies; but their sweet high-pitched giggles and friendly bubbling personalities draw everyone's attention, even as they gasp in slight embarrassment at the sight of the two enormous beauties.

If a person in the row behind the one which the girls are standing in, happens to accept their offer of a "*STRAWbellie,*" the girls have no hesitation in leaning over the gentleman in front of them, (it's always a gentleman) and pushing their ample cleavages into his face while they stretch to hand the fruits over. This dicey position also ensures that the person seated behind gets into very personal contact with the sisters abundant thonged, fishnet-clad rears, and elicits screams of hilarity from the people around; especially those who are seated in close proximity to the event!

All this vulgar behavior of course delights the audience no end, and the sisters welcoming attitude probably only leaves about half the men in the audience hoping they don't have to go through the friendly fun!

While some people are fixated on the girls and their flirtatious antics, other members of the cast are also interacting with the audience. A male and female 'pair' try to draw out the couples seated on sofas in front of the stage by asking them suggestive questions, while Raven, the handsome young man with a Mohican haircut and tattoos, is transformed into an exotic creature who strides around the theater on the sexiest pair of legs imaginable and rivets unwavering stares upon whomever takes his fancy in the audience.

To describe what happens in detail would spoil the show for those who have not seen it; but from the moment it officially opens with the unrelenting throb of exotic songs and rhythms, to the arrival of MC,

Joey Arias, *The Mistress of Seduction* who expertly guides the audience through the entire production with his unrestrained comments and caustic innuendo, no one can say they are not either shocked, entertained or both by *Zumanity*.

This is a show for adults only, but it is certainly not a production where one would take a prudish person, a grandparent or one's boss. It aims to astonish and titillate, and also to throw light in an entertaining way on some of the more bizarre forms of sexuality, and though it is comically vulgar and blatantly suggestive at times, it is not crude.

The main theme is discovering love; sometimes in the most unlikely places and ways, and sometimes with the most unusual people; the true human zoo that exists on this earth, whether or not everyone find it acceptable.

One of the most touching acts is a story of unrequited and unattainable love between a small person, played by Alan Jones, and a tall blonde goddess, played by Olga Vershinina. They are both amazing aerial artists, but Jones puts just enough pathos into his role to make it feel real, and one wants to see the act time and again in the hopes that he may eventually realize his desire.

The entire story of the production, written and directed by the brilliant Canadian Rene Richard Cyr, in collaboration with Dominic Champagne, relates the human condition in a series of touching, sensual, hedonistic and hilarious themes. The "taboo" subjects are handled with either sensitivity or humor and only the most straitlaced amongst us would be insulted, though the producers of the show make it as clear as they can on their website and publicity material what the show is all about, lest anyone be offended.

~~~~~~~~~~~

Just before their curtain call, Augie and Margo were exhilarated. An "It's now or never" attitude had already processed its way through their minds, and they were prepared and ready, if not a little impatient, to get on stage.

Their eager attitude would have to wait though for, unlike in their past career, their appearance was now to be in the 'closing' not 'opening' position; although they would be brought to the attention of the audience by Joey Arias in the first half of the show.

They looked fabulous! Margo had been allowed to keep her own hair – no grey or subdued look for her- and it was cut in its normal style, very similar to the young hostesses who seat the audience. She was dressed in a black cocktail dress and coat and black high-heeled shoes. Augie looked handsome in a dark lounge suit and a shirt and tie, with his hair slicked back and the recognizable soft curls at the top of his collar.

A few minutes before the show they were brought by a hostess to their seats in the audience, a few rows back from the stage, and for most of the performance they melted into the background.

Joey Arias, who refers to himself as a 'she male,' was an impressive and highly entertaining Master of Ceremonies as he introduced the audience into his world of pleasure, which is replete with a genderless phantom, an African tribal dancer, a nature-defying contortionist, an autoerotic aerial act, lotharios and male/female acts in a variety of combinations; flying through the air, swimming underwater, discovering themselves inside a cage or body to body in a dazzling hand balancing act inspired by positions from the *Kama Sutra*.

Without giving away the integrity of the show, those are some of the acts in *Zumanity*; each of them brilliant in its own way and performed by some of the best and most disciplined entertainers in the world today.

~~~~~~~~~~~

Augie and Margo, once seated, waited to be drawn into the show by Joey, and from the word 'go' they felt confidence in his guiding role. They had seen Joey perform enough during rehearsals to know that if a sentence was forgotten or a miss-step was made, he would fill in the blanks and keep their role in play. The dancing part was second nature for them and they had no need to be concerned, but interacting with the audience and extracting a few laughs was new territory.

As it happened, no lines were forgotten and everything went well. The audience was charmed by the lovely couple who were at first reluctant, but then gracious enough to go on stage to do a waltz.

As they performed on, and turned the waltz into a salsa, the audience gasped in astonishment. For a few dazzling moments, Augie and Margo held them in the palms of their hands, and then, when the rest of the cast came down the stage to join them they burst into loud applause.

The uplifting feeling that the producers were looking for at the end of the show had been achieved. Everyone clapping and cheering: delighted with the outcome of the show; that two perfectly average people from the audience could still be in love after fifty years of marriage, and enjoying life and each other.

As they filed out of the theater, snatches of conversation could be heard:

"And then didn't the couple show them?" "They were great!" "Who were they?" "Do you think they . . . . ?" "Augie and Margo who?"

Augie and Margo felt good about the first performance and calmly returned to their dressing room to await the next show; they were already focused and back in the saddle!

By the next day, with two successful shows under their belts, Augie gained a little confidence in his ability to ad lib, and Margo knew exactly when to project her voice. They then discovered how just a small tweak could gain a big reaction! This time at the end of the show the audience became elated, started stomping their feet and calling out, "Au*gie*, Au*gie*, Au*gie*!"

And that is exactly how it happened and how it remains for them; twice a night, five days a week!

~~~~~~~~~~~

On this day, at this time of writing, Augie and Margo will have been dancing with *Cirque du Soleil* for exactly one year! They are happy and contented and love being back in show business, although to quote Margo, *"The hardest thing about being in the show is sitting down."*

They are in their element back in Vegas! It only took a few weeks in town for them to know that they wanted to stay. This was where so many good things happened for them, and the memories are happy and overwhelming; they feel they belong.

Their famous and dear friend, Eddie Villela, founder of the incredible Miami Ballet, has a favorite saying, *"It's not the leap – it's the landing."* And in that regard Augie and Margo have landed safely on both feet. A new and beautiful home has just been constructed for them, complete with a dance studio, (will this couple never stop?) The only item they feel is missing is Sammy's Rolls Royce, which they would love to have had parked in their driveway.

Ed Villela has great wit; he humorously retorts to occasional critics after his shows, *"Don't speak to me like that, you don't know who I used to be."* The same can be said for Augie and Margo, and they still *are*. The dynamic duo, known as the premier opening act in the entertainment business is still going strong with a closing one.

Maxwell Hyman and his *Palladium* helped launch two dancers who brought theatrical movement and style to the world of Latin dance, and were described many times as being one of the most successful dance teams of all time.

A photograph, a signed limited edition of 500, titled *"Crowd – Palladium Ballroom, 1955"* by William Klein, the Master photographer, sells now on the internet for $590. Klein, who describes himself as having 'A devouring hunger for faces, bodies and crowds,' used the *Palladium* image in his celebrated series of shows in New York; titled *Life is Good and Good for You*. It need hardly be said that Augie and Margo Rodriguez wholeheartedly agree!

****

THE END

.... The Opening Act